A DAILY WALK WITH GOD

Smyth & Helwys Publishing, Inc.
6316 Peake Road
Macon, Georgia 31210-3960
1-800-747-3016

The devotions quote from the following Bible translations: Common English Bible (CEB),
English Standard Version (ESV), King James Version (KJV), *The Message* (MSG),
New American Standard Bible (NASB), New International Version (NIV),
New King James Version (NKJV), and New Revised Standard Version (NRSV)

Cover photo by Kyle Mills/Unsplash

Library of Congress Cataloging-in-Publication Data

Names: Hensley, Christopher J., author.
Title: A daily walk with God / by Christopher J. Hensley.
Description: Macon, GA : Smyth & Helwys Publishing, Inc., [2021] | Includes
bibliographical references and index.
Identifiers: LCCN 2020048546 (print) | LCCN 2020048547 (ebook) | ISBN
9781641732901 (paperback) | ISBN 9781641732918 (ebook)
Subjects: LCSH: Devotional calendars.
Classification: LCC BV4811 .H47 2021 (print) | LCC BV4811 (ebook) | DDC
242/.2--dc23
LC record available at https://lccn.loc.gov/2020048546
LC ebook record available at https://lccn.loc.gov/2020048547

christopher j. hensley

A DAILY
WALK
WITH GOD

Lancy,

May you be encouraged and

nourished.

Chris Henry

Dedicated to

My wife—
I am humbled by your love and support of me and my endeavors.

My children—
I hope and pray that you journey with God as God has, is, and will forever journey with you.

My parents—
Thank you for building my foundation on solid rock.

CONTENTS

January 1
NEW BEGINNINGS

"In the beginning was the Word, and the Word was with God, and the Word was God." —*John 1:1 (NIV)*

With the turning over of another year on the calendar comes the feeling of a new beginning, a fresh start with a new set of dates, calendars, and events. This newness can be both exciting and overwhelming. The turning of the calendar brings the hope of freshness and renewed energy and focus, often coming out as resolutions to better yourself. On the flip side of that coin, you might find that with the beginning of another year come thoughts of deadlines quickly approaching, children growing, graduation drawing near, or age getting the better of you.

No matter what thoughts are evoked within your mind at the beginning of a new year, a new project, a new relationship, or any other new venture, remember that God is there too. In the John's Gospel, we are reminded that the Word, or Jesus Christ, was there in the beginning with God the Father, before time began, before creation, and before anyone was ever considered a possibility. Take comfort in knowing that the Savior of humanity has existed for all eternity and continues to exist even now at the side of God the Father.

As you begin this New Year today, pause for a moment and allow the Presence of God to overwhelm you in a time of prayer and meditation. Pray that God will guide your path. Pray that you will have the humility to follow God throughout this New Year and into the new adventures that will present themselves to you as you journey into a new beginning.

January 2
GOD'S GREAT LOVE

The LORD's lovingkindnesses indeed never cease, For His compassions never fail. They are new every morning; Great is Your faithfulness. —Lamentations 3:22-23 (NASB)

Every day we get up and begin our routines of preparing for the day ahead: for work, school, or whatever lies before us. Each of these days brings different challenges and struggles as well as rewards and blessings. In these verses from Lamentations, believers in God are reminded of the one blessing that is constantly being renewed with each new day—the compassion (mercy) of God.

Not only is the compassion of God renewing every day, but God's love for us is so great that we cannot be consumed by evil. Do not be confused; we can and will suffer in this life. Sometimes we will be pushed beyond our breaking point, but the blessing of God's continued compassion is this: though we are pushed and battered by the challenges of daily life, we will not be totally consumed by the evil in this world, for consumption of that sort means having oneself removed from the Presence of God. Our God, though, is too faithful to God's people to allow us to be removed from the Divine Presence. For an example of God's faithfulness, we need look no further than Jesus Christ.

The Lord's love for each of us is overwhelming. It is something that cannot fully be grasped or understood. As you look forward to the events that are scheduled for the day ahead, pray that God will remind you of God's renewed mercies or compassion for you. Remember that God's great love for you prevents you from being consumed by evil if you will only allow God to protect you through faith in Jesus Christ.

January 3

INTIMACY WITH CHRIST

One of his disciples—the one whom Jesus loved—was reclining next to him . . . . —John 13:23 (NRSV)

Jesus and his disciples were reclining at the table during the celebration of the Passover meal and what would become known as Jesus' Last Supper. To truly appreciate this passage and the intimacy Jesus shared with his disciples, it is important to understand that they were all lying on the ground, maybe on top of cushions, and as they were reclining, their feet were angled away from the table with their heads near to their neighbor's chest—so near that John was able to incline his head and whisper to Jesus the question, "Lord, who is it?" (v. 25).

John, also known as the disciple whom Jesus loved, was sitting with his head relaxed against the bosom of the Savior of humanity. Implied in their seating arrangements is a level of intimacy that is easily lost on the modern reader. Jesus and his followers were sharing in an intimate and meaningful moment. The intimacy here is a stark contrast to the abandonment that Jesus will experience in just a few hours according to the Gospel accounts.

This intimacy that the disciples were sharing with Jesus Christ pales, though, in comparison to the intimacy that a genuine believer in Christ may share with our Lord, even without the physical closeness John experienced while he felt the rising and falling of Jesus' chest as he breathed. It is difficult to imagine, but our intimacy with Christ is deeper. Allow that to sink into your mind today: you are closer to Christ than even John could have been at the Last Supper, and praise God for this intimacy that is so glorious! You too are reclining with Christ today.

January 4
PRAISE IN SORROW

And he [Job] said, "Naked I came from my mother's womb, and naked shall I return. The LORD gave, and the LORD has taken away; blessed be the name of the LORD." —Job 1:21 (ESV)

Suffering is a part of everyone's life. For many it is a constant companion, closer even than a best friend or a spouse. For others it is only an acquaintance, visiting every few years and departing just as quickly or quietly as it appeared. No matter how close you are to the emotions that suffering brings to the surface of life, you have likely been affected by suffering in several ways throughout your experiences.

Job was a righteous man, a man who did not sin against God, and a man who made sacrifices to God on behalf of his ten children just in case they had sinned. One day he was placed in a difficult situation; all his vast wealth was stolen or destroyed and his children were killed by a collapsing house. Naturally, Job was suffering at this moment in his life. His response, though, reflected his faith in God; he praised God even in the midst of great sorrow.

There is nothing wrong with asking "why?" during moments of sorrow. Neither is there anything wrong with becoming angry or hurt and expressing those emotions in a healthy way. However, room and time should always be made to offer praise to God, even in the moments of our greatest pain and sorrow. For believers in Christ, this moment of sorrow is fleeting, and though it appears to be insatiable in its consumption of our joy, it too shall pass. Sorrow may be a close companion at times, but God is far more intimate with you and desires that you be intimate with God in your time of trouble.

January 5

SLOW DOWN

[Martha] had a sister named Mary, who sat at the Lord's feet and listened to his teaching. But Martha was distracted with much serving. And she went up to him and said, "Lord, do you not care that my sister has left me to serve alone? Tell her then to help me." —Luke 10:39-40 (NIV)

Life is chaotic, full of demands and expectations that we must meet within certain deadlines. Martha's life had suddenly gotten chaotic; Jesus and his disciples were visiting at her home in Bethany, and she was frantically preparing a meal in the kitchen to feed her guests.

There is nothing wrong with feeding our guests when they have made time to visit with us in our home. This is what a good host or hostess does. However, when we busy ourselves so much that we miss truly wonderful and meaningful opportunities in life, then we fail in a greater sense than if we had not fed our guests anything at all.

Mary, Martha's sister, had the right idea. She sat at Jesus' feet and learned from him, basking in his presence and enjoying the moment. Sometimes life gets so busy that we miss meaningful moments like visiting with friends or family because we're working in the kitchen. Sometimes we miss the opportunity to have a deep and meaningful conversation with our significant other because of the soft glow of a smartphone or television screen. Other times we miss the simple joy of God's creation as we rush to take the children to school or try to make it to the bank before it closes.

Slow down today. Give yourself a little more time to enjoy creation on your way to work. Sit with your significant other. Most importantly, commune with God today, taking note of God's love for you.

January 6
EPIPHANY

Today in the city of David there has been born for you a Savior, who is Christ the Lord. —Luke 2:11 (NASB)

Merriam-Webster defines epiphany as "a sudden manifestation or perception of the essential nature or meaning of something." Within the context of Christianity, epiphany is the celebration of the manifestation of God in flesh or the recognition of the arrival of the Messiah. For the Israelites, the Messiah would bring about restoration.

For Christians, the theme of restoration is no less important than it was for our spiritual forebears, the Israelites. We long to be fully restored in relation to God, our Creator and Savior. This restoration comes through Jesus Christ, the Son of God and the promised Messiah of our Old Testament.

Some two thousand years ago, the Magi discovered the manifestation of God in flesh, brought him gifts, and worshiped him. We too worship him and celebrate as the shepherds of Luke 2 celebrate—by praising God for the fulfilled promised of restoration.

On the liturgical Christian calendar, the season of Christmas lasts for twelve days before being capped by today, Epiphany. As this season ends once again, be encouraged to continue to celebrate the wonderful gift of restoration to God through Jesus Christ. Epiphany is the endcap. It is the celebration of a prophecy hundreds of years in the making finally being fulfilled: the prophecy of the coming Messiah, the Anointed One of God who came to forgive us our sins and free us from death. Reflect on the realization of who Jesus truly is this day and commune with God, thanking our Savior for faithfulness.

January 7

SPIRITUAL EXERCISE: LECTIO DIVINA
(DIVINE READING)

On this day you are invited to practice a spiritual exercise, a "divine reading" of a select passage of Scripture. Please follow the guide provided as you meditate on the passage.

> The LORD is my light and salvation; whom shall I fear?
> The LORD is the stronghold of my life; of whom shall I be afraid?
> When evildoers assail me to eat up my flesh, my adversaries and
>   foes, it is they who stumble and fall.
> Though an army encamp against me, my heart shall not fear;
>   though war arise against me, yet I will be confident.
> One thing I have asked of the LORD, that will I seek after; that
>   I may dwell in the house of the Lord all the days of my life,
>   to gaze upon the beauty of the Lord and to inquire in his
>   temple.
> For he will hide me in his shelter in the day of trouble; he will
>   conceal me under the cover of his tent; he will lift me high
>   upon a rock. —Psalm 27:1-5 (ESV)

- Read the passage twice, pausing between each reading for a moment of silence. Identify key words as you read through the passage without elaboration.
- Read the passage again, pause for silence, and answer the following question: Where does the content of the reading touch my life today?
- Read the passage once more, again pausing for silence, and complete this sentence: I believe God wants me to . . . .

January 8
THE IMPORTANCE OF COMMUNITY

Jesus went up on a mountainside and called to him those he wanted, and they came to him. —Mark 3:13 (NIV)

Human beings are social creatures. Even those of us who are introverts require some level of community to maintain a healthy life, whether we admit it or not. Because we are social, isolation is used as a form of punishment in prison; the thought of being completely isolated from one another is truly terrible and terrifying. We crave community and companionship. Even Jesus desired to have companions throughout his earthly ministry.

Today's verse is the beginning of Mark's account of Jesus calling the twelve disciples and the beginning of the formation of the messianic people of God. Out of this first community sprang forth the early church known as the Way—later, Christianity. All Christians are part of this same community that Jesus first formed on a mountainside in Galilee in the early stages of his ministry on earth. As members of that community, we have a responsibility to continue to actively participate in it.

Regular and active participation with fellow believers is good not only for our mental and emotional health but for our spiritual health as well. Get involved, or stay involved, in some way, shape, or form with other believers in Jesus Christ. Follow his lead by building one another up, discipling one another, and enjoying life with each other. We would be mistaken to believe that Jesus was a stiff and staunch teacher all the time; he must have enjoyed life and celebrated with friends. He did attend weddings, after all! You go and do likewise: enjoy the community that surrounds you in the faith.

January 9

AN ESCAPE FROM TEMPTATION

No testing has overtaken you that is not common to everyone. God is faithful, and he will not let you be tested beyond your strength, but with the testing he will also provide the way out so that you may be able to endure it. —1 Corinthians 10:13 (NRSV)

The temptation to claim that God will never put more on our plates than we can handle is great, but it is dangerous. God does not control temptation, but God does offer to God's people an escape from temptation. When facing a moral "fork in the road," we can always find a righteous path that leads away from sin and temptation. This path of righteousness may not be easy, popular, or even socially acceptable according to the fallen world around us, but it is the path of God.

When you face temptation throughout your daily walk, remember this verse and pause to consider the path God is offering that will lead you out of the sinful temptation. We worship and believe in a God who is mighty, patient, and willing to assist us when we stumble or are about to stumble. Look to God for guidance through temptation, and look also to the people God has placed in your life who may have experience that could assist you. The moral dilemmas and temptations that we face in modern society are as old as sin; they may simply look slightly different. The blessing in that is this: our God has plenty of experience helping people facing those dilemmas and temptations and will help you in your moment of temptation. You need only to look to God's guidance.

As you journey throughout your life today, seek God's guidance and allow God's vast knowledge and wisdom to see you through your dilemmas and temptations.

January 10

PHARISAICAL PERFECTION

For I say to you that unless your righteousness surpasses that
of the scribes and Pharisees, you will not enter the kingdom of
heaven. —Matthew 5:20 (NASB)

In order for any of us to enter the kingdom of heaven and stand in the full presence of God, we must be perfect, without blemish, following every iota of the Law with the zeal of the strictest of Pharisees. The reality is that this is impossible. Jesus was teaching in the first, and most famous, of his great discourses throughout the Gospel of Matthew: the Sermon on the Mount. It may be hard to imagine, but Jesus was a bit facetious at times, and this could qualify as a snarky moment.

The Savior of humanity knew that none of us could be righteous enough to enter the kingdom of heaven; Paul would go on to explain that no one is righteous (Rom 3:10). It would be troubling to know that no matter how righteous we are and how closely we follow God's commands, it will never be good enough—except that salvation has been given through Jesus Christ.

While it is true that you will never be good enough according to your own merit to enter the presence of God, Jesus Christ sits at God the Father's right hand, interceding on behalf of all who genuinely believe in him as their Savior. Your faith in Christ will be rewarded more than your attempts to be a good person. Praise God today that, as God passes judgment over your life, you are looked at for your faith in the Son before you are looked at for your behavior. Do not hold yourself, or anyone else, to Pharisaical perfection, but instead rely on the mercy of God the Father through the Son.

January 11

THE PEOPLE OF GOD ARE BLESSED

All you who fear GOD, how blessed you are! how happily you walk on his smooth straight road! —Psalm 128:1 (MSG)

Those who walk in the ways of God are blessed, but what are those ways? Love, joy, peace, mercy, grace, forgiveness . . . the list could easily continue. Central to these qualities is faith in Jesus Christ as God's Son and the Savior of humanity. For people living post-Pentecost, such faith is central to walking in the ways of God and fearing, or respecting and honoring, God.

The blessings God pours out onto his people come directly through the Son, and they are different forms of the ways God's people should follow: love, joy, peace, and so on.

The duty of God's people, and the way to receive these blessings, is first to have faith in Jesus Christ. That faith results in the outpouring of the blessings given by the Father through the Son. Throughout your daily journey, allow the blessings of love, joy, peace, mercy, grace, and forgiveness to pour from you as water pours from a fountain, pure and free. These are the blessings that matter, and these are the blessings that the people of God have been given, but not to hoard or hide under a basket. What good are blessings that are not shared? One of the most irresponsible things a person of God can do is to be a spiritual miser, hoarding their blessings and not using them to uplift their spiritual siblings or share the gospel of Jesus Christ. Be encouraged to continue to walk in the ways of God and share the blessings that God pours out onto you.

January 12

LISTEN TO THE WISDOM OF GOD

. . . but those who listen to me will be secure and will live at ease, without dread of disaster. —Proverbs 1:33 (NRSV)

All too often in life, it is easy to hear the words of one who has more experience, greater wisdom, or is simply smarter than we may be and yet fail to heed their advice. Often, we find ourselves hastily answering, "Yes, I understand," or "I know how to do this!" before we dive headfirst into a project that quickly gets out of hand because of our lack of understanding, skill, or experience.

By the time we realize that we have bitten off more than we can chew, it is embarrassing to return to the one who offered advice at the beginning and ask for further assistance, especially given that we ignored their advice in the first place. However, if our mentor or guide is worth their salt, they will be patient and allow us to swallow our pride, letting that be the end of the shame.

God is similar to earthly mentors; God is wise and willing to share this wisdom with God's people if they will only listen. In this section of the book of Proverbs, Divine Wisdom is speaking to the reader and imploring them to heed the advice and wisdom that comes from this Holy source. As you go about your business today, heed the advice and calling of the Holy Spirit. This Divine messenger provides wisdom to those who attune themselves to hear the Divine voice of reason. Trust in this wisdom, and allow it to guide and protect you from making a fool of yourself. When faced with a difficult decision or challenge, lean on Divine Wisdom rather than your own, and you will be better equipped to make the correct decision and always give God the glory for this guidance.

January 13
FAITH LIKE A CHILD

Jesus said, "Let the little children come to me, and do not hinder them, for the kingdom of heaven belongs to such as these."
—Matthew 19:14 (NIV)

How easy it is for a child to believe in something that is difficult to explain or beyond the modern methods of detection. The faith of a child is wonderful, and adults are called to have this same type of faith when it comes to a relationship with God through Jesus Christ and the Holy Spirit. This faith is difficult to maintain when facing the many questions asked of Christianity today, but it is rewarded when believers meet God face to face.

In the meantime, until the day we meet our Savior, we are called to have faith in Jesus Christ like a child has faith: fearlessly and readily. That is not to say there cannot be questions about God and God's intentions, methods, and motivations, but we cannot allow our desire for cold, hard facts to override our faith in God and Christ.

Jesus invited the children to come to him so that he might bless, teach, and minister to them. Jesus did this so we might learn that we too must come to him as the children did, in faith and with excitement. We then must share our faith with enthusiasm to bring more children to know Jesus Christ as their Savior. Hold on to your faith as a child holds on to their beliefs, but continue to nurture your faith throughout your life and allow it to mature. Run to God in prayer today, and climb onto the Divine lap as a child climbs onto their earthly father's lap. Bask in God's presence.

January 14

SPIRITUAL EXERCISE: THE JESUS PRAYER

"Lord Jesus Christ, Son of God, have mercy on me, a sinner."

This prayer, known as "The Jesus Prayer," finds its roots scattered throughout Scripture. The tax collector prayed, "God, be merciful to me, a sinner!" (Luke 18:13). Paul taught the members of the church in Thessalonica to "pray without ceasing" (1 Thess 5:17). Peter preached to the crowds, "let it be known to all of you and to all the people of Israel that by the name of Jesus Christ of Nazareth . . . there is no other name under heaven given among men by which we must be saved" (Acts 4:10, 12).

The idea behind this spiritual exercise is to practice continual prayer. Practice a breathing technique as you repeat the words of this little prayer: inhale as you recite "Lord Jesus Christ, Son of God," and exhale as you recite, "have mercy on me, a sinner." Recite this prayer throughout your daily routine, practicing the breathing technique alongside the recitation. It is easiest to breathe correctly with a mental recitation as opposed to a verbal recitation. While you do so, focus on the words. You are praying to Jesus Christ, who is both Lord of your life and the Son of God, a holy title that separates him from anything else in this world. You are also asking that Jesus have mercy on you because you are a sinner and have fallen short of God's expectations. This mercy comes from the Son of God, the only one who can give it to you in the first place.

January 15

CHRIST DIED FOR SINNERS

But God demonstrates His own love toward us, in that while we were yet sinners, Christ died for us. —Romans 5:8 (NASB)

How difficult is it for you to do something for someone you know and love? The likely answer is that it is not difficult to do something, even if it means getting out of your comfort zone, for someone you love. How difficult is it, then, to do something for someone you do not know or perhaps for someone you might consider to be an enemy, undeserving of your assistance? The likely answer is that it is difficult to do something for those people.

The truth is that God did something difficult for a bunch of people who do not know God, do not want to know God, or even hate God and everything that God represents. Christ died for them. What's amazing is that all people in this world who have ever lived and ever will live and live today are sinners—all of us—and yet Jesus died on our behalf.

An incredibly wonderful feeling overwhelms those who are believers when they reflect on this passage. Read and know that God did not spare even God's own Son to save a creation that was disobedient, troublesome, and unfaithful. As you go about your daily activities, reflect on the reality that God loves you so much that God's own Son was worth the price of ensuring that you would one day see God's face, even while you were a sinner. Do not take this gift for granted, but instead share it with others whom you encounter today and allow them an opportunity to know salvation despite their sins. Take a moment today to praise God for God's great love of you.

January 16

SIN IS MISSING THE MARK

. . . for all have sinned and fall short of the glory of God . . .
—Romans 3:23 (ESV)

Archery is a skill that is focused on releasing an arrow into a target accurately. A skilled archer may be able to do this from a great distance and even in unruly weather conditions such as high wind or rain. However, for an archer to be successful their equipment must be pristine, their bow must be flexible yet strong, the string must not be frayed, and the arrows must be straight. If any one or more of these pieces of equipment are not in good order, then the difficulty of making an accurate shot increases unnecessarily.

When we sin, we are much like an archer who is using a bent arrow; it may fly, but we are uncertain as to whether it will hit the target or something else in that general direction. Out of a sinful heart fly bent arrows of hate, cruelty, lust, fear, and so on. These sinful things fly in all directions, inflicting great harm on ourselves and on those around us. When we sin, we miss the mark just as an archer misses when using poor equipment.

Thankfully, though, we have a master bowyer and fletcher who is willing to provide us with artfully crafted equipment that will ensure that we cannot fail. Jesus Christ died and was resurrected so that all who believe in him would have salvation and be rescued from sin and from missing the mark. When we rely on him throughout our lives, we will draw arrows of righteousness, peace, and grace from our quivers. Look to him today and rely on his grace for the moments when you loose a rogue arrow of sin from your heart and miss the mark.

January 17

BEING CONTENT

. . . for I have learned in whatever state I am, to be content . . .
—Philippians 4:11b (NKJV)

Being content is not something the owners of corporations that sell various trinkets would want for the masses of people who see their advertisements. Advertisements of all kinds show individuals or groups getting excited by whatever item is being advertised—a car, the latest electronic device, the newest fashion, or even a popular carbonated beverage.

Paul was writing to the Philippian believers and had received a gift from them so that he might continue in his ministry efforts. However, Paul explains that he had learned something important in his life. He had experienced moments with plenty of resources and moments with limited resources. Throughout all these moments, the apostle had learned that there is no need to fret over what is lacking or to hoard what is in excess; we only need to be content in the moment in which we find ourselves immediately.

If we allow the world to drive us, we will always be left wanting more. We will inevitably face an unquenchable thirst to have more things, a bigger house, a nicer car, or whatever else we may desire. The flip side is true too; if we find that we are lacking in the base essentials of life, we will be consumed with the desire to meet our needs, feed our bellies, quench our literal thirst, and provide shelter. Both extremes may lead to anxiety and a lack of trust in God. Practice being content throughout your daily journey, and recognize the Divine peace that enters into your life through this practice today.

January 18

HOLY GROUND

"Do not come any closer," God said. *"Take off your sandals, for the place where you are standing is holy ground."* —*Exodus 3:5 (NIV)*

The location of the burning bush was ordinary. There was nothing special about the ground itself. However, the presence of God within that bush made the ground and everything else holy. For Moses and others throughout the Old Testament the places where they experienced the presence of God were deemed holy because God was in those places.

Christians, people of the New Testament, believe in the continued presence of the Holy Spirit, the third person of the Trinity. This Spirit is with all believers everywhere they go in their lives, and therefore all ground that we trod is holy ground because the presence of God goes with us and is in each place. The presence of God may not manifest itself in your life today as a burning bush and command you to remove your footwear, but rest assured that the presence journeys throughout this life with you today.

Do not be intimidated by this constant presence, but be encouraged. Encouraged to face each of the challenges life throws at you today with confidence. Encouraged to walk with joy and peace as your companions because the God of joy and peace dwells not in a bush but within your very being. Praise God today for the gift of making all ground holy, for this means that God's presence is there, and that means God is with you always. Rest easy in that knowledge today as you face your daily journey.

January 19
DEVOTED TO TEACHING

They devoted themselves to the apostles' teaching and fellowship,
to the breaking of bread and the prayers. —Acts 2:42 (NRSV)

The early church and the first believers had devoted themselves to ensuring that the membership would continue to mature and grow spiritually and faithfully. One thing they did was study the teaching of the apostles, which included Jesus' earthly teachings that are recorded in the four canonical Gospel accounts found in the New Testament as well as the teachings he shared with his disciples during the various resurrection appearances.

The goal of a believer in Jesus Christ is to continue to grow in knowledge and maturity; that is done through the active practice of Jesus' teachings throughout a person's life. These teachings include loving God above all, loving neighbor and enemy alike, being faithful and fruitful in sharing the gospel, and avoiding hatred, lust, and sin in general.

Let the example of the early church, learning from the apostles' teachings, be a guide for you today and every day. Devote yourself to greater scriptural and spiritual knowledge and maturity through active learning from personal readings of Scripture, small group studies, and active participation in communal worship experiences. These things are all gifts from God that allow us to continue to grow closer to the Divine and closer to our fellow believers.

January 20

JOHN THE BAPTIST? ELIJAH? CHRIST!

"Who do people say that the Son of Man is?" And they said, "Some say John the Baptist, others say Elijah . . . ." He said to them, "But who do you say I am?" Peter replied, "You are the Christ, the Son of the living God." —Matthew 16:13b-16 (ESV)

Jesus was privately communing with his closest disciples, having recently sparred with the Pharisees and Sadducees regarding a sign from heaven. Jesus begins by testing his followers, asking them who the people think he is, and the disciples make a list of potential identities that others have associated with Jesus. While it is undoubtedly flattering to be associated with each of these figures, none of them carry the worthiness to defeat sin and death.

Jesus then asks the disciples directly who they think he is, and Peter, as usual, speaks up and declares that Jesus is more than a prophet and greater than Elijah or John the Baptist; he is the Christ, the Anointed One, the Son of the living God. There is so much packed into this response from Peter. Jesus is the Son of the living God. Unlike the pagan gods of the cities and regions surrounding them, specifically in Caesarea Philippi, God is alive, and Jesus is God's unique Son. The title "Christ," or "Messiah," means Anointed One and points to Jesus being the one whom the prophets of old said would come and bring salvation to those who believe.

The significance of this passage cannot be missed: our hope, future, and salvation rests on this divine man—this man who is both human and divine, this man who is the Christ, your Savior, the Son of the living God. Reflect on the true identity of Jesus Christ today, and thank him for his identity because it means salvation for all who believe.

January 21

SPIRITUAL EXERCISE: PSALM OF PRAISE

Today, simply reflect on Psalm 98. What does the Spirit tell you through these words? Do you find it easy to offer praises to God today? If not, then commune with God and listen for the Divine voice. Can you identify what is preventing your ability to offer praises?

> *Oh, sing to the LORD a new song, for he has done marvelous things! His right hand and his holy arm have worked salvation for him.*
> *The LORD has made known his salvation; he has revealed his righteousness in the sight of the nations.*
> *He has remembered his steadfast love and faithfulness to the house of Israel. All the ends of the earth have seen the salvation of our God.*
> *Make a joyful noise to the LORD, all the earth; break forth into joyous song and sing praises!*
> *Sing praises to the LORD with the lyre, with the lyre and the sound of melody.*
> *With trumpets and the sound of the horn make a joyful noise before the King, the LORD!*
> *Let the sea roar, and all that fills it; the world and those that dwell in it!*
> *Let the rivers clap their hands; let the hills sing for joy together*
> *before the LORD, for he comes to judge the earth. He will judge the world with righteousness, and the peoples with equity.*
> *—Psalm 98 (ESV)*

January 22

WE ARE JARS OF CLAY

But we have this treasure in clay jars, so that it may be made clear that this extraordinary power belongs to God and does not come from us. —2 Corinthians 4:7 (NRSV)

We are but jars of clay, molded, glazed, and fired in the kiln by our potter, our creator. Like jars that are made of clay, we are fragile in nature. Whether it is literal in that our bodies are easily broken, damaged, or riddled with disease, or mental, or emotional, or even spiritual wounds—we are easily damaged. The cracks and fractures that we accumulate over a lifetime may cause us to be less attractive, and they can be formed by the sins that we commit.

Some of these cracks can been seen on the surface of our lives, while others remain hidden from prying eyes, although we know that they are indeed present. Our cracked condition is both tragic and wonderful. It is unfortunate that we are damaged because of sin, but it is fantastic that God may still use these broken clay vessels to share his gospel of grace and mercy with the world.

When we are believers in Christ, it is not the vessel that should draw attention but the treasure held within the vessel. When we hold the Light of Christ within our lives, it shines through the cracks in the clay that makes us up. It is the treasure that is most important to us and to those around us. The mercy of God outshines the cracks that are visible in our lives. Be encouraged today to share your faith in Jesus Christ with another person. Also remember that God's great love for you, embodied in Jesus Christ, has turned your cracks, your sins, into examples of his mercy for others to embrace. Embrace the treasure of grace that dwells in you today.

January 23

CONFESSION IS GOOD FOR THE SOUL

If we confess our sins, He is faithful and righteous to forgive us our sins and to cleanse us from all unrighteousness. —1 John 1:9 (NASB)

Confession of sins is a healthy exercise for all believers to continue to practice throughout their lives. Confession provides many positive rewards for a believer, including serving as a time of reflection, encouraging humility, remembering the need for grace and mercy, and receiving forgiveness and purity from God through Christ.

There is a good deal of confessing going on in Christianity. First and foremost, we confess that Jesus Christ is our Lord and Savior. Following that, there is continued confession that we have sinned against God and our neighbor. This latter form of confession is what the author of the letter was referring to: confession of sin. This type of confession yields wonderful rewards and should not be disregarded or overlooked. However, the flip side of the coin is that we should avoid punishing ourselves in some horrific act of mortification of the flesh such as seen practiced by Silas in the popular film *The Da Vinci Code*.

As you face your day, be encouraged to go to the Lord in prayer and confess the sins that you have committed. Avoid beating yourself up; instead, be appreciative to our God that, though he is fully aware of your sins, he is willing to forgive each of them and purify you, making you righteous and worthy of entering God's presence. God loves you and desires you to be a humble follower of his Son, Jesus. God desperately desires to forgive you and make the relationship you have with him whole through forgiveness of your sins.

January 24

YOU CANNOT SERVE BOTH GOD AND . . .

No one can serve two masters. Either you will hate the one and love the other, or you will be devoted to the one and despise the other. You cannot serve both God and money. —Matthew 6:24 (NIV)

Many things in this life compete for our devotion and attention. Some things rightly deserve our attention: our spouse/significant other, our children, our jobs, our friends, our church family, and so on. None of these, though, should override our devotion to God. All these things come in second to God, or so they should.

While money is often viewed as the greatest master in this world, and it certainly is near the top, it is not alone in tempting believers away from serving God first in their lives. Even the things in this life that God has blessed us with and that are promises for various biblical characters can be different masters to serve, including our families and the church.

As you go about your activities today, take some time to give thanks to God for the many blessings he has placed in your life, no matter how great or small. Be on guard, however, recognizing that the blessings in this life pale in comparison to the blessings God has for you in paradise. Remember that the masters of this life demanding that we serve them are hollow and meaningless. They cannot give to you the same peace, love, and salvation that God has offered through his Son, Jesus Christ. Thank God today for your family, your shelter, and your financial resources. Be thankful most of all that God is your true master, that God is a gracious and loving master to all who faithfully serve the Divine.

January 25

GOD IS SAVIOR AND REDEEMER

I will deliver you out of the hand of the wicked and redeem you from the grasp of the ruthless. —Jeremiah 15:21 (NRSV)

In the original context of this verse, God was speaking through the prophet Jeremiah to the people of Judah and Jerusalem. An enemy, the Babylonian army, was encroaching on the people of God, and hope seemed to be lost. Gloom and doom had been prophesied, and the people had been unfaithful to God.

We too live in a world that seems to be lacking in hope. Enemies surround us in all forms: terrorism, fear, financial instability, and the list goes on. But we have a silver lining that encompasses this dark cloud of the world in which we live. Believers in God have the hope of deliverance from the wickedness and cruelty. These things that threaten to overwhelm us, that appear to have already overwhelmed the world in which we live, are no match for our God.

The wickedness and cruelty of this world that are embodied by international terrorism, national financial instability, and local hatred and mean-spiritedness threaten us every day and sometimes indeed overwhelm us; however, our God promises to deliver us from these things. Look to God today, despite what is reported on the various news media outlets, despite what threats are made and what disasters appear to loom over the horizon. Look to God and trust that his grace and mercy will see you through these trials and tribulations. Trust him today and give him praise because these wicked and cruel things are not the end. They hold no true power over you. Remember that God is your redeemer and savior from these evil things, and find peace in his divine presence today.

January 26

STRENGTH TO
THE WEARY

He gives strength to the weary, and to him who lacks might He increases power. —Isaiah 40:29 (NASB)

The sources of weariness are innumerable and often overwhelming: school, job, or career responsibilities, relationship conflicts, volunteer work, lack of Sabbath or time away from the daily grind. Any one of these alone can cause weariness to overwhelm us, include illness, injury, or simply a lack of restful sleep, and we have enough examples here to make us weary.

But God is a God of rest and restoration; he is willing and able to help each of his people be strengthened and renewed as we feel weary and worn down. We must be willing to participate in the process of renewal, however. Our God will give us strength, but we must slow down and allow time in our lives to commune with him and receive this renewal.

Take time today to get away from all the things that busy your mind and body. Rest in the presence of God. This will be the most difficult aspect of being renewed and given strength in the face of your weariness: to put away all distractions in your life. Isolate yourself today if only for a few moments, and enter into a time of prayer and communion with God. Turn off your phone, television, and/or computer, remove yourself as best as you can from the busyness of life, and if you need to, recite the Jesus Prayer to focus your mind. Enjoy the presence of God at some point today, and be refreshed and strengthened to go and face the challenges that life throws at you. The sources of weariness may be innumerable, but the source of strength is divine and is always there to renew his people.

January 27
EVIL LIKES THE DARK

When your eyes are healthy, your whole body also is full of light.
But when they are unhealthy, your body also is full of darkness.
—Luke 11:34b (NIV)

Everywhere we look, light and dark appear to be the mascots of good and evil. In literature, the hero stands in the light while the villain hides in the shadows. In movies, lighting effects tend to place the "good guy" in a sort of spotlight shining above and somewhat behind them while the "bad guy" is partially hidden by grim shadows and poor lighting. This is all done intentionally to give us a clear, albeit somewhat subtle idea as to who we should root for and who should be booed.

Scripture is no different in terms of its use of light and darkness as themes of good and evil. Perhaps, if pressed, the many authors and directors who use similar archetypes would cite the Bible as inspiration.

Regardless of secular entertainment's source for this idea, we see that Jesus is using light and darkness to teach his disciples about being his followers. John describes Jesus as the life and light of men (John 1:4), and as such, when he dwells in our lives, his light shines from us and others will know that there is something different about those who follow him. This difference is that Jesus' followers act out of love, peace, patience, mercy, and righteousness while the world around them acts out of selfishness, cruelty, impatience, and evil. This evil likes the darkness because it is able to hide and then strike without warning. It cannot, however, stand against the Light of Christ. Allow the Light of Christ to shine from your life this day and conquer the evil that attempts to sway you away from him.

January 28

SPIRITUAL EXERCISE: GUIDED PRAYER

You are encouraged to enter a time of prayer and meditation. Are there burdens weighing on your heart or mind today? If so, take them to God. Petition him to give you wisdom and guidance to face those challenges today or soon.

Is there strife in your life between family members, friends, coworkers, or fellow church members? If so, ask that the Lord of mercy and peace will overwhelm each person involved in the situation. Pray that God will soften the hearts of all involved and open each mind to be willing to hear each other out with the goal of settling the problem.

Do you have questions regarding your faith? Approach the God of all things, asking him to grant you clarity and to ease your heart and mind concerning your faith in him.

Suggested Scripture: James 1:5; John 15:12-13; Psalm 13

Suggested Prayer:

O Gracious God,
I thank you for your Son and my Savior, Jesus Christ. I ask that
you grant me the wisdom necessary to make the decisions that
reflect my faith in you and that would serve as examples of your
presence in my life. Please allow me to find resolutions for any
negative conflict that exists in my life between myself and others.
Grant each of us peace in our relationships. I ask that you also
strengthen my faith in you alone. Grant me a greater under-
standing of who you are and of the relationship we have together.
In Christ's name I pray, amen.

January 29

BE STRONG IN THE FAITH

Be watchful, stand firm in the faith, act like men, be strong.
—1 Corinthians 16:13 (ESV)

Many things in this life would attempt to erode our faith: evil, temptation, hardship, strife, and many more. However, our faith should be firmly rooted in Christ, so much so that we are able to withstand the world's attempts to wear us down and bash our faith into irreparable pieces.

Paul, the writer of our text from 1 Corinthians, uses the phrase "act like men," which was common throughout the Septuagint (the Greek translation of the Hebrew Bible or Old Testament). This phrase was meant to encourage listeners to remain faithful in the face of adversity and to act with bravery, courage, strength, and obedience to the Lord. All of this was built on faith in God's power, no matter the challenges or circumstances being faced. The Corinthian Christians were being encouraged to face their challenges with strong faith in God. We too, whether man, woman, girl, or boy, are called to this same strong faith in God's power despite our challenges and difficulties in life.

Be encouraged today to face the challenges in your life with a strong faith that is deeply rooted in Christ. Our God is a God whose power exceeds all things and who is above all things, and therefore we are right to trust in him and maintain strong faith in him. When you feel weak in faith, go to God in prayer, with patience, and seek his face through communion with him. Remember the rewards of faith in God through Christ: eternal life in paradise away from the things that would try to erode our faith in the first place.

January 30

LIFE WITH GOD BRINGS LIFE WITH LOVE

Whoever does not love does not know God, for God is love.
—John 4:8 (NRSV)

The God of Christianity is a God of love, and this is revealed through God's grace, mercy, and forgiveness given to all who genuinely believe he sent his Son to live, die, and be resurrected on the third day for the sins of humanity. This is not his only attribute, but it is a core part of the gospel message. By default, Christians should be a people of love. A genuine believer in Jesus Christ will be a person who is changed from the core of their being outward to reflect this decision. This change is one that was made possible by God's love for the believer, and it is revealed through the believer's ability to love their neighbor selflessly.

Once you become a believer, it does not mean you are only capable of loving other people. If that were true, then I would not be a genuine believer. We are not changed instantaneously into someone who is overflowing with love for everyone else, but we are equipped to share the love of Christ and God with the rest of humanity. We are equipped because the God of love has sent his Spirit to dwell in all who genuinely believe, and when we allow the Spirit to work in our lives, this love flows from us like water from a fountain, freely and for all.

Do not be discouraged when you do not have love for all people all the time; this is a result of the sinful state of the world in which we live. However, do be encouraged to practice this great and unconditional love with all whom you encounter in your daily activities. God is a God of love, and we, imperfect as we may be, are called to reflect that love into all the world throughout our lives.

January 31

GOD DESIRES THAT WE BE MERCIFUL

For I delight in loyalty rather than sacrifice, And in the knowledge of God rather than burnt offerings. —Hosea 6:6 (NASB)

God is merciful to humanity; this was revealed through Jesus Christ primarily, but we see it also as a theme throughout the Old Testament. Hosea 6:6 reveals to us that God wants his people to show mercy to one another before he wants us to make sacrifices to him or, for the modern reader, to worship him.

The world in which we live is a cruel and merciless place, a place where advancement at the cost of relationships is common, a place where the "me, myself, and I" mentality reigns supreme. This is not the way of God, and neither should it be the way of his people.

God has revealed to the world how merciful he truly is in sending his Son to die in place of humanity, to bear the burdens of sins he did not commit and suffer a cruel death that should have been reserved for all of us. This mercy grants each believer in Christ an eternity of peace, love, and joy in the presence of our God.

Because of this wonderful show of mercy, we too are expected to show mercy. As you encounter others throughout your life, remember the mercy that God has first shown to you—mercy that was undeserved and yet free. As you remember this mercy, be encouraged to share it with others as well. Reveal that you are indeed a follower of the One True God who has shown humanity the greatest mercy of all by showing those around you undeserved mercy as well.

February 1

TRUE WORSHIP, NOT A SHOW

For I desire steadfast love and not sacrifice, the knowledge of God rather than burnt offerings. —Hosea 6:6 (ESV)

One of the deepest desires of God is that God's people, those who genuinely believe in Jesus Christ as their Savior, would worship him sincerely, without the fluff of false worship or going through the motions of a given worship service at a local church building. The temptation to offer pseudo worship, going through the motions, is great indeed. Any one of us faces this temptation every time we gather with our fellow believers for worship. We may sing the songs, we may tithe, and we may even take notes during the homily that is offered, but there is something missing, and that is honest worship of God.

The people whom God was addressing through the prophet Hosea had failed to offer true worship. They were going through the motions of offering sacrifices to God without any sense of real worship and praise of God. Not only that, but the people were also guilty of idolatry, worshiping the false gods of the surrounding people groups.

Steeped in a secular society, we are tempted to commit idolatry in various ways. We also face the temptation to offer a form of lip service to God that we attempt to pass off as real worship. We may fool those who sit near us during communal worship, but our salvation does not rest on convincing our pastor, neighbor, or family that we worship God; it rests on truly accepting God's grace through Christ and then knowing and worshiping God. Be encouraged to offer God genuine worship, for this is the least we can do considering our salvation and God's infinite grace.

February 2

KNOCK, KNOCK

Here I am! I stand at the door and knock. If anyone hears my voice and opens the door, I will come in and eat with that person, and they with me. —Revelation 3:20 (NIV)

Jesus appeared to John and dictated seven letters to be sent to seven different churches throughout Asia Minor. One of those letters was bound for Laodicea. This church had a reputation for being lukewarm in their spiritual lives. With this lukewarm attitude in mind, Jesus offered a message in the letter addressed to the believers in Laodicea: "If you welcome me [Jesus] in, I will be with you."

The knocking on the door is Jesus knocking on the hearts of those who claim to believe in him as their Savior. It is a reminder that he is still searching for his people and that he desires to have a relationship with you, if only you will welcome him into your life as you would a beloved family member or friend.

Jesus is seeking after you today. Will you open up to him and allow him to be close to you? The imagery of eating together with Jesus depicts an intimate setting. Picture the Last Supper that Jesus had with his disciples, the intimacy they shared in that last meal together before his crucifixion. This is what Jesus seeks with you: an intimacy that is deep and rich. An intimacy that is beyond anything that words may express. Open the door of your life today and allow Jesus into your most secret places. Dine with our Lord and Savior on this day, enjoying your intimate relationship with him.

February 3

GOD IS YOUR STRENGTH

My flesh and my heart may fail, but God is the strength of my heart and my portion forever. —Psalm 73:26 (NRSV)

We are made of flesh and blood, finite beings that have limits. Because we have limits, we will eventually become weary; our fleshly bodies will fail, and we will "give out" as the saying goes. This type of failure is brought about by our inability to continue to move forward. Be it physically, emotionally, mentally, or spiritually, we have reached our limits. These failures reveal themselves in many ways: literal physical weaknesses, the inability to focus, emotional stress, and the temptation to sin.

These limitations and failures do not apply to our God, though; he transcends human frailty, limitations, and weaknesses. The psalmist offers a wonderful reminder that though we may fail in our weaknesses and lack the strength or ability to continue to press on, God is able to provide strength to those who lean on and trust in him.

As you go through your daily activities, you may become weary and your flesh may fail; worry not in these moments of weakness, and look instead to God. Seek his strength to see you through your life and, most importantly, seek his strength to see you through temptation. No matter how life wears you down or what saps your strength, causing your flesh to fail, always look to God's strength. God is the greatest source of strength for his people no matter the circumstances: the death of a loved one, the loss of a job or home, or the daily grind of life. Allow God to be your strength always.

February 4

SPIRITUAL EXERCISE: FASTING

When we think of fasting, the image that pops into the minds of many people is a break from food and perhaps even water. Many of the world's religions practice a fast from food and drink during high holidays. Some denominations of Christianity do, too. Fasting need not be limited to food, however. An individual may fast from anything that requires time during their regular routine. The purpose of fasting is not simply to abstain from whatever you are fasting from. There is much more to fasting than that.

When an individual fasts from food, for instance, during the time that would be spent eating a meal or snack the individual instead meditates, prays, reads Scripture, or uses some other method to strive to encounter the Divine.

Jesus fasted, and so did many other figures from Scripture in both the Old and New Testaments. While they fasted from food, that is not necessarily the path you have to take. You are encouraged to fast today. Start small. Perhaps fast from social media for the remainder of the day, or skip supper tonight, or plan to fast from one meal tomorrow. When you fast from something that normally takes time in your day, spend that time with God in prayer, reading Scripture, meditating on your relationship with the Divine, and worshiping God. Consider what it might mean to introduce fasting into your routine, whether daily or once a week. What would that look like? If this is an exercise that has benefited you, consider incorporating the spiritual discipline of fasting into your regular walk of faith.

February 5

CONQUER EVIL WITH GOOD

Do not be conquered by evil but conquer evil with good.
—Romans 12:21 (author's translation)

In the world of humanity, it is easy to see that evil exists; even nonreligious people, when pressed, may confess that there is evil in this world. Evil manifests itself in many ways. On the global scale, we bear witness to war, terrorism, natural disasters, sex trafficking, and many more evils. On a localized scale, we bear witness to sickness, depression, racism, sexism, death, and more.

While the global-scale evils may not be conquered by any one individual, the localized evils may be taken head on. Reflect for a moment on your daily life. Is there an evil that constantly reveals itself to you? Perhaps it manifests itself as hatred for another group of people based on race, gender, socioeconomic class, sexual orientation, or some other subgrouping. Perhaps the evil is manifested in a lack of concern for others. If you wrestle with such feelings, then pray that God will give you the strength to eradicate this evil in your life.

If, on the other hand, this evil manifests itself in the life of someone you encounter regularly, pray that God will allow you to be an example of Christ's love to that person and ask that Christ's goodness will pour from you in such a way that will truly conquer that evil. While we cannot conquer evil by our own effort, we *can* conquer evil with the goodness of Christ. Be encouraged to shine Christ's goodness in your life today and serve as a beacon of Christ's hope in an otherwise bleak world.

February 6

DIVINE COMPULSION

And He said to them, "Why is it that you were looking for Me?
Did you not know that I had to be in My Father's house?"
—Luke 2:49 (NASB)

Not much is known about Jesus' life prior to the beginning of his earthly ministry. Only Luke's account says anything about his childhood beyond his birth. There, we learn that he was compelled to be in the temple in Jerusalem. Upon reading Luke 2:49, it would not be incorrect to put emphasis on the word "had." Jesus *had* to be in his Father's house and doing his Father's work.

This same divine compulsion drew Jesus to pray early in the mornings, to be baptized, to share in the Passover meal with the man who would betray him, and eventually to die on the cross.

This divine compulsion that drove Christ throughout his earthly ministry is the same compulsion God has to love you. As you go through your life today, facing the various challenges that appear along your path, remember that God is driven to love you and embrace you. Remember that you are valuable in the eyes of God. Your worth was proven through the compulsion Jesus felt in his life, even as a young man of twelve years old. Jesus was compelled to be near God and do the work that God the Father had placed in his life. That work was to bring salvation to humanity and into the lives of those who would believe.

The same compulsion that drove Christ to the temple and the cross still drives his people today. What is God compelling you to do in your life to serve and honor him?

February 7

THE PEOPLE OF GOD

*For this is the covenant that I will make with the house of Israel
after those days, declares the LORD: I will put my law within
them, and I will write it on their hearts. And I will be their
God, and they shall be my people. —Jeremiah 31:33 (ESV)*

The people of the old covenant, the Israelites, had a special place in God's heart. They were his and he was theirs; nothing would come between God and his people, except their unfaithfulness. A new covenant was necessary to mend the relationship between human and Divine—a covenant that would redefine the relationship, offer greater intimacy, and bring salvation.

The passage from which Jeremiah 31:33 is drawn looks forward to that new covenant between God and his people. The idea of God writing on the hearts of his people is intimate, reflecting God's desire not only to be known by the people but also to be with the people.

Christians now live under that new covenant, where God is our God and we are his people. This idea that we are God's people is not an idea of possession but of intimacy and love. We are in a relationship with God that goes beyond all understanding.

Remember today that you are God's and he is yours. The relationship you have with God is one of deep love. As you go about your business today, you are encouraged to reflect on what it means to be a part of God's people of the new covenant, to be in an intimate relationship with the God of the universe. What a blessing it is to be counted as a part of God's people through the new covenant of Jesus Christ.

February 8
I WAS HUNGRY

I was hungry and you fed me . . . . —Matthew 25:35a (MSG)

The call of a Christian is not limited to the spiritual aspects of life, including faith in Jesus Christ. While faith will indeed allow you to be totally united with God in paradise forevermore, your life should reflect that faith. In Matthew 25, Jesus is teaching that those who feed the hungry of this world are also feeding him. The Food Aid Foundation estimates that there are about 795 million people in the world who do not have enough food to lead a healthy and active lifestyle ("Hunger Statistics"). That is about one in nine people in the world. While most of these people live in developing countries that may be far away, there are still ways to ensure that you are living out your faith by helping to end their hunger.

Perhaps you do not need to look as far away as a developing country; perhaps you know of hungry people in your own area. Maybe you are one of those hungry people. Whatever your situation, you are encouraged to begin to prayerfully consider how you might help those who are hungry and do not get enough to eat. Pray that God will help you find a local charity that seeks to ease the burden of hunger in your area or around the world. Many food banks, soup kitchens, and food pantries require regular donations and volunteers to assist in their quest to help the needy of this world. Jesus teaches his followers to act out their faith by feeding the hungry and caring for those who cannot care for themselves. Be encouraged to act on your faith today.

February 9
GOD IS MINDFUL OF YOU

When I consider your heavens, the work of your fingers, the moon and the stars, which you have set in place, what is mankind that you are mindful of them, human beings that you care for them? —Psalm 8:3-4 (NIV)

It is easy to become overwhelmed when you look around at creation, whether you are beholding something as grand as the night sky with the winking stars, pondering the enormity of space, or you are studying a leaf that has sprouted from a tree in your yard, noticing the veins and curves of the little sign of life.

No matter what part of creation catches your eye and causes you to pause, it is a creation of God's; he is above all and in all. However, no matter how beautiful, intricate, or awe inspiring, this is nothing compared to you in the eyes of God. As Psalm 8 continues, it describes how humanity is a little lower than God but is above all the rest of creation. What a blessing it is to be considered a part of God's favored creation.

As you go about your journey today, remember this blessing: God considers you, along with all of humanity, above all the rest of creation. You are valued in the eyes of God as someone with whom he would commune. While it may seem that you are small in comparison to the rest of the vast creation, you are important in the eyes of God. You may never know why God shows you favor, but understanding that is not as important as relishing in the fact that God considers you so important that he would send his Son to die so you could have peace and life for eternity. Thank God today for the wonderful gift of considering you the pinnacle of all creation.

February 10
JUSTICE FOR ALL

But let justice roll down like waters, and righteousness like an ever-flowing stream. —Amos 5:24 (NRSV)

The Old Testament prophets were primarily concerned about the idolatry of the people of Israel and their unfaithfulness to God. However, there was another concern that occupied the prophets throughout their ministries and writings: injustice, particularly when it concerned the poor and their treatment at the hands of those who were higher up on the socioeconomic ladder.

This concern is equally burdensome today, removed some two millennia from the last pen stroke that saw Scripture put to paper. The world in which we live is corrupt and fallen, and nothing will see it restored to its original point of perfection short of Christ's return. However, in the "here and now," it is part of the calling of all Christians to seek justice for those who are burdened by the corrupt world. Primarily those are still the poor but also widows, the elderly, orphans, and anyone else may fall into this category of being burdened by the world. Amos spoke of justice and righteousness flowing like water. The imagery brings thoughts of being cleansed and refreshed by this outpouring. Be encouraged by Amos's words that came from God.

While you may not be able to impact the world on a global scale today, seek justice in your own walk. Extend a hand of generosity, compassion, and love toward someone today when you may not have done so before. Remember that Christ has extended you that same hand, and as his follower, you are to embody that sort of action in the world as his representative and ambassador to those whom you encounter.

February 11

SPIRITUAL EXERCISE: GUIDED PRAYER

Do you feel called to go into the world and share the gospel of Jesus Christ with someone? If so, have you answered that call? Go to God in prayer and ask that he will guide you to the person in your life who needs to hear the gospel or needs a reminder of the love God has for them.

While not all Christians are called to be pastors, missionaries, or other full-time ministers, all Christians are called to minister in some way, shape, or form. Pray that God will encourage and equip you to answer his call to minister to someone in your life, to build a relationship with someone that is based on love and care for them.

Suggested Scripture: Matthew 28:16-20; Acts 8:26-40

Suggested Prayer

> *Creator of all things,*
> *I thank you for Jesus Christ and my salvation. I ask that you grant me the knowledge, tact, and ability to minister to those around me. Heighten my senses and make me aware of those who suffer and need the gospel of Jesus Christ. Grant me all that is necessary to be the salt and light that you have called me to be throughout my journey in this life. Make me into a faithful and devoted disciple, and mature me in such a way that I will be the sharpest tool I can be for the tasks you have placed in my life. These things I pray in the blessed name of Christ and through the Holy Spirit, amen.*

February 12
LIFE'S NOT ALL SMILES

*And the LORD afflicted the child that Uriah's wife bore to
David, and he became sick. . . . On the seventh day the child
died. —2 Samuel 12:15b, 18a (ESV)*

David had sinned against Uriah, Bathsheba, and God. The punishment
of this sin was the death of the first child born to David and Bathsheba.
Many in this world who are labeled "pastor" try to fool their listeners into
thinking that God does not want anything bad to befall them. That God
will bless his faithful with wealth, health, and happiness like a magical genie
or an overly zealous parishioner passing out handfuls of candy during the
fall festival.

God does not operate in that fashion. God does not put a hedge of
protection around his people, ensuring that they will be guarded from all
harm. Do not be fooled by this aspect of the prosperity gospel. Instead of
praying that God will protect you from the storm, pray that God will help
you to grow from the storm.

David suffered the loss of a child. This is something many Christian
parents suffer even today. Scholars and theologians have attempted to
answer the question of why these evils occur if an all-good and all-powerful
God exists, and no answer seems to satisfy. This study is called theodicy.

As you journey through life, remember that God has never promised
to protect you from all harm or heartache. Remember that life is not all
smiles, but also remember that one day there will be nothing but smiles as
we see the face of our Savior and enjoy the full presence of the Triune God.
Weep today, for tomorrow all of your tears will be dried and your burdens
lifted.

February 13

CLEANSED

Come now, and let us reason together, though your sins are as scarlet, they will be as white as snow; Though they are red like crimson, they will be like wool. —Isaiah 1:18 (NASB)

Stains are often hard to remove. There is a full line of products specifically made to remove stains from clothing, from furniture, from carpets, and so on. Each of these products claims to be better than their competitors. Each advertises that they remove stains without much fuss. Some of them may live up to the hype, but none of them are equipped to remove stains from the human soul.

There is a huge difference between the colors red and white. If one were to wash a load of white clothes with a red item, the result would be pink socks and undershirts. On the other hand, if one were to spill a little bleach on a red shirt, the result would be a red shirt with white spots. As Christians, this sort of discoloration is exactly what has happened.

The sins that you commit profane your soul, making you unworthy to enter into the presence of God. However, when you place your faith in Christ, you will be cleansed. The red that has stained your soul is removed as if by a supernatural stain remover. It is revealed that the red uniform you have been wearing was white; your sin dyed it red. God's love, through Christ, has cleansed you and made you pure, like white wool. Be encouraged to continue to deepen your faith and grow in your relationship with God through Christ, for it is through this relationship that you are truly cleansed and made pure.

February 14

BE CONCERNED WITH WHAT YOU CONTROL

And the LORD said, "You pity the plant, for which you did not labor, nor did you make it grow, which came into being in a night and perished in a night." —Jonah 4:10 (ESV)

Too often it is easy to become depressed over various things in this life that are out of your control. No matter where you fall on the political spectrum, the politicians in control often disappoint us. It is easy to become worked up over various laws that do not align with your beliefs or to become bent out of shape at government spending and budgeting.

Jonah was upset that God had spared the people of Nineveh from divine wrath and anger. In response to God's compassion, Jonah became angry and went out of the city and sat under some shade. While Jonah sat, God allowed a vine to grow and offer more shade to the disgruntled prophet. However, God also caused the scorching sun and dry wind to wither the vine. This displeased Jonah to the point that he was ready to die.

God reminds Jonah in today's verse that the existence of the vine is out of the prophet's control. So too is sparing the people of Nineveh, no matter how sinful they have been prior to their repentance.

As you journey through life today, avoid becoming frustrated with the things that are clearly out of your control. Instead of expending time and energy on your frustrations, use those resources to worship God and share the gospel of Jesus Christ with those around you. Use your time wisely and focus on what you can control, specifically living as a Christian.

February 15

PAGING THE SPIRITUAL DOCTOR

On hearing this, Jesus said, "It is not the healthy who need a doctor, but the sick." —Matthew 9:12 (NIV)

Jesus had just called Matthew to be one of his twelve disciples. Matthew (Levi) was a tax collector and seen as a traitor by many of his fellow Jews. Tax collectors were employed by the oppressive Roman government, which was a terrible thing in and of itself. On top of that, many tax collectors charged higher taxes in an effort to make more money for themselves. This made tax collectors some of the worst "sinners" of Jesus' day in the eyes of society.

The Pharisees were naturally upset that this rabbi was associating with known "sinners" and traitors. Jesus, though, responded to the Pharisees' protests with a simple reminder that the sick need the doctor, not those who are well. In other words, sinners need salvation, not the righteous.

The truth of the matter is this: all are spiritually sick. We all need a spiritual physician. Jesus is the one who is willing to go into the home of a person who is so spiritually sick, so far gone in unrighteousness, that others have given up hope. The Pharisees had given up hope on Matthew and his friends, but Jesus was willing not only to visit with Matthew but also to make him a disciple.

If you have been hurt by the church or others who call on the name of Christ, perhaps they look at you as though you are too far gone in your sinful life. Know that Jesus has not given up on you. Know that the spiritual doctor has the cure for all spiritual diseases and that we are all spiritually sick. Turn to Jesus today and thank him for offering you his cure.

February 16
THE LORD OF PEACE

Now may the Lord of peace himself give you peace at all times in all ways. The Lord be with all of you. —2 Thessalonians 3:16 (NRSV)

Paul is offering a benediction for the people of Thessalonica. The purpose of a benediction is to offer encouragement for the people who are on the receiving end of such words.

Paul offers these words to all the believers within the collective church at Thessalonica. The intended purpose is to give the recipients of the letter hope that God will continue to make his presence known in their lives and to offer to them a sense of peace that comes only from the Divine who holds power over chaos and strife. This peace is unique and different from any that this world has to offer. Christ is the God of peace, the one through whom all believers may know peace one day. Paul's prayer is that his fellow believers may know Christ and his peace. Even nearly two thousand years removed from Paul's writings, we may also receive the same peace that the apostle to the Gentiles spoke of: the peace of Christ.

As you go about your daily journey, seek the Lord of Peace. Do not be overburdened by life on this day. Take moments throughout your daily activities to be still and silent before Christ. Allow him to calm your mind, spirit, and body, especially if you feel overwhelmed by your responsibilities today. Remember that the Lord of Peace is on the side of his followers and will offer ultimate peace when we see his face. In the meantime, we may find momentary peace as we commune with him.

February 17
A CALL TO PEACE

Let the peace of Christ rule in your hearts, to which indeed you were called in one body; and be thankful. —Colossians 3:15 (NASB)

Jesus Christ is the Lord of Peace, and as his followers Christians should exhibit peace throughout their lives. The attitude of peace comes directly from the Lord of Peace and should replace any negative feelings Christians have toward others. Ideally, the attitude of peace should override attitudes of anger, hatred, bitterness, cruelty, jealousy, and so on.

The attitude of peace should serve as an overriding force in our relationships with other people. This is how Christians *should* behave; however, that is not always the case. Christians are called to live a life of peace with other people, no matter the differences—be they racial, socioeconomic, political, geographic, cultural, or even religious. Christians are to be a people of peace.

This is a tall order for many people. Being peaceful with everyone we encounter is not always the easiest option. In light of that reality, you are encouraged to remember this calling to peace by the Lord of Peace. Remember also that Christ will offer his followers peace when life presents difficulties. Take comfort in the knowledge that though this is a difficult task, the Lord of Peace will equip you for it through continued prayer and discipline. Allow the peace of Christ to rule in your life, to take charge over your thoughts and actions, and in this way you will grow closer to Christ and shine the Light of Christ into the lives of the people you encounter.

February 18

SPIRITUAL EXERCISE: PSALM OF PRAISE

This is a day on which you are encouraged to simply reflect on the following psalm. What does the Spirit tell you through these words? Do you find it easy to offer praises to God today? If not, then commune with God and listen for the Divine voice. Can you identify what is preventing your ability to offer praises?

> Praise the LORD! Praise, O servants of the LORD, praise the
>   name of the LORD!
> Blessed be the name of the LORD from this time forth and
>   forevermore!
> From the rising of the sun to its setting, the name of the LORD is
>   to be praised!
> The LORD is high above all nations, and his glory above the
>   heavens!
> Who is like the LORD our God, who is seated on high,
> Who looks far down on the heavens and the earth?
> He raises the poor from the dust and lifts the needy from the ash
>   heap,
> To make them sit with princes, with the princes of his people.
>   He gives the barren woman a home, making her the joyous
>   mother of children.
> Praise the LORD! —Psalm 113 (ESV)

February 19
YOU ARE FORGIVEN

Then He said to her, "Your sins are forgiven." —Luke 7:48 (NKJV)

"Your sins are forgiven." These are simple yet profound words. If care is not exercised, these words may lose their potency and power. The woman to whom Jesus spoke was a "sinner." What those sins may have been is left to the imagination of the reader, yet she was unwelcome in the home of the Pharisee whom Jesus was visiting, and her actions were astounding to the onlookers. She had come to anoint Jesus' feet with perfume and then to kiss and wash them with her tears and hair.

Jesus' response to the woman's actions, actions motivated by love, was to forgive her sins. The motivation for Jesus' entire life—from his childhood through his ministry and to the cross—was love. This love is for the entire world, for each person who has lived, is living, and ever will live. This love is for you.

This love that Jesus has for you also holds forgiveness for your sins. No matter how great or small you may consider your sins to be (there is no ranking system), Jesus has forgiven them if you have faith in him. Take comfort in the truth that Jesus loves you and has forgiven all your sins. You are encouraged to insert your own name into Luke 7:48 and repeat it to yourself. Savor every word as you do so, and allow the peace of Christ to overwhelm you as you reflect on those blessed words that carry the greatest news you will ever hear. You are indeed forgiven of your sins.

February 20

DEATH IS SWALLOWED UP

On this mountain he (God) will destroy the shroud that enfolds all peoples, the sheet that covers all nations; he will swallow up death forever. —Isaiah 25:7-8a (NIV)

Death is often seen as the ultimate end. It is something that is not understood, that is feared, and that is even considered to be a taboo topic of conversation in some circles. It is a mystery wrapped up in uncertainty and fear. The fear is the result of uncertainty. However, for the Christian, death is truly only a gateway, a transition from one life to the next.

Christians have been given some certainties about death, the first of which is that it has been swallowed up, defeated, no longer to be a tormentor or a great, unknown thing that is to be feared. Why fear something that has been defeated? To use a favorite word from a favorite character from a well-known science fiction series, it is "illogical" to fear that which can do no harm, and death can no longer harm us.

This does not take away the sadness of losing a loved one, a dear friend, or a family member. However, if we are believers in Christ, we possess something great: victory over death. Prior to the actions of Christ on the cross and the empty tomb, death was understood as something that separated us from God. All, except a select few in the Old Testament, were doomed to die one day, and on that day, they would be separated from God, entering the place of the dead or Sheol. However, God has swallowed up death, defeating this enemy and removing the fear that surrounds it. Praise God today that this enemy no longer holds eternal sway. Instead, it has become a gateway that leads into the presence of God.

February 21

FAITH THE SIZE OF A MUSTARD SEED

And the Lord said, "If you had faith like a grain of mustard seed, you could say to this mulberry tree, 'Be uprooted and planted in the sea,' and it would obey you." —Luke 17:6 (ESV)

It would be a remarkable sight to witness a tree lifting itself out of the ground and leaping into the ocean. That is completely unnatural to everything we know about this world. What a marvelous visual Jesus has provided. Imagine having that power within you simply through having enough faith, which Jesus tells his audience is as small as a mustard seed.

No trees, to this author's knowledge, have taken the plunge into the deep in this manner. Perhaps Jesus is not making a literal declaration. What, then, would be so marvelous as to match this power of terraforming? To love others the way we love ourselves.

The context of Luke 17 discusses sin, faith, and duty. It is the duty of all Christians to love God and to love others. Nothing in this world could match the miraculous power of commanding nature to do your bidding other than to love your neighbor as yourself. This world needs Christians putting their faith into practice, not by pushing political agendas or by decorating the town for Christmas but by loving other people, both fellow Christians and non-Christians.

Do something miraculous with your faith today. Command a tree to leap into the sea! Do something unnatural to the world in which we live, and love those whom you encounter today.

February 22

FROM ONE KINGDOM TO ANOTHER

He has rescued us from the power of darkness and transferred
us into the kingdom of his beloved Son . . . . —Colossians 1:13
(NRSV)

Within Christian theology is a great divide between two kingdoms: that of darkness and that of light. We see this represented in Christian art, poetry, music, and other mediums. It is played out not only in Christianity but also in other world religions and even in secular entertainment with light vs. darkness, good vs. evil, and so on.

The divide between the kingdom of darkness and the kingdom of light is as clear as the divide between high noon and midnight. The mental picture is intended to be clear for the reader of the letter to the Colossians; we are in a place of darkness prior to our salvation through faith in Jesus Christ. However, now as people of belief and faith, we are rescued from that kingdom of darkness and brought to our new home, the kingdom of light, the kingdom of Jesus Christ, the Son of God.

If you are a Christian, then you are a child of the Light. This means you no longer belong in the darkness. Now you carry within you the Light of Jesus Christ. Take comfort in the reality that you have been rescued from the darkness of sin and death and have a permanent place in the kingdom of Light, the kingdom of Christ. God has plucked you from your former life, though some scars may remain. You are encouraged to find joy in the fact that God considered you enough to encounter you where you were, in that place of darkness, and bring you into a place that will ensure that you will one day enjoy his presence to the fullest extent possible.

February 23

WHOM SHALL I FEAR?

The LORD is my light and my salvation; Whom shall I fear?
The LORD is the defense of my life; Whom shall I dread?
—Psalm 27:1 (NASB)

Fear is a poignant emotion that motivates those affected to react quickly and often with little thought to the consequences of their actions. Psychologists have determined that humans, and other species, often react to stimulus with a fight or flight reaction.

The truth for Christians is that we need not react to situations with fear. While our natural and primal reaction may indeed be to run away in fear of some event, we need not fear whatever has happened. We need not fear other people either. There is nothing that someone or something else may do to us that would remove us from the presence of God. While we may be killed or severely injured in this life, and that may cause us concern, the truth is that bodily injury is only temporary, even if it is a life-long injury, and death is only a gateway into eternity with God in paradise.

Other, less dangerous situations may evoke fear as well—giving a presentation in front of a group, starting a new job, moving to a new school or town, or any number of changes or challenges in life. Do not be overcome by the fear that these events may bring to the surface. Instead, remember that God is with you. He is your stronghold in all situations, and he is the light that will guide you. Take comfort and be encouraged today and every day, as God is your companion throughout your journey.

February 24
CHRISTIAN UNITY

. . . that all of them may be one, Father, just as you are in me and I am in you. May they also be in us so that the world may believe that you have sent me. —John 17:21 (NIV)

There is great diversity among Christians. Denominational lines divide Methodists from Baptists, Pentecostals from Episcopalians, Catholics from Presbyterians, and so on. Even within those lines there is division. There are American Baptists, Southern Baptists, Cooperative Baptists, Primitive Baptists, and more. Some denominational lines blur, and we see pockets of Christians like the Baptist-Pentecostal hybrids, or "bapticostals," that interweave two or more traditions into one. While this diversity should be celebrated as a sign of the rich history of the church, we should not allow these differences to cause us to be divided in our worship of and work for God.

Jesus was praying in the Garden of Gethsemane prior to his arrest. Specifically, he was praying that all of his future followers would be unified just as God the Father and God the Son are unified. This unification is intimate; there is nothing more closely united than the Triune God, three persons in one. This is the type of unity that Jesus was praying that his followers, all Christians, would have with one another.

Be encouraged to find common ground with your fellow believers today, especially those whom you cannot seem to agree with on some issue beyond what is central to the Christian faith. Things like the mode of baptism, political alignment, what football team to root for, or what color the carpet should be are minor issues and should not drive a wedge between you and your fellow believer no matter their denominational alignment. Identify what unifies rather than what divides.

February 25

SPIRITUAL EXERCISE: LECTIO DIVINA
(DIVINE READING)

On this day, you are invited to practice a spiritual exercise, a "divine reading" of a select passage of Scripture. Please follow the guide provided as you meditate on this passage.

• Read the passage twice, pausing between each reading for a moment of silence. Identify key words as you read through the passage without elaboration.
• Read the passage again, pause for silence, and answer the following question: Where does the content of the reading touch my life today?
• Read the passage once more, again pausing for silence, and complete this sentence: I believe God wants me to . . .

> Nevertheless, I am continually with you; you hold my right hand.
> You guide me with your counsel, and afterward you will receive me to glory.
> Whom have I in heaven but you? And there is nothing on earth that I desire besides you.
> My flesh and my heart may fail, but God is the strength of my heart and my portion forever.
> For behold, those who are far from you shall perish; you put an end to everyone who is unfaithful to you.
> But for me it is good to be near God; I have made the LORD God my refuge, that I may tell of all your works. —Psalm 73:23-28 (ESV)

February 26
GOD WILL HOLD YOU

Fear not, for I am with you; be not dismayed, for I am your God. I will strengthen you, yes I will help you. I will uphold you with My righteous right hand. —Isaiah 41:10 (NKJV)

Humans need physical contact throughout their lives. Being held in a hug is one of the most wonderful feelings for many people; it may even make you feel better emotionally if you were to hug a loved one and be hugged in return. Virginia Satir, a psychologist, once said that people need four hugs a day for survival, eight for maintenance, and twelve for growth. While this is not a literal or physiological truth, it is true that hugs reinforce relationships and make people feel better.

God understands this reality. While God does not physically hold his followers in his arms, you will never be out of God's care. Even during the Israelites' plight in exile, which they brought upon themselves through their unfaithfulness, God was still with them, holding them even though they surely felt abandoned. The same was true for Israel's prophets, the men of God who were faithful and delivered difficult messages. God held them too.

In Isaiah 41, God is promising Israel that he will help them in their time of need and be with them during their plight. God is with all of his people throughout their lives and no matter their circumstances. Find comfort in this today: the same God who held the Israelites and their prophets, the same God who was with Peter, Paul, James, and the other disciples, is with you and is holding you today. No matter what you face, whether your load is heavy or light on this day, find peace in the truth that God holds you with his righteous hand.

February 27

BLESSING IN LIGHT OF OPPRESSION OR ABUSE

Blessed are the poor in spirit: for theirs is the kingdom of heaven.
—Matthew 5:3 (KJV)

Aside from the Lord's Prayer, the Beatitudes are perhaps the most well-known verses within Jesus' Sermon on the Mount found in Matthew 5–7. They fall under the category of wisdom literature within Scripture. While they should not be understood as absolute truths that serve as blanket statements, encouragement may still be drawn from these wonderful words.

The first Beatitude (Matt 5:3) targets people who know their need for God: the poor in spirit. This is not to be understood as a Christian whose relationship with God is not as strong as another's. Instead, Jesus is focusing on the condition of absolute need and dependency on God because of a continued oppression or abuse at the hands of another or a particular situation in life.

For those who have recognized their need for God, the kingdom of heaven is theirs. This kingdom or dominion of God is present in their lives even now.

Take heart today, and be encouraged to recognize your own need for God in your life. Upon this realization, you too will experience the dominion of God or the kingdom of heaven. This does not mean all will be well and that the difficulty you face today will be diminished or cease all at once. But you can strive to find a sense of peace that comes from the knowledge that your situation is indeed temporary and that the dominion of God is eternal.

February 28
PUT AWAY MALICE

Put away from you all bitterness and wrath and anger and
wrangling and slander, together with all malice . . . .
—*Ephesians 4:31 (NRSV)*

In a world dominated by the impulses of humanity, it is easy to fall victim to our own desires and impulses that demand we act with cruelty and malice. It is easy to act out of impulse, lashing out in bitterness, wrath, anger, etc. toward another who, in our perception, has offended us. And, truly, perception is reality to our minds.

However, Paul, the author of the letter to the Ephesians, knew that this was not the way of Christ, though it was, and still is, indeed the way of the world. How then should a Christian, literally *little Christ*, respond to the various offenses or situations in which the world responds with malice? By putting these things away!

How easy it is to say those words, and yet how difficult it is to put malice away, to bite back against bitterness, wrath, anger, etc. Yet this is our calling as followers of Christ: to put these things away and replace them with love, joy, mercy, and forgiveness.

You are encouraged to begin a concentrated effort of actively putting malice away. Do not become disappointed in yourself for failure in this practice; instead, ask for forgiveness and continue to move forward. Practice replacing the negative knee-jerk reaction with a more positive reaction that is bathed in the light and seasoned with the salt of Christ.

February 29 (Leap Day)

SPIRITUAL EXERCISE: THE SPIRITUAL DISCIPLINE OF REFLECTING ON CHRISTIAN SYMBOLS

Symbols are an important addition to worship and the Christian experience. You are encouraged to meditate on a favorite religious image or a dearly held religious symbol on this day. Whether your image is that of the cross, the empty tomb, the bread and wine of Communion, or some other symbol of Christianity, meditate on the power of this image in your life. What does it mean to you? How does it affect the way you carry yourself through challenges? Is it a source of strength and support?

Here are some examples of religious symbols and images within Christianity:

- The cross
- Water
- Wine and bread
- The fish
- A boat
- Salt
- A candle
- Sheep or shepherd
- Stained glass

As you reflect on these images, what thoughts and feelings are evoked? Are they positive or negative? Why do you think they bring about those specific feelings in you? Are symbols an important part of your Christian experience? If not, has this exercise aided you in your journey today?

March 1

TAKE UP KINDNESS

Be kind and compassionate to one another, forgiving each other,
just as in Christ God forgave you. —*Ephesians 4:32 (NIV)*

Kindness toward one another is a simple concept that has been passed down for countless generations. In the children's movie *Bambi*, the mother of the character Thumper, the rabbit friend of Bambi, reminds her son that if he has nothing nice to say, then he has nothing to say at all. Clearly this fictional rabbit mother was wise to share this with her child. The idea of being kind to others is taught to children but too often left in a children's lesson book, failing to translate to true-to-life situations.

Even among fellow Christians, there is disconnect between this age-old teaching and our actions. No matter the cause for our failure to exhibit kindness, we must strive to overcome this failure.

Paul teaches us that we are to be kind to one another and forgive one another, as God has shown us kindness and forgives us through his Son and our Savior, Jesus Christ. To show kindness on the same level as our divine Creator is a human impossibility. However, we may strive to follow this divine example and even, as we ask for it, be equipped to practice such kindness and forgiveness.

Be encouraged to seek to forgive others today, specifically those who have wronged you personally, whether intentionally or not. Seek to embody divine forgiveness and kindness, and remember the words of Paul, who wrote them long before Thumper's mother shared a similar truth with her son. Remember that forgiveness came to us from God and through Christ first, and reflect on that today as well.

March 2

ABUNDANT LIFE THROUGH CHRIST

I came that they may have life and have it abundantly.
—John 10:10b (ESV)

An abundant life is full of meaning. It is fulfilling because of the relationships that are shared and experienced. Do not be confused: an abundant life through Christ is not one that is full of material possessions such as new cars, big houses, and fat bank accounts. By all accounts, Jesus himself likely lived in abject poverty.

Instead, an abundant life through Christ is centered first on the relationship you have with God, built on Christ and the Holy Spirit. This abundant life is then filled with meaningful relationships with other people as well as with meaning for yourself.

Christians are encouraged to seek meaningful and healthy relationships with others. We are communal creatures. Even the most introverted of us need some social interaction. Meaningful relationships with others help make life in the here and now more pleasant. We should not only tend to our human relationships but should also seek a meaningful and rich relationship with God.

An abundant life is one that sees fulfillment in the people who surround us, in the simple things that we do, and in our relationship with God. Seek to recognize your abundant life today. If you seek it and have trouble finding it, spend some time with God today and identify those who are most important to you. Make a plan to spend time with them soon.

March 3

SPIRITUAL EXERCISE: THE SPIRITUAL DISCIPLINE OF SLEEP

Sleep may seem like an odd spiritual discipline; however, as both Scripture and science suggest, sleep is good for us. The National Sleep Foundation has recently widened the recommended hours of sleep that a person needs to remain healthy. For example, it is recommended that a teenager get between 8–10 hours, whereas previously it was recommended that they get 8.5–9.5 hours. The recommended hours vary for different age groups and developmental stages, but the National Sleep Foundation recommends that everyone aim to get ample sleep ("National Sleep Foundation Recommends New Sleep Times").

Scripture teaches that Jesus himself required sleep, and he got it. Even as his disciples panicked during a storm on the sea, Jesus slept peacefully. In Mark's account, Jesus tells his weary disciples to rest after being sent out to do ministerial work and preach the gospel. God even rests and makes it a law to rest on the seventh day, the Sabbath.

Today you are encouraged to go to bed earlier than normal. Begin to rearrange your schedule in such a way that allows you to get more sleep. Turn off your phone, television, and computer. Remove yourself from high-stress situations. Make a list of things to do tomorrow and then set the list aside, not picking it up again until you wake for the next day. Do whatever you can, within reason, to make time to sleep more this week, and begin to make this a habit. God designed humanity to need sleep for nearly one third of our lives. Take advantage of that design and get some sleep.

March 4

THE SON OF GOD

*Now when the centurion and those with him, who were keeping
watch over Jesus, saw the earthquake and what took place, they
were terrified and said, "Truly this man was God's Son!"*
—Matthew 27:54 (NRSV)

The death of Jesus was accompanied by the tearing of the temple curtain
and an earthquake, which is specifically mentioned in Matthew's account.
These physical representations of the removal of the barrier between
humanity and God—and the way they demonstrate God's mourning—
must have been potent for those who witnessed them. Clearly, even a
group of Gentiles (non-Jewish pagans) recognized that there was something
special about Jesus.

This identity that the Gentiles recognized made, and continues to
make, Jesus special. His identity as the Son of God is crucial to the faith
that is Christianity. A divine realization overcame these individuals as they
witnessed the physical death of Jesus Christ, and they experienced a revelation that echoes Peter's confession of Jesus as the Christ earlier in the
Gospel account (Matt 16:16).

Jesus' identity as the Christ makes him important to believers still to
this day. Jesus, though, is not just the Christ; he is the Son of God. Jesus'
divine identity has given you the opportunity to enter into the presence
of God the Father. No longer are we separated from his divine glory. No
longer are we limited because of our sinful nature. Instead, we have been
given the greatest gift of all, a gift that will be realized fully when we leave
this life: the gift of eternity in the full and complete presence of God. Savor
that gift today, and remember that God's great love for you drove him
to the cross so that the divide between humanity and the Divine may be
bridged for all eternity.

March 5

JESUS PRAYED FOR YOU

My prayer is not for them alone. I pray also for those who will believe in me through their message . . . . —*John 17:20 (NIV)*

Did you know that you are mentioned in the Bible? That Jesus prayed for you before he was arrested? Perhaps your name is not found literally on the lips of Jesus, but he prayed for you if you believe in him as your Savior. On the night that Jesus was betrayed, we find that he prayed for himself, for his immediate disciples, and for all who would believe in him through the work of his disciples.

As a Christian, you are an indirect product of the work of the disciples of Jesus Christ; therefore, Jesus prayed for you before he was crucified. This is a marvelous thing to realize. The Savior of humanity lifted you up to his Father and our Creator. Jesus prayed that all of his followers would be unified and that each believer would eventually come to the place where he is going—the eternal presence of God the Father.

What a blessing to have had Jesus Christ pray for you. Find comfort in the knowledge that Jesus thought of you prior to his death. Be encouraged by this today, and seek to find peace in all situations, knowing that Jesus not only prayed for you but is interceding in the presence of the Father on your behalf. Know that the Holy Spirit is with you, a follower of Christ, in this moment. May this truth bring you peace today, and may you never forget that you are so loved by God that he not only sent his Son to die for your sins but also heard his Son's prayers for you on the night of his death.

March 6

FROM MOURNING TO COMFORT

Blessed are those who mourn, for they shall be comforted.
—Matthew 5:4 (ESV)

Life provides a plethora of reasons to mourn: the death of a loved one, the loss of a job, a traumatic event, the loss of a beloved pet, and the list goes on. All of these events can lead to painful emotional responses that may be summarized in one word—*mourning*. We mourn when we lose something valuable and important to us. Mourning is inevitable for all people in this life. However, for Christians there is a promise that one day our mourning will cease and we will be comforted.

Jesus' Beatitudes, those paradoxical sayings that kick off the Sermon on the Mount, offer words of comfort to those who are suffering in some way, shape, or form. Particularly, Jesus promises that our mourning will indeed come to an end.

Are you mourning today? If so, take comfort in knowing that this will not last forever, although it may certainly feel as though it will when you are immersed in the crisis. If you are not currently mourning, take a moment to thank God that you are not facing such a burden right now, and pray that God will encourage you and remind you of his presence when you do mourn. Remember that your mourning shall pass, and one day all mourning will be overwhelmed by the peace and presence of the Triune God.

March 7
CHRIST'S EXAMPLE

For to this you have been called, because Christ also suffered for you, leaving you an example, so that you should follow in his steps. —1 Peter 2:21 (NRSV)

Jesus is the epitome of the suffering servant ideal. His earthly ministry revolved around the shadow of the cross and what would immediately preface that terrible chapter within his life. Suffering, though, is not something many people in this world approve of in any way. Most people avoid it if possible. According to the logic of our flesh, that makes sense. However, according to the logic of the Christian faith, that does not compute.

The context of this verse is Peter's way of encouraging believers who were facing terrible suffering and persecution for their faith. This level of persecution is foreign to most Western Christians in the twenty-first century. Beatings and other forms of harassment were common for the early Christians. Christ, though, suffered first and left a blueprint for his followers to use. While it is unwise to actively pursue suffering in this life, it is impossible to live a completely protected and sheltered existence devoid of all suffering.

As you journey throughout life, do not be intimidated by the different kinds of suffering that you may face. Do not shrink away from it, either; instead, follow in Christ's footsteps. Recognize the moments of suffering in your life as opportunities to reflect the light and hope of Christ into the lives of those who witness your suffering. Use your pain as a moment of life-changing ministry for those around you. Acknowledge your feelings, and then embrace the reality that Christ too knows suffering.

March 8

WHAT FRUIT ARE YOU KNOWN FOR?

"Make a tree good and its fruit will be good or make a tree bad and its fruit will be bad, for a tree is recognized by its fruit."
—*Matthew 12:33 (NIV)*

What kind of fruit do you produce? Honest self-reflection is beneficial to identifying those fruits; so too are honest friends and family members. Take a moment now and reflect on the last twenty-four hours. What kinds of fruit did you produce? How would others react if they were to sample your fruit? Would they bite into a bitter fruit that has soured? Or would they be pleasantly surprised at the sweet freshness of your produce? No matter how you identify your fruits, you are encouraged to measure them against the fruit of the spirit mentioned in Galatians 5:22-23.

Are you filled with love for God and others? Joyful? Peaceful? Patient? Kind? Or do you withhold love from others? Are you filled with anger? Prone to antagonize others? Impatient? Malicious? The most likely answer is that you produce some good fruit and some bad.

Keeping your reflection from the last twenty-four hours in mind, be encouraged to replicate the good fruit that you produced and discard the bad fruit. To do this, you must reflect on what helped you produce the bad fruit. What attitudes led you to react to situations in a way that produced bad fruit? Work on changing those attitudes. Go to God in prayer and communion, seeking strength for the coming hours and days so that you may produce only good fruit. Find a trustworthy and confident believer who may be able to help hold you accountable to producing good fruit and tossing out the bad.

March 9

SPEAK THE TRUTH
IN LOVE

*. . . but speaking the truth in love, we are to grow up in all
aspects into Him who is the head, even Christ . . . .*
—Ephesians 4:15 (NASB)

An old saying goes something like this: "The truth hurts." Well, this author
wants to suggest something to push back against that saying. Is it the truth
that hurts, or is it the method used to reveal the truth that hurts? It's likely
that both are probably hurtful. The truth often reveals a weakness or failure
in our own lives, while the methods used to reveal that truth to us can be
as painful as the failure.

Paul was reminding the church in Ephesus that unity in the Body
of Christ is paramount, and part of that unity is being honest with one
another. However, honesty, while exceedingly important, can indeed be
hurtful. Therefore, it is important that those who seek to be honest speak
with a loving and peaceful tone. The message itself will already be painful
to hear, so it behooves Christians to offer that truth in love. This does not
mean we compromise the truth; we should still share it, but we can offer it
in a way that the recipient understands that we tell them the truth in love,
not in malice or anger.

Be encouraged today to seek to share the truth with others in love. Go
beyond simply sharing the truth in love; share everything that you do in
love. As Paul teaches the Corinthian believers, "Let all that you do be done
in love" (1 Cor 16:14, NRSV).

March 10

SPIRITUAL EXERCISE: PSALM OF PRAISE

This is a day on which you are encouraged to reflect on the following psalm. What does the Spirit tell you through these words? Do you find it easy to offer praises to God today? If not, then commune with God and listen for the Divine voice. Can you identify what is preventing your ability to offer praises?

> *I will bless the LORD at all times; his praise shall continually be*
>   *in my mouth.*
> *My soul makes its boast in the LORD; let the humble hear and*
>   *be glad.*
> *Oh, magnify the LORD with me, and let us exalt his name*
>   *together!*
> *I sought the LORD, and he answered me and delivered me from*
>   *all my fears.*
> *Those who look at him are radiant, and their faces shall never be*
>   *ashamed.*
> *This poor man cried, and the LORD heard him and saved him*
>   *out of his troubles.*
> *The angel of the LORD encamps around those who fear him, and*
>   *delivers them. —Psalm 34:1-7 (ESV)*

March 11

CONFESSION LEADS TO RECONCILIATION

I acknowledged my sin to you, and I did not cover my iniquity;
I said, "I will confess my transgressions to the LORD," and you
forgave the iniquity of my sin. —Psalm 32:5 (ESV)

Confession is one of the most difficult things to do in this life, for numerous reasons. We often find confession difficult, whether we want to admit it or not, because it implies a level of guilt on our part. When we confess, we admit that we were wrong, have made a mistake, or hurt someone, and no one likes to be wrong.

However, in the Christian context, as well as any context when we think about it, confession leads to reconciliation—or at least it opens the door for reconciliation to be a possible outcome. On the other hand, without confession there can be no reconciliation. We cannot come to terms with a failing or a wrong if we cannot own up to the failing or wrong that we've committed.

When we come to the place where confession is necessary and then follow through with that act, we are assured that God will offer forgiveness to us. What a wonderful assurance to know beforehand that your confession will lead to a pardon! Celebrate today, knowing that, though you are indeed in need of confessing some wrong to God, you will be forgiven. You are encouraged to strive to emulate this in your relationships with others. If you have been wronged, seek to respond to the other person when they confess as God has responded to your own confessions. If you need to confess to someone else, do so and open the door so that reconciliation may enter into your relationship with the other person.

March 12

CHRIST'S GRACE IS SUFFICIENT

. . . but he said to me, "My grace is sufficient for you, for power is made perfect in weakness." So, I will boast all the more gladly of my weaknesses, so that the power of Christ may dwell in me.
—*2 Corinthians 12:9 (NRSV)*

God's grace, the grace of Jesus Christ, is sufficient for us even in our weaknesses. It is truly a remarkable concept that even in our weakness Christ is strong. It is difficult to understand and even more difficult to put into practice. This author certainly hates to admit weaknesses. It is no one else's business that I must seek assistance to do anything beyond the most basic car maintenance, such as changing windshield wipers and putting air in the tires. However, in our weakness someone else is allowed to show their strength.

In our spiritual weakness, our sinful state, our failings as children of God, Christ is allowed to shine as our Savior and as the one who intercedes on our behalf in the presence of God the Father. Not only does Christ shine in the presence of God the Father; Christ shines as our Savior and guide in our lives in the here and now, and others whom we encounter along this journey can see his light in us.

As followers of Christ, it is imperative that we strive to allow Christ to shine in our weaknesses. In doing so, we should not attempt to hide our weaknesses—weaknesses more pressing than being unable to change the oil in your car; weaknesses like depression, spiritual doubt, addiction, marital strife; and the list goes on. Does that mean we should celebrate these weaknesses and flaunt them? No. However, we shouldn't seek to hide them. Rather, we should be comforted in knowing that our weaknesses make room for Christ's strength.

March 13

GOD'S JUSTICE

. . . he does not treat us as our sins deserve or repay us according to our iniquities. —Psalm 103:10 (NIV)

God is not a just God. God does not always agree with what is morally right. If God did conform to the dictionary's definition of the word *just* (morally right and fair), then we all would receive our just punishment for our sins and would be condemned to an eternity outside of the Divine presence. However, as it stands in light of Christ, God certainly does not conform to that definition.

Rather than being a just God, the God of Christianity is merciful. God does conform to the dictionary definition of *merciful* (showing compassion and forgiveness). Since we believe in a merciful God rather than a just God, we have greater reason to celebrate and worship this God. This may seem like an issue of semantics, but in the strictest sense God is not a just God but rather a merciful God, and praise him for that!

Since we who have faith in Jesus Christ as our Savior do not receive the punishment that we justly deserve, let us take a moment to praise God today. You are encouraged to pause and praise God that he is merciful rather than just. Praise God that your sins have been dealt with on the cross and that you no longer bear the immense spiritual weight of an eternity outside of the presence of God. Celebrate today and encourage others to join you in this celebration.

March 14

DRAWING NEAR TO GOD

Draw near to God and he will draw near to you. —James 4:8a
(ESV)

In this portion of his letter, James is reminding his readers that their relationship to God is not simply a one-way street. To have a relationship with God, the individual must be an active participant. God does not desire that we be puppets, reacting when our strings are pulled and dancing to his delight. God wants a meaningful and rich relationship with his people. This occurs only when we approach him in faith through Jesus Christ.

Notice that James points out that we must initiate the relationship. We must first draw near to God, and then God will draw near to us—an interesting point by the author of this letter. Humanity's relationship with the Divine is not compelled or forced by the Divine; rather, it is a movement initiated by humanity.

What is the significance of this point? Simply that we are encouraged to initiate the relationship. This does not mean that we have any real work to accomplish in ensuring that the relationship may begin. We must remember that God has already done the work necessary by bridging the gap of sin with his Son, Jesus Christ. The work is done. We simply need to take the first step, following the path that Jesus has blazed into the full presence of God the Father. We then have the assurance of James that as we set out on this journey toward the Divine, God will rendezvous with us and we will complete this journey. Be encouraged to initiate that relationship on a daily basis through prayer, meditation, Scripture reading, and practicing spiritual exercises.

March 15

HEALING TO THE NATIONS

. . . On each side of the river stood the tree of life, bearing twelve crops of fruit, yielding its fruit every month. And the leaves of the tree are for the healing of the nations. —Revelation 22:2b (NIV)

Too often when Christians think of the book of Revelation, there is great uncertainty. Thoughts of the end times, suffering, a lake of fire, Satan, and the mark of the beast emerge in our minds. Self-proclaimed prophets attempting to make a profit off these fears and uncertainties push their books and feed off the anxiety evoked by various tragedies around the world. The point of the book of Revelation gets lost amid all the hullabaloo in attempting to make sense of the various visions regarding the end of the world and the return of Christ.

Instead of seeking the signs of the return of the Savior, you are encouraged to remember that, no matter when or how it will occur, when Christ returns we who believe will be blessed beyond our wildest imaginations. John spends a great deal of time at the conclusion of this book describing what paradise looks like. This author believes that, no matter how magnificent John made it sound, his description pales in comparison to what we have to look forward to. However, the tree whose leaves are for the healing of the nations is a wonderful image. Take a moment to get away from the bad news that is broadcast via the various news outlets, and reflect on this hope that one day this negative news won't even be a bad memory. All the hurts, the famine, war, suffering, disease, sex trafficking, poverty, and so on will be no more, and we who believe will all be healed.

March 16

DO NOT RESIST AN EVIL PERSON

But I say to you, do not resist an evildoer. But if anyone strikes you on the right cheek, turn the other also . . . . —Matthew 5:39 (NRSV)

How do you respond to someone who does not behave as a Christian ought to behave, whether they are or are not a fellow Christian? The easy answer is to quote Jesus' words from the Sermon on the Mount, "turn the other cheek." The difficulty lies in the reality that this teaching is easier said than done.

While we are to love others and treat them as we would like to be treated, we cannot assume that they will respond in kind. With enough life experience, most people can testify that the world is full of those who do not love others and will not treat others the way that they would like to be treated.

Accepting this reality is the first step in being able to turn the other cheek when someone spites you. Whether it is a literal strike against your cheek, an emotional attack, or some other slight against you or your person, you can learn to turn the other cheek and respond in such a way that you emulate Christ's teachings of love and treat others the way you would like to be treated. When evil people, or those whose behavior is evil, reveal themselves to you, be encouraged to resist them, knowing that you can only control your own behavior. As a follower of Christ, you are taught to love those people and treat them as you want to be treated. Avoid malice, avoid vengeance, and remember that you may be the only example of Christ's love that they may see today or even this week.

March 17

SPIRITUAL EXERCISE: LECTIO DIVINA
(DIVINE READING)

On this day, you are invited to practice a spiritual exercise, a "divine reading" of a select passage of Scripture. Please follow the guide provided as you meditate on this passage.

• Read the passage twice, pausing between each reading for a moment of silence. Identify key words as you read the passage without elaboration.
• Read the passage again, pause for silence, and answer the following question: Where does the content of the reading touch my life today?
• Read the passage once more, again pausing for silence, and complete this sentence: I believe God wants me to . . .

> The LORD is my shepherd; I shall not want.
> He makes me to lie down in green pastures. He leads me beside
>   still waters.
> He restores my soul. He leads me in paths of righteousness for his
>   name's sake.
> Even though I walk through the valley of the shadow of death,
>   I will fear no evil, for you are with me; your rod and your
>   staff, they comfort me.
> You prepare a table for me in the presence of my enemies; you
>   anoint my head with oil; my cup overflows.
> Surely goodness and mercy shall follow me all the days of my life,
>   and I shall dwell in the house of the LORD forever.
> —Psalm 23 (ESV)

March 18

HOW MANY TIMES SHOULD WE FORGIVE?

Then Peter came and said to Him, "Lord, how often shall my brother sin against me and I forgive him? Up to seven times?" Jesus said to him, "I do not say to you, up to seven times, but up to seventy times seven." —Matthew 18:21-22 (NASB)

What a bizarre question the leading disciple asked. It almost seems as though Peter was searching for a limit to the forgiveness he might offer so that he could know when to stop forgiving. Admittedly, we cannot say what Peter's motivation was, and it is dangerous to put thoughts into his mind. However, we may note that Peter's question brings a striking answer from Jesus.

How many times is it okay to forgive someone when they keep sinning against us? This is a fair question, something all Christians have wondered or will wonder about at some point in their journey.

Jesus answers plainly, "not seven times but seventy-seven," or as some translations say, "seventy times seven." No matter the exact amount, Jesus is teaching his disciple that there is no limit to the amount of forgiveness that his followers ought to pour out. When reflecting on our own spiritual journey and the amount of forgiveness we have requested from God, it is easy to see that there should be no limit to the amount of forgiveness we pour into the lives of others. God willingly continues to pour out forgiveness into our own lives. Be encouraged to offer forgiveness to someone in your life who needs it. Do not be hindered by the question of whether they deserve forgiveness because, honestly, do any of us *deserve* forgiveness?

March 19

JESUS PRAYED IN A SOLITARY PLACE

Very early in the morning, while it was still dark, Jesus got up,
left the house and went off to a solitary place, where he prayed.
—Mark 1:35 (NIV)

In a world of social media, cell phones, and Wi-Fi, it is difficult to find a truly solitary place, though not impossible. Solitude is not only a good way to find peace and quiet in the busyness of this life but is also an opportunity to commune with God in an environment that is free of distractions. It is well documented throughout the Gospel accounts that Jesus was not an isolationist or a hermit; he shared in fellowship and celebrations, enjoyed the wedding in Cana, and experienced communal sorrow at the death of Lazarus. However, Jesus also understood that regular communion with God is necessary for a healthy spiritual life. This communion comes easiest when there are no other distractions.

Be encouraged to begin setting aside time to commune with God. You have started by choosing to read this devotion for today. Now go beyond these pages, dive into the Scriptures, and spend some time in prayer, both in petition and in listening. Seek to carve out time in your routine to be with God on a conscious level, and practice this enough that you reach a point where you are no longer "carving" time out of your schedule but have made it a part of your daily routine. Follow in the steps of Christ and make it a point to commune with God in a solitary place daily. Escape from the regular distractions of your life and commune with the God who loves you and desires a meaningful relationship with you through Christ, who is our perfect example.

March 20

PRAY FOR THOSE WHO PERSECUTE YOU

But I say to you, love your enemies, bless those who curse you, do good to those who hate you, and pray for those who spitefully use you and persecute you . . . . —Matthew 5:44 (NKJV)

I was introduced to a mental exercise from a friend of mine during a Clinical Pastoral Education unit. Close your eyes and picture someone who angers you, someone you may even hate. It could be a bully, a coworker, a classmate, anyone. Once you have given this some thought and identified the person that you cannot stand, remember that God loves them. Allow that thought to truly sink in for a moment. Let the idea marinate a while.

After a few moments of thinking about this person whom you loathe and recognizing that they are indeed loved by God, what are you thinking? What are your thoughts about this person now? Have your original thoughts or feelings changed after meditating on how they are a loved creation of God? Do not be overly concerned if your feelings haven't changed in this instant; few things change that quickly.

Continue to do this exercise today, remembering that this person or group is loved by God, just as you are. Pray for this person today. Pray for peace in your relationship, for reconciliation if there are strained feelings, or at least that God will soften your hatred toward this person. As you do, remember that our hatred toward others builds walls of division that do not allow the light and love of Christ to shine forth from our lives into theirs. Be challenged and encouraged by this exercise today.

March 21

A LISTENING PRESENCE

The LORD God has given Me the tongue of disciples, That I may know how to sustain the weary with a word. He awakens Me morning by morning, He awakens My ear to listen as a disciple.
—Isaiah 50:4 (NASB)

One of the most difficult things to do in a situation of high anxiety or crisis is to listen to the person in the midst of that crisis without offering our own advice, making thin connections to their situation from our own lives, waiting for a break in their conversation so that we might reply, or otherwise making light of their situation by dismissing it as a non-crisis event. It is true that not all have been blessed to be good listeners, but in a genuine relationship with another person it behooves us to listen attentively to their concerns.

Isaiah spoke of being given the ability to listen to others, and this is a skill that all believers should hone. Christians have a powerful tool at their disposal if only we will use it: to listen carefully and without passing undue judgment on those who suffer. To listen is to open the door of care, which in turn opens the door for Christ to enter that situation.

Be encouraged to be a good listener to someone today. Ask that God will open your ears to listen and open your other senses to perceive those around you who may need a listening ear. What better way to shine the Light of Christ than to meet someone where they are and lend a listening ear? This, after all, is the beginning of ministry—to hear the burdens of another.

March 22

THE END RESULT OF OUR WORK

That is why we labor and strive, because we have put our hope in the living God, who is the Savior of all people, and especially of those who believe. —1 Timothy 4:10 (NIV)

Paul was writing to his young friend and coworker in mission and ministry. Here he is encouraging Timothy to be a good and faithful servant of Christ, trained to resist all that is ungodly, for this is the end result of our work—to have hope in the living God who has given salvation to all who believe.

This should be our motivation. It should drive us to accomplish all that we set our minds to, to be good servants of God in sharing the hope of salvation in and through the one, true, living God.

In this life of social media, twenty-four-hour news programming, and a plethora of other distractions motivated by constant going and moving, it is easy to be overwhelmed and place our faith in the back of our minds, turning to God only in moments of crisis or strife. However, you are encouraged to continue to train yourself daily, spiritually speaking, and focus on the end goal of entering into the full presence of God one day. In the meantime, resist losing focus and becoming trapped in the wrong spiritual and emotional state of giving one of life's many distractions a place of honor above God. Distractions from our end goal are not new to the current generation; they have been around since before the time of Paul and Timothy and continue to plague Christians. Find comfort in your focus on the end goal, as it is far better than any of life's distractions claim to be.

March 23

FROM POOR IN SPIRIT TO THE KINGDOM OF HEAVEN

"Blessed are the poor in spirit, for theirs is the kingdom of heaven." —Matthew 5:3 (ESV)

The Beatitudes are wonderfully simple and wonderfully paradoxical at the same time. The poor in spirit, those who mourn, and those who are meek are all blessed in ways that do not compute according to the flesh. Who, though, are the poor in spirit, and what is the kingdom of heaven that is promised to them? The poor in spirit are those who are aware of their life situation. It is a situation that is troubling, burdensome, and depressing. Essentially, the poor in spirit are those who may be oppressed in some way, whether that oppression is motivated by race, gender, class, education, religion, or anything else that makes the person in question different from the majority.

This oppression is sinful and contrary to the gospel of Jesus Christ and the intended purpose of humanity. Perhaps you are among the millions, if not billions, of people who suffer from oppression daily throughout the world.

If you find yourself suffering today, whether from overt oppression or some other evil or cruelty in this life, be encouraged to take comfort in the presence of God. You are promised that you will inherit the kingdom of heaven, which, simply put, is reconciliation. You will be fully reconciled and will one day enter the full presence of God. In the meantime, seek comfort in the presence of God in the here and now. If you are not being oppressed, be encouraged to be a shelter to someone in your community who needs a reminder of God's love in their life.

March 24

SPIRITUAL EXERCISE: GUIDED PRAYER

Do you ever struggle with confessing your sins? Is it difficult for you to admit a failing? Does the thought of having to confess make you uncomfortable? Are you carrying the burden of an unconfessed sin? While confession may be difficult, requiring a certain level of spiritual maturity and a bit of self-awareness and humility, it is good for the soul. That may feel like a meaningless and hollow adage, but there is truth to be found in the saying, "Confession is good for the soul."

Our burden is lifted when we confess our guilt of a sin or wrongdoing. It leads to forgiveness. Many Christian denominations believe that to be absolved of our sins, we must first confess. Whether you share this sentiment or not, you are encouraged to enter a time of prayerful confession to God today.

Suggested Scripture: Matthew 6:9-13; 1 John 1:9

Suggested Prayer:
> *Loving God,*
> *I approach you with the knowledge that I am unworthy of this opportunity but grateful to you for your assurances of forgiveness through Jesus Christ. I confess to you that I have sinned against you or another of your favored creation. I ask that you cleanse me of this sin and give me the endurance and strength necessary to avoid further failings. I thank you for your unending forgiveness in Christ, amen.*

March 25

SOMETHING PROFOUND HAS HAPPENED

But when Simon Peter saw it, he fell down at Jesus' knees,
saying, "Go away from me, Lord, for I am a sinful man!"
—Luke 5:8 (NRSV)

Something profound has occurred in Peter's life: he has recognized that Jesus is special. In Luke's account of the gospel of Jesus, this profound occurrence follows Jesus' demonstration of his power over nature in the miraculous catch of fish as he calls his first disciples.

The profound realization in Peter's life, though, is not about fish; it centers on Jesus' identity. Granted, Peter will later have another profound moment when he confesses that Jesus is the Christ, yet another example of a profound occurrence in a series of profound occurrences throughout his life. Peter's reaction to this profound realization was to worship Jesus and declare his own sinfulness. Peter wasn't sure exactly who this man was, but he did know that there was something special about Jesus. The initial reaction of this first disciple was to fall at Jesus' knees and declare himself unworthy to be in Jesus' presence, both through word and deed.

What a powerful image we have of Peter falling to Jesus' knees and offering worship and honor to this man from Nazareth, a man whose identity was not yet fully known by this fisherman from Galilee. It is significant that Peter calls Jesus "Lord" in this passage because it elevates Jesus to a state of leadership and authority over Peter, a place where all Christians should elevate Jesus as we simultaneously lower ourselves in humility to Jesus' knees. Be encouraged to lift Jesus up and humble yourself throughout your journey today.

March 26

EVERYTHING NEEDS TO REST

. . . but on the seventh year you shall let it rest and lie fallow, so that the needy of your people may eat; and whatever they leave the beast of the field may eat. You are to do the same with your vineyard and your olive grove. – Exodus 23:11 (NASB)

The Scripture reveals that God was and is intentional with God's people. Throughout the Old Testament, there are numerous instances of God leaving specific instructions for the people, whether in various dietary laws, dimensions for the tabernacle or the temple, or even how to make war. God had a set way of doing things and high expectations for the people who followed God. The same was true even for the land that the people farmed.

Not only were the people to set aside at least one day out of the week to rest and relax; the land itself was to be allowed to rest every seventh year. This seems odd, but it turns out that this is good for the soil as well as for the worker.

Most in our society are busy. Our schedules are full, and our planners overflow with things to do. Our minds often are swimming with the various activities that we must accomplish throughout any given day.

You are encouraged to pause today, recite the Jesus Prayer or simply take a few deep breaths, and stop everything that you are doing. Take time to rest and remember that this is a part of God's plan. While work is good, being busy for the sake of being busy is counterproductive and not befitting a Christian.

March 27

WHAT IS REQUIRED?

*He has shown you, O mortal, what is good. And what does the
LORD require of you? To act justly and to love mercy and to walk
humbly with your God. —Micah 6:8 (NIV)*

The overwhelming message for many of the Old Testament prophets
revolved around being faithful to God and, even more so, ensuring justice
for the poor and downtrodden. God, through the prophets, calls out the
wealthiest of Israel and Judah for their lack of compassion on the poor and
their unrighteous behavior.

This verse brings those two themes together: faithful journeying with
God and concern for those who are lower on the social and economic
ladder. A faithful follower of Christ ought to have compassion and concern
for the well-being of all humanity. This verse, not unlike the two greatest
commands first introduced in the Pentateuch and then reiterated by Jesus
in the Gospels, summarizes neatly the expectations of the followers of God.
God has revealed to his people what is good and what is right. We know
the actions that will further ensure that we are doing what is expected. The
good that we are expected to do follow in the verse—do justice, love kindness, and walk humbly with God.

This is not always easy. Admittedly, it is easier to follow our own path
that does not always seek justice for all, is not always kind, and does not
walk humbly with anyone, let alone God. You are encouraged to seek what
is right today and every day. Form new habits, beginning with humbly
walking with God everywhere you go.

March 28

THE LORD GOES BEFORE YOU

It is the LORD who goes before you. He will be with you; he will not leave you or forsake you. Do not fear or be dismayed.
—Deuteronomy 31:8 (ESV)

The people of Israel had been wandering for forty years with Moses at the lead. They were preparing to enter the promised land, but a change of leadership was in order before proceeding. Joshua must have been intimidated at the prospect of stepping into the sandals of Moses, the man who had, through the power of God, freed the Israelites and led them in worship of God over the last four decades.

Moses, nearing the end of his life and handing the reins over to his successor, knew that Joshua needed a few words of encouragement. Moses was able to speak to the younger man out of personal experience. God had not abandoned Moses through the various trials of his life, and neither would God abandon Joshua. God had not only been with Moses but had led Moses and the people and would continue to do so with Joshua as his human mediator.

God has not stopped leading his people; his presence is with all who believe right now. The Spirit of God may not manifest itself as a pillar of smoke or fire, but rest assured that the Spirit goes with you in your times of sorrow as well as your moments of joy. Take comfort today in the reminder that you are being led by the Spirit of God and that the Spirit not only fills you but surrounds you in your journey through this life.

March 29

THE FELLOWSHIP OF THE WAY

And they continued stedfastly in the apostles' doctrine and fellowship, and in breaking of bread, and in prayers. —Acts 2:42 (KJV)

Fellowship is an important aspect of faith. Christianity is not a religion that is intended to be practiced in solitude, at least not in permanent solitude. Moments of isolation are important and even encouraged, but they should be limited in length and frequency. Even introverted people need to have fellowship with others.

The early church knew and understood well the importance of fellowship with one another. Theirs was a hostile environment that saw persecution from all sides. The fellowship was deep, meaningful, and rich. It revolved around sharing in the study and learning of the gospel of Jesus Christ, the breaking of bread together, and communing with God together in prayer.

All of these are still practiced by the church today, some two thousand years removed from the earliest events in the New Testament. You are encouraged to seek a fellowship of like-minded believers if you are not already part of a local church body. If you are, seek to deepen your fellowship with your brothers and sisters in faith. Remember that solitude is sometimes necessary to help us orient ourselves to God and commune with God on a personal level, but fellowship is still a necessity in our spiritual experience and our journey with God.

March 30
GOD BECAME FLESH

And the Word became flesh and lived among us, and we have seen his glory, the glory as of a father's only son, full of grace and truth. —John 1:14 (NRSV)

Prior to this instance in human history, the Divine had indeed dwelt among the people of God; however, his presence was limited to clearly defined spaces such as the holy of holies in the temple or to naturally occurring, albeit divinely manifested, phenomena such as fire and clouds. Never had God dwelt with the people in the flesh.

What a beautiful reminder that God, the Divine being that is above all fleshly understanding, took on flesh to live alongside humanity. Undoubtedly, as he was wrapped in flesh, Jesus experienced many highs and lows associated with the flesh, from joys like the wedding at Cana to lows such as the death of Lazarus. As the Christian theologian and comedian Grady Nutt explained, it is easy for us to forget that Jesus, in all of his divinity, was indeed human too. Jesus experienced two natures, the Divine and the human.

It is far too easy to fall into the trap of forgetting the simple truth that Jesus was human too! There is comfort in remembering this truth, that Jesus experienced things in a similar way to you. Jesus experienced joy, pain, weariness, hunger, and sorrow. He probably laughed, and he got angry. The point is that the Divine experienced the human experience. This makes God more relatable. However, in our attention to Jesus' humanity, we dare not forget his divinity. Take comfort today in Jesus' human experiences, and bask in his divinity.

March 31

SPIRITUAL EXERCISE: REFLECTING ON THE CROSS

The cross is a simple shape that has helped to define a huge portion of the modern world and has influenced humanity over the last two thousand years. For many Christians, the cross is the center of their faith. In my experience, it is seen as a beautiful paradox. On the one hand, it was a terrible means of execution, both brutal and effective. On the other hand, it is a sign of hope to many who otherwise feel hopeless.

Chances are high that, even if you do not attend a local church fellowship regularly, you have seen a visual depiction of the cross on which Jesus was crucified. Whether that depiction was large or small, made of wood or metal, hung around someone's neck or on their wall, or stood at the top of a church steeple, you probably know what a cross looks like.

On this day you are encouraged to meditate on the image of the cross. If it helps you to look at a cross, do so. What thoughts come to your mind? What images? What feelings? Do you have any new revelations regarding the cross and what it means to you as a Christian? Use the remainder of this page to make notes about your experience in this exercise.

_____

_____

_____

_____

April 1

BEAUTIFUL PARADOX

We always carry around in our body the death of Jesus,
so that the life of Jesus may also be revealed in our body.
—*2 Corinthians 4:10 (NIV)*

Paul offers an interesting connection between life and death. What a paradox to explore. The overall feel of this entire passage is of paradox, of opposite extremes meeting one another. Paul presents an idea where Christians are carrying both the life and death of Jesus Christ in our lives.

Why both, though? Why not simply carry the cross? Or, conversely, why not carry the empty tomb? The answer is simple: Christians cannot focus too much on either Jesus' death or Jesus' life without entertaining the idea of the other. It is through Jesus' life that we are given examples and teachings on morality, on carrying ourselves in this world, on interacting with other believers and nonbelievers. And it is through Jesus' death that we are given salvation and eternal life, access to the complete presence of God the Father.

It is in Jesus' life that we are taught how to live, and it is in Jesus' death that we are given the opportunity to live. That is why we carry not only the cross but also the empty tomb. Be encouraged today to mull over this wonderful paradox of both life and death. Consider how truly wonderful it is to carry this paradox around with you as a believer in Jesus Christ. The life and death of Christ are central to our beliefs and, more than that, are central to God's love of us.

April 2
HELP MY UNBELIEF

Immediately the boy's father cried out and said, "I do believe; help my unbelief." —Mark 9:24 (NASB)

Unbelief or doubt is a difficult concept to come to terms with, especially for those who are believers. We often loathe to admit it when doubt creeps into our lives. We question God's goodness. Is God all knowing? Is God all good? Can God be both? Can God be one or the other? Does God even exist at all? Where is God during this struggle that threatens to overwhelm me? Does God even care?

Many believers are afraid to entertain these questions and would perhaps even denying having them at all. We must seek God, even in moments when it feels as though God is nowhere to be found. Often, amid various crises, when our unbelief seems to be at its strongest, we can find glimpses of the Divine in the people who are caring for us. A visit, a casserole, a card, a phone call or text, or a silent embrace may carry with it the unspoken groans of the Holy Spirit (Rom 8:26).

Unfortunately, there is no easy or quick fix to the crises in our lives or to the situations that bring about unbelief, doubts, or questions. Thankfully, if we are discerning enough to notice, God is patient and surrounds us with resources to encourage and uplift us. Be encouraged to seek the resources God has given to you to help you face your moments of unbelief and doubt. Take comfort in the knowledge that you are not alone in your unbelief.

April 3

DISCIPLINE IS
A BLESSING

*Behold, blessed is the one whom God reproves; therefore despise
not the discipline of the Almighty. —Job 5:17 (ESV)*

Being disciplined is not necessarily fun. It is not only difficult for the one
being disciplined but, especially if there is a child involved, also difficult
for the one doing the disciplining. A mantra of the parent is "This is going
to hurt me more than it hurts you." As a parent myself, it is hard to deny
my child something or to discipline them in such a way that causes them
to be upset.

However, the end goal of any reasonable act of discipline is to teach the
one being disciplined to avoid in the future the behavior that led to being
disciplined in the first place. God, not unlike a loving parent, is willing
to discipline God's children. Job, one of the most famous individuals in
Scripture when it comes to suffering, is introduced to this idea by one of
his friends. Eliphaz introduced the idea of discipline to Job. While it is
debatable that Job required discipline, it may be understood that, when
God does indeed offer discipline to God's people, the people ought to pay
careful attention.

Within the context of the new covenant through Jesus Christ, it is not
necessary to believe that God would ever discipline the faithful followers the
way that Job, at least through the eyes of Eliphaz, was disciplined. Rather,
it is important for faithful Christians to understand that God desires that
we learn from the difficult moments in our lives. Treat every moment as a
learning opportunity. While God's hand is not heavy in terms of being a
Divine disciplinarian, the lessons of life are truly important and are most
easily learned when we face challenges like Job's.

April 4
DON'T FORGET . . .

Do not neglect to do good and to share what you have, for such sacrifices are pleasing to God. —Hebrews 13:16 (ESV)

Doing good and sharing what you have are two major practices of Christianity. Even so, they seem to be elusive for many people. Admittedly, it's tough to do good all the time, and it's even more difficult to share our possessions with others. Western society is loath to share possessions with others who have not "pulled their weight" or "earned their keep."

Too often it is easy to forget to do good to others and share what we have. We busy ourselves with our own lives and schedules, and when we do that, other people are placed on the back burner of our minds. We might even get frustrated by them when we perceive that they are in our way.

You are encouraged to slow down and remember today that there are indeed others in this world. Those other people need reminders of the presence of God in their lives. Be a reminder of the presence of God in the here and now. Don't forget that you, as a follower of Christ, are called to do good in this life and to share what you have with others. These two practices within Christianity are remarkably effective at showing the light of Christ in this world. Be encouraged to do something good for someone else, and, if you are able, share what you have with someone so that they see and feel the presence of the Holy Spirit within your life as this presence pours forth into their own life.

April 5

A BLANKET OF LOVE

Above all, keep loving one another earnestly, since love covers a multitude of sins. —1 Peter 4:8 (ESV)

Love is like a blanket that warms the heart and soul. It is also like a blanket in the sense that, when we practice love, we cover several sins that we and others have committed. When we are sinned against and yet return the offense with love, we are giving a wonderful gift to the person who has offended us. What an amazing feeling to offer to the person who has slighted you a blanket of love that covers their sins. Instead of the shame and guilt associated with their offense, they are greeted with the warmth of forgiveness.

Then, when you are the guilty party, the one who has sinned against another person, and you react in love rather than indignation and defensiveness, you open the door to forgiveness from the offended party. This may not happen immediately—or at all—but when you confess in love and humility, the door is open for forgiveness and mercy to flow. When we practice covering sin with a blanket of love, we are practicing a Divine behavior.

You are encouraged on this day to practice throwing a blanket of love over the sins that others commit against you. You are also encouraged to be humble and practice confession in love when you sin against other people. Be patient with others. Do not expect others to cover your sins with a blanket of love as quickly as you may cover theirs, but do not withhold that love from them.

April 6

DO NOT FEAR

. . . Jesus said to Simon, "Do not be afraid; from now on you will be catching people." —Luke 5:10b (NRSV)

Fear has the potential to be an all-consuming emotion. It can paralyze us, freezing us as we notice something bad is about to happen. It can cause us to flee from a situation when that is not necessary. Fear can cause us to buck against something or someone when we do not understand all the details of the situation or we feel that we are being mistreated. Fear can also cause us to flee from our calling in life.

Peter had witnessed Jesus' power over nature. He still did not know Jesus' identity as the Christ, but he understood enough to recognize that, because of his sinfulness, he did not need to be in Jesus' presence. Peter was afraid and Jesus knew it. Jesus also knew that Peter had a special calling in his life, a calling from which Jesus could not let his soon-to-be disciple flee. Peter was going to be one of the greatest evangelists and missionaries that the church had ever known, but he would not get there if he fell into the trap of fear.

Peter was afraid, not of Jesus but of being a profane person in the presence of one so righteous. Jesus, though, knowing what to say and when to say it, expelled Peter's fear and affirmed him by offering these comforting words: "Do not be afraid." What a blessing to be offered this simple phrase. Its simplicity betrays its weighty impact.

You too need not fear. Be comforted by the presence of Christ in your life today. Despite your failings and sins, Jesus has approached you and said, "Do not be afraid." Fear not; Jesus knows your sins and yet desires a relationship with you.

April 7

SPIRITUAL EXERCISE: GUIDED PRAYER

Do you ever struggle with offering forgiveness to others? Are you withholding forgiveness from another person in your life right now? The truth of the matter is that this is a human reaction to being hurt. However, this human reaction is still sinful and wrong. Take a few moments to honestly reflect on your life and relationships. Try to identify whether you are indeed withholding forgiveness from anyone.

Perhaps you are not withholding forgiveness. If this is true, that is wonderful, but resist the temptation to become prideful about it. Instead, pray that you never fall into the temptation of withholding forgiveness, and pray for those who struggle with this issue.

Suggested Scripture: Genesis 50:15-20; Matthew 6:14-15

Suggested Prayer:
> *Merciful God,*
> *Thank you for not withholding forgiveness from me, even at the cost of your own Son's life. Please grant me the strength, wisdom, and grace to offer forgiveness to others, even when they would not admit to any wrongdoing or receive my genuine offer of forgiveness. Please give me the ability to forgive others as you already have, continue to do, and will forever forgive me of my sins. These things I pray to you in the name of Jesus Christ, amen.*

April 8

THE STONES WILL LIFT
UP THEIR VOICES

Some of the Pharisees in the crowd said to Jesus, "Teacher, rebuke your disciples!" "I tell you," he [Jesus] replied, "if they keep quiet, the stones will cry out." —Luke 19:39-40 (NIV)

Jesus arrived at Jerusalem in what has become known as the "Triumphal Entry." During this moment, Jesus rode a donkey into the city of David and thereby fulfilled Old Testament prophecies regarding his identity as the Son of David, one worthy to sit on David's throne. In response to this visual symbol, the disciples began shouting their praises to Jesus. The other Gospel accounts include the crowds in this praise. The Pharisees responded by asking that Jesus calm his disciples down and make them silent. Jesus answered them with a beautiful image: that if the disciples fell silent, then the stones would cry out their praises to Jesus.

This is truly a beautiful image, particularly since it involves parts of nature that cannot sing for lack of vocal cords and a mouth. These inanimate objects would become livelier than the disciples if the closest followers of Christ suddenly lost their voices. This is a powerful word concerning the identity of Jesus of Nazareth.

You are encouraged to offer up praises to Jesus in your own way today. Do not be outdone by the stones, trees, and birds outside. While nature itself is always offering up praises to the Creator, it is especially meaningful to God when the favored creation, humanity, freely offers up praise to our Savior.

April 9

THE SERVANT OF
THE LORD

*"Behold my servant, whom I uphold, my chosen, in whom my
soul delights; I have put my Spirit upon him; he will bring forth
justice to the nations." —Isaiah 42:1 (ESV)*

Isaiah is sometimes known as the Messianic prophet. Many of the prophecies found within the pages of the Old Testament book that bears his name deal with the Jewish Messiah. Today's verse is found at the beginning of what is called a "servant song." There are four such "songs" within Isaiah. They all talk about the coming Messiah.

The Messiah would be a servant to God the Father. Indeed, the Christian Messiah, Jesus, though being the second person of the Trinity, does play a role that is subservient to God the Father; Jesus prays that God the Father's will be done, not his own. The idea that God the Son is servant to anyone is sometimes troubling, even if it is to God the Father. However, Christians may rejoice in the idea that Jesus, the Servant to God the Father, indeed fulfilled that role perfectly. Without this perfect submission, there would not be an adequate atonement for the forgiveness of the sins of humanity.

Pause today and ponder the servant role of Jesus Christ. This role is filled to overflowing with humility. The God of the universe lowered God's self to a servant role in order to rescue humanity from the muck and mire of sinfulness. Offer praises to God that the ultimate Servant has rescued you from absolute separation.

April 10

THE ABSURD POWER OF GOD

For the message about the cross is foolishness to those who are perishing, but to us who are being saved it is the power of God.
—1 Corinthians 1:18 (NRSV)

The idea that humanity could be rescued from sinfulness by someone hanging on a cross seems absurd. Making this declaration of faith in the presence of a nonbeliever, particularly one who is convinced that Christianity is wrong, opens the door for criticism or worse, depending on your location in the world. However, when we recognize the truth of Christianity—that God does indeed love humanity, that God does indeed exist, and that God does indeed desire a deep and meaningful relationship with humanity through God the Son—we see the true power of God on display as Christ hung on the cross.

By going to the cross, Christ displayed the full extent of the Divine power of God. Nothing would stand in the way of God revealing the Divine to humanity. Nothing would stifle the love of God. Nothing, not even death, would defeat the saving grace of God.

For Christians, the season of Lent/Easter is an important time for reflection. We reflect on the true power of God that was displayed on the first Good Friday. We reflect on the power of God that had apparently been defeated on Holy Saturday. And we rejoice over the power of God that was fully displayed when the tomb was found empty. Reflect today on the absurd power of God, this power that makes no sense to the non-Christian world, and rejoice because that power was displayed for you.

April 11

FROM SHAME TO THE THRONE

Looking unto Jesus, the author and finisher of our faith, who for the joy that was set before him endured the cross, despising the shame, and has sat down at the right hand of the throne of God.
—Hebrews 12:2 (NKJV)

There was great shame in being crucified on the cross. The individuals were likely naked, with their arms and legs spread so all could see. They were nailed to the beams that made the cross. Their bodies were exposed, contorted, and beaten, and they were dying in an excruciatingly painful manner, likely from suffocation after exhaustion overwhelmed them.

If this were not enough, Jesus suffered this torturous death not because he deserved it but because he was offering salvation to all who would believe in him as the Son of God. God does not deserve this type of treatment, being scorned and beaten. Yet Christ endured it all to ensure that any who would believe in him as the Son of God would have an advocate sitting at the right hand of God the Father, who is on the throne of paradise.

Be encouraged today to seek comfort in the knowledge that Jesus, God the Son, endured such shame to ensure that you have an advocate. Christ's shame was temporary, but it was well worth suffering to ensure that you have salvation. Remember that Christ's life and death were for the purpose of bringing salvation to all who would believe in Christ. Christ endured great shame and dishonor for the sake of all of humanity. Rest in the assurance that you have salvation because of Christ's temporary shame and eternal glorification at the right hand of God the Father.

April 12

ULTIMATE COMPLETION

When Jesus had received the wine, he said, "It is finished." Then
he bowed his head and gave up his spirit. —John 19:30 (NRSV)

The life of Christ had apparently come to an abrupt and terrible end. The religious leaders of the Jewish community who had viewed Jesus as a threat were likely relieved. The Messianic prophecies from Old Testament prophetic books like Isaiah had been fulfilled. Jesus, the Son of God, had died for our sins.

Jesus gave himself up to be crucified and gave up his spirit as he hung on the cross. Christians come to this portion of Scripture with mixed feelings. On the one hand, it is appropriate to mourn that Christ had to die, especially in such a horrific fashion, to forgive our sins. On the other hand, we may rejoice that our sins are indeed forgiven.

There was great intentionality in the events of what we call Good Friday. God intended for the Son to die. Christ submitted to the will of God the Father the night before his crucifixion as he prayed in Gethsemane (Matt 26:39). The Divine plan of salvation came to its ultimate completion. As Jesus' lifeless body hung on the cross, our lives were spared a fate worse than crucifixion. We were instead assured, through this act of Divine love and sacrifice and our faith in this event, of eternal life and salvation from our sins and the Divine judgment that would have fallen squarely on our shoulders had Christ not intervened. Be encouraged on this day to rest in the knowledge that your salvation has been assured through your faith in Christ, who completed the Divine plan of salvation.

April 13

A DARK DAY OF REST

On the Sabbath they rested according to the commandment.
—Luke 23:56b (ESV)

The disciples, the women who had been following Jesus, and the other followers of Christ rested on the Sabbath. Joseph of Arimathea had taken Jesus' body on that Friday and placed him in a tomb. There was not enough time in the day to truly prepare Jesus' body for a proper Jewish burial according to their customs, so they waited in mournful rest.

How painful and dark this day must have been for the initial followers of Jesus, those who had built a deep and meaningful relationship with him and had followed him for those last three years. They shared meals with him, likely camped with him under the stars, bore witness to all his miracles, heard all his sermons and teachings, and were even empowered to heal the sick and drive out demons. These individuals mourned and hid in fear of the Jewish leadership who had orchestrated the crucifixion of their rabbi and friend.

You are encouraged to enter a time of quiet reflection today. Reflect on Jesus' death: what it meant for humanity and what it means for you individually. Consider what it must have been like to be one of those first followers on the first full day after Jesus' death. Consider also the great love that God has for you.

April 14

SPIRITUAL EXERCISE: LECTIO DIVINA
(DIVINE READING)

On this day you are invited to practice a spiritual exercise, a "divine reading" of a select passage of Scripture. Please follow the guide provided as you meditate on this passage.

- Read the passage twice, pausing between each reading for a moment of silence. Identify key words as you read through the passage without elaboration.
- Read the passage again, pause for silence, and answer the following question: Where does the content of the reading touch my life today?
- Read the passage once more, again pausing for silence, and complete this sentence: I believe God wants me to . . .

> *On the first day of the week, very early in the morning, the women took the spices they had prepared and went to the tomb. They found the stone rolled away from the tomb, but when they entered, they did not find the body of the Lord Jesus. While they were wondering about this, suddenly two men in clothes that gleamed like lightning stood beside them. In their fright the women bowed down with their faces to the ground, but the men said to them, "Why do you look for the living among the dead? He is not here; he has risen! Remember how he told you, while he was still with you in Galilee: 'The Son of Man must be delivered over to the hands of sinners, be crucified and on the third day be raised again.'" Then they remembered his words. —Luke 24:1-8 (NIV)*

April 15

CHRIST HAS RISEN

"He is not here, for he [Jesus] has risen, just as he said. Come, see the place where he was lying." —Matthew 28:6 (NASB)

Jesus Christ, the Son of God, has risen from the dead and now lives forevermore at the right hand of God the Father, interceding on behalf of all who believe in him. Jesus' death was only one part of the Messianic prophecy. The rest was fulfilled on that first Easter Sunday when the women found the empty tomb where Jesus' body was supposed to be.

Easter Sunday is arguably the greatest day on the Christian calendar. While it may not receive the same amount of attention from the retail stores as Christmas does, Easter is the day on which all of humanity, particularly those who believe in these events, received the greatest gift of all: salvation from sins and the assurance of eternal life in the full presence of God. This is unparalleled. Nothing compares to the gift of a risen Savior and all that his resurrection has accomplished.

Jesus Christ was brutally killed. Scripture records that he did indeed die on the cross. However, that was not the end of the story. Christ's death brought about an intermission of sorts. His resurrection brings about the fulfillment of the Old Testament's prophecies and seals the new covenant in his blood, that is, the forgiveness of all sins of those who believe in these events and the promise of eternal life. Celebrate this today. You have eternal life because your Savior, Jesus Christ, lives and is interceding on your behalf in the presence of God the Father.

April 16
GRACE OVER LAW

But to him who does not work but believes on Him who justifies the ungodly, his faith is accounted for righteousness . . . .
—Romans 4:5 (NKJV)

Obeying the law is expected of all reasonable citizens of any community. Adhering to the laws saves one the trouble of paying fines, spending time in court, or, worse yet, spending time in prison. Laws also help to maintain order and avoid chaos in the here and now. However, when it comes to our spiritual lives and that which is to come, adhering to a set of laws doesn't accomplish our goal of making us righteous enough to enter the full presence of God.

In this passage in the letter to the Roman church, Paul emphasizes that Abraham was justified and forgiven of his sins, not because of anything that he had done but because he had faith in God. Abraham was the perfect convert from a pagan religious tradition to a follower of the One True God. Abraham simply exercised faith in God, without any previously established laws, and was forgiven of his sins.

When it comes to our own faith, we have a decision to make. Will we exhaust ourselves trying to adhere perfectly to the laws of God? Or will we be content to exercise faith in God through Christ and allow that faith to justify us? Remember, no matter how faithful you think you are to the law of God, it is never going to be faithful enough to ensure everlasting life and peace in God's presence. You are encouraged to seek the grace of God. Yes, there is merit in the laws of God, and they are good to follow. However, they will not save you; only the grace of God will save you. Seek this grace rather than strict legalism.

April 17

TRUTH THROUGH UNCLEAN LIPS

"What do you want with us, Jesus of Nazareth? Have you come to destroy us? I know who you are—the Holy One of God!"
—Mark 1:24 (NIV)

The demon-possessed man was presenting the gospel, but he was presenting it through unclean lips. The Greek word for *evil* may also be translated as *unclean*. It is often used to describe the kinds of spirits that inhabited those whom the New Testament describes as demon possessed. In this case, the demon-possessed man was identifying Jesus as the Christ before it was the appropriate time to do so. Thus, unclean lips were sharing the truth.

The same thing occurs today. People whose motivations are impure will share the truth of Jesus Christ. As Augustine explained, the danger is that the truth may be distorted by these unclean lips. When we notice that there are those who are presenting the truth with impure motives, motives not given to them by the Holy Spirit, we must be careful.

It is imperative that Christians be discerning, able to recognize when someone is distorting the truth of Christ to push their own agenda(s) or perhaps to fatten their own pocketbooks. You are encouraged to deepen your spiritual life, to broaden your understanding of the Triune God, and to prepare yourself to recognize distortions in the presentation of the gospel of Jesus Christ. Remember that the truth of the gospel itself is absolute, but we should inspect carefully the messenger who brings us that truth. Remember Paul's teaching: weigh against Scripture everything that is taught in order to find the truth, particularly when that teaching centers on Scripture and the gospel of Jesus Christ.

April 18

REMOVE YOUR YEAST FIRST

Clean out the old leaven so that you may be a new lump, just as you are in fact unleavened. For Christ our Passover also has been sacrificed. —1 Corinthians 5:7 (NASB)

When worked through a large batch of dough, a small bit of yeast affects the entire batch. In this context, Paul was talking about a specific person who was sinning. Paul encouraged the Corinthians to expel this person from the church until he had repented and ceased his sinful behavior. This was the yeast. The sins of this man were a threat to the entire church community in Corinth. It is not a bad thing to remove yourself from someone or something that is sinful; doing so helps you to avoid falling into a similar trap.

The challenge that we face as Christians in situations like this is failing to perform spiritual self-reflection before we target the person who is clearly sinning. Christians have, unfortunately, been labeled hypocrites. That label is earned. Too often in our collective history, Christians have been quick to point a finger at someone else for their open sin in order to avoid having our own sins identified.

You are encouraged to perform some self-reflection today. Where is there yeast in your life? Where does sin persist? What type of sin continues to plague you? Reflect on your spiritual life and repent. Make a 180-degree turn and flee from that sinful habit. This leads to spiritual maturity and removes the yeast of sin from your life. When you do this, you will be better equipped to assist your fellow believers when they are stuck in a sinful habit, struggling with their own yeast.

April 19

JESUS' COULD NOT ABANDON HIS REASON FOR COMING

"Now my soul is troubled. And what should I say—'Father, save me from this hour'? No, it is for this reason that I have come to this hour." *—John 12:27 (NRSV)*

Jesus had a specific reason for coming to this world. There had to have been a reason for God to come and live this earthly life, incarnated in human flesh. The reason was to live, minister to the people of Israel, teach of the coming kingdom of God, die, and rise from the dead to forgive the sins of those who confessed faith in these events.

When Christ came to this life, the Divine and human entities slammed into one another full force. Christ, as orthodox Christian theology teaches, maintained a dual nature, that of God and that of human being. This empowered Christ to experience all the temptations, struggles, and joys that come with being human, including the temptation to abdicate his responsibility to serve the will of God the Father.

Although Christ evidently faced this temptation, as he faced others following his baptism while in the wilderness, he did not succumb to the temptation to flee from his reason for coming to this life. Christ knew that his purpose was to offer salvation to humanity. Christ also knew that salvation would not come unless he went to the cross and died. What a terribly difficult place for any human being! Thankfully, Jesus was also Divine in nature and was compelled to follow the will of God the Father. He completed his duties as the Savior of humanity in dying on the cross and rising from the dead to bring hope, meaning, and true joy to the lives of those who believe in these events as they are recorded in the Gospel accounts.

April 20

JESUS' PEACE OVERCOMES THE WORLD

I have said these things to you, that in me you may have peace. In the world you will have tribulation. But take heart; I have overcome the world." —John 16:33 (ESV)

So many things in this life threaten to disrupt any sense of peace that we may have. Financial difficulties; disappointments at school or work; arguments with family, friends, or coworkers; crushing news from a doctor's appointment; the death of a loved one or a dearly loved pet. If you are a parent, then the burdens of rearing a child may plague your heart and mind. Perhaps your child is struggling to make friends. Maybe they didn't make a team or first chair. There is a plethora of situations in life that threaten to disrupt our peace.

The truth of the matter is that we may never find peace in the here and now. Or if we do, that peace is fleeting, here one moment and gone the next. However, the peace that Christ offers overcomes all things in this life. Christ's peace is everlasting, it is fulfilling, and it has overcome the troubles of the world.

What does this mean? Simply put, no matter the troubles in which you are embroiled, the peace of Christ will find you and offer you comfort and rest. Unfortunately, that peace will not be fully realized until we cross over into what is to come, but as we practice our faith, we will have opportunities to encounter glimpses of that future in the here and now. Be encouraged to seek Christ's peace in the here and now through your faith rather than seeking to make peace on your own terms.

April 21

SPIRITUAL EXERCISE: PSALM OF PRAISE

This is a day on which you are encouraged to reflect on the following psalm. What does the Spirit tell you through these words? Do you find it easy to offer praises to God today? If not, then commune with God and listen for the Divine voice. Can you identify what is preventing your ability to offer praises?

> The LORD is merciful and gracious, slow to anger and
>   abounding in steadfast love.
> He will not always chide, nor will he keep his anger forever.
> He does not deal with us according to our sins, nor repay us
>   according to our iniquities.
> For as high as the heavens are above the earth, so great is his
>   steadfast love toward those who fear him;
> as far as the east is from the west, so far does he remove our
>   transgressions from us. —Psalm 103:8-12 (ESV)

April 22

FEELINGS OF ABANDONMENT

My God, my God, why have you forsaken me? Why are you so far from saving me, so far from my cries of anguish? —Psalm 22:1 (NIV)

It is easy to look to this psalm and imagine the psalmist crying out to God with clenched fists waving frantically about in the air. This is the psalm Jesus quoted while hanging on the cross. Considering that image, it is easy for us as readers to get the feeling that there are moments when God is far off, when God has abandoned God's people. Do not lose heart.

When the world and life's circumstances seem to overwhelm you, when things of this life seem to push God far away and the Divine presence is no longer felt in your walk, take courage. This is admittedly easier said than done. It is easy to find courage when we are surrounded by a reliable support system. Soldiers of antiquity, when standing shoulder to shoulder, would face insurmountable odds because they knew that they were not alone.

Jesus quoted this psalm when it appeared that all was lost. Christians who face situations where the Divine presence may not be readily felt may also quote this portion of the psalm. Do not be lulled into this way of thinking. Jesus did not quote this portion of Psalm 22 because God the Father was absent. Rather, Jesus quoted this psalm to acknowledge that God's will was being done. Reflect on your life circumstances, particularly those that are difficult. What might you be able to learn of God and your relationship to the Divine through those circumstances?

April 23

TRANSITION

They divide my clothes among them and cast lots for my garment. But you, LORD, do not be far from me. You are my strength; come quickly to help me. —Psalm 22:18-19 (NIV)

Jesus begins to quote the psalmist's words from Psalm 22 while hanging on the cross. It could have been, as many suggest, that Jesus felt like God the Father's presence had left him as he hung, suffering on the cross. More likely, Jesus viewed the psalm as a sort of prophecy, a word of connection between the Messiah and the psalmist of old.

The Twenty-Second Psalm begins with a word of woe and, apparently, a word of concern that God is no longer present to assist the psalmist through a certain chapter in life that was filled with suffering. However, as the psalm continues, a transition takes place from that word of woe to a potentially prophetic word and then on to assurances that God is indeed present with the psalmist amid suffering.

There will undoubtedly be moments in the life of every believer that seem void of any Divine presence. Do not be discouraged; this is only an illusion. God's presence is with you all the time. Find comfort in this knowledge. God is not far from you. None of your troubles will ever separate you from God. Be patient in those moments when God feels distant, and wait for God to make the Divine presence known. Allow that time of transition to take place, and seek to learn something of God and yourself in that moment.

April 24

THE TRUTH OF PSALM 22

From you comes the theme of my praise in the great assembly; before those who fear you I will fulfill my vows. The poor will eat and be satisfied; those who seek the LORD will praise him—may your hearts live forever! —Psalm 22:25-26 (NIV)

The truth of Psalm 22 is revealed as the reader delves further into the text. When one reads the first few verses, or even reads Jesus' quote of this psalm in the context of his crucifixion, it is easy to understand why one would assume that Jesus feels as though he is left alone on the cross.

The truth is much greater than the empty and alone feeling that is attributed to the Savior. Rather than being alone, Jesus, knowing the psalm in its entirety, knew that God the Father was present even in that moment of great suffering. Though it may have appeared that the Divine presence had taken a back seat to the suffering in the moment, that was false.

What sort of suffering are you experiencing right now? Or what has been the most recent event that you have suffered through? Did it feel as though God was absent? Did you recognize that you were not alone? Or are you recognizing that truth now? God is not absent in our moments of strife and agony. God is with us. In the crucifix, our Catholic brothers and sisters lean on a powerful visual symbol of God's joint suffering with humanity. Does the presence of God, even amid our suffering, make that suffering any more bearable? Not always. Despite this, remember that God is with you, no matter your suffering. Remember also that God has suffered and likely suffers for the sake of humanity even now. God is not an absent God. God is present with us in our pain. I pray that this offers some comfort to you when you do suffer.

April 25

ANGRY TO BED, ANGRY TO RISE

Be angry, and yet do not sin; do not let the sun go down on your
anger . . . . —Ephesians 4:26 (NASB)

Anger is a potentially dangerous emotion. Yet at the same time it can be a righteous response to certain evils in this world. In the case of the verse for today, anger is not necessarily a sin in and of itself; however, Paul is encouraging the Christians in Ephesus to deal with their anger before the day is over.

The issue at hand was not that the people were angry. It was how they dealt with that anger. Evidently, they were not dealing with the anger and were carrying it with them to bed and, most likely, into the next morning. When we allow our anger to remain with us, even well beyond that which triggered the anger, it becomes toxic and unhealthy.

Paul's point is that when we carry our anger with us, while it may not start out as a sin, the longer it ferments in our hearts and minds the less righteous it becomes—if it even started out as righteous anger to begin with. We must understand that anger itself is not a sin; it is what we do with that anger. When we get angry about a situation, a person, or something else and do not address the cause, then we are fueling an unhealthy or toxic habit that breeds dysfunction and further problems. Be encouraged to face what causes you to become angry. More than facing it, deal with it and come to peace with it. Help others to understand what they did or said that made you mad so that they may grow from the experience too. Avoid holding on to your anger for an extended period.

April 26

REJECTING THE TRUE KING

. . . and the LORD said to Samuel, "Listen to the voice of the people in all that they say to you; for they have not rejected you, but they have rejected me from being king over them."
—1 Samuel 8:7 (NRSV)

The Israelites desperately wanted to conform to the nations around them. Everyone else had an earthly king sitting on a throne, but the Israelites had judges who would execute the commands of God and lead the people according to how God led the individual judges. This pattern went on for many generations, from Moses to Samuel. However, the people wanted to fall in line with the "heathen" nations—as the Hebrew language puts it—around them.

Samuel had a visceral reaction to this rejection and took it personally. God responded with Divine wisdom and helped Samuel recognize that the people were not rejecting their last judge but were rejecting the One who led that judge. The Israelites were fooled by the world around them into rejecting God as their sole leader. Instead, they wanted to fit in according to the political climate of their world. It is dangerous to conform to this world and reject God our King.

Be encouraged to avoid rejecting the King of kings for some finite earthly king who will only disappoint in the long run. Avoid following the example that the Israelites offered in rejecting God's leadership for the leadership that would eventually abuse the people. Avoid also taking things too personally when someone around you does indeed reject God in their lives.

April 27

DIVIDED KINGDOMS FALL

"How can Satan cast out Satan? If a kingdom is divided against itself, that kingdom cannot stand." —Mark 3:23b-24 (ESV)

This is one of the most famous verses in all of Scripture. It has been reworded and attributed to Abraham Lincoln, who said it during his presidency regarding a divided nation. Jesus and Lincoln are right: a divided kingdom or nation or house cannot stand. Here, Jesus is responding to the accusation that he is Beelzebub, as he has exercised authority over demons.

Jesus points out the obvious—that Satan cannot succeed if Satan drives out the demons from their hosts and stymies the demonic efforts to trip humanity. Satan cannot succeed anyway, but why would anyone intentionally hurt their own efforts? It makes no sense. Take this to heart. As Lincoln knew, it does not apply only to Jesus about Satan.

Are you having an issue with someone who is close to you? Are you fighting with your spouse? Is there heartache in your relationship with your children or parents? Do you and your siblings fail to get along? Avoid looking too much into the relationships of others. Do not worry about your spouse's relationship with your mother; you cannot control that relationship. What you can control is how you behave in your own relationships. Reflect on your relationships and how you carry yourself as you interact with others. If you have a conflict, think about what you are contributing to encourage that conflict. Seek resolution, remembering that your conflicts will not be resolved and there will be no real sense of peace in your relationships unless you face the problem. Seek God's wisdom as you strive to end the conflict.

April 28

SPIRITUAL EXERCISE: COUNT YOUR BLESSINGS

You are invited to enter a time of reflection over your life. Often, when reflecting and thinking about our lives, we dwell on the negative. We think things like this: "I don't make enough money." "If only I had that house." "I should have gotten that degree." "I wish I had the time to do that thing." Insert any perceived failure or desire here.

Instead of focusing on these perceived failures or unfulfilled desires, reflect on the blessings you have in this life. Think of the meaningful relationships in your life, the essentials that you might take for granted—even that clunker of a car that leaks, skips, or sputters but still gets you to your destination in one piece. Use the remainder of this page to count your blessings, and thank God for each one as you write them down. Revisit this page in a few days, weeks, and even months and reflect on the list you've made. What additions can you make?

_____

_____

_____

_____

A DAILY WALK WITH GOD

April 29

DISCERNMENT IS
IMPERATIVE

*But the LORD said to Samuel, "Do not consider his appearance
or his height, for I have rejected him. The LORD does not look at
the things people look at. People look at the outward appearance,
but the LORD looks at the heart." —1 Samuel 16:7 (NIV)*

Within the overall passage of 1 Samuel 16:1-13, the Hebrew word translated most often as *to see* appears four times. Often it is understood as literally referring to the sense of sight. However, twice in this passage it is meant to be read and understood as *to have discernment*. To discern simply means to understand something that is difficult.

Samuel sought to anoint the second king of Israel after Saul's kingship had not panned out. Samuel met with Jesse, the father of David, and his sons. David's seven elder brothers were physically impressive to Samuel, each appearing as though he would make a good king. This was part of what hindered Saul: he was a physically impressive and imposing man, but that did not equate being a good king. Eventually, God revealed that David was to be the next king, and Samuel anointed the young shepherd.

Discernment is a crucial skill that is imperative for right decision making. As followers of Christ, we must be discerning in all aspects of life. Recognizing how we ought to behave in difficult situations and knowing the right things to say and do when we assist others require discernment. Seek to be discerning in your life today.

April 30
PRIVATE LESSONS

. . . and He [Jesus] did not speak to them without a parable; but
He was explaining everything privately to His own disciples.
—Mark 4:34 (NASB)

Jesus taught many people through word and deed; however, the most pointed and clearly articulated lessons were reserved for his disciples, the ones who were closest to him. Those individuals had a great opportunity to learn from the Son of God. Modern Christians are privy to those private lessons too, since they are recorded in Scripture.

In these private lessons, the disciples were given a clearer understanding of Jesus' parables and actions. Following these private lessons, the first twelve disciples were instructed to go and share what they had learned. These private lessons were not reserved only for those first disciples; they are for all who call on Christ in genuine faith.

Jesus taught many things. Chief among his teachings is the summary of the Law: love the Lord your God with every part of your being, and love one another as you love yourself. That is not the entirety of Jesus' teachings. John himself says that all the books of the world would not contain everything Jesus taught.

Since you and I are blessed to be included in those private lessons between Jesus and the disciples, let us take them to heart. We are blessed with the gift of the Holy Spirit to help us make sense of Jesus' teachings that we have in our Scriptures. Apply those teachings to your life today, and every day, and ensure that you are the salt and light that Christ has taught you to be.

May 1

HUMAN PANIC VS. DIVINE CALM

*But he was in the stern, asleep on the cushion; and they woke
him up and said to him, "Teacher, do you not care that we are
perishing?" —Mark 4:38 (NRSV)*

Prayer is often a tool used by the faithful in times of crisis. It can and is a
wonderful practice in our daily walk when we are not being tossed about by
the chaotic storms of life. But when life goes haywire and we are neck deep
in a tumultuous situation, we panic. When we no longer feel as though
we have control over situations, we begin to wonder if God is with us or,
if God is indeed present, why the Divine does not seem to care about us.

If we can get beyond the false idea that God is not with us or does not
care, we can avoid panicked prayers and panicked faith. When we are in
a panic, we may misunderstand those around us who remain calm as not
caring about us or our situation. This is not true, especially for those closest
to us. Even more so, it is not true about God.

To the disciples who were fighting against a terrible tempest, Jesus
appeared to be unconcerned for his followers as he was sleeping in the back
of the boat during the storm. This is an easy conclusion to come to when
we are panicked by a crisis; our loved ones seem aloof and unconcerned
when they do not share in our panic. The truth is that both our loved ones
and, more importantly, God are with us, supporting us, loving us, and
helping us. Remember that the disciples were not spared going through the
storm. Seek to avoid panic when facing crisis; rather, turn to the Divine
peace and presence that permeates all situations in your life.

May 2
SPACE TO GRIEVE

David took up this lament concerning Saul and his son Jonathan
.... —2 Samuel 1:17 (NIV)

David's best friend had been killed in battle, and so had the king of Israel. Second Samuel 1:17-27 is a funeral dirge, a lament that is unique in Scripture. Though psalms and poems of lament outnumber all other genres of psalm and poetic writing, the dirge is not found in the book of Psalms. The dirge has no theological language and no mention of God, though it is extremely important within the pages of Scripture.

Why, you might ask, is such a psalm so important within Scripture when it does not mention God or hold any real theological nugget? It is important because of the raw humanity on display here. David experiences great anguish, suffering the pain and agony of losing his greatest friend, Jonathan, one whom he viewed as a brother—perhaps even closer than a brother since they were indeed in-laws.

David and all of Israel needed the space to grieve the loss of their king and prince. David had a violent and turbulent relationship with Saul throughout the last half of the first book of Samuel. Most Israelites were ignorant of that aspect of their king's personality—his jealousy. David, following the format of a dirge, only gave a glowing eulogy of Saul and Jonathan, though his real pain was over Jonathan's death. Take some time to acknowledge the grief in your life. If you do not have any grief currently, allow others in your life the space they need to express their grief as David expressed his own.

May 3
HOMETOWN ZERO

"Is not this the carpenter, the son of Mary and brother of James and Joses and Judas and Simon? And are not his sisters here with us?" And they took offense at him. —Mark 6:3 (ESV)

Jesus had been traveling about, teaching and preaching, performing miracles of healing, exorcising demons, and calming storms. He had returned home and was teaching in the synagogue. Most folk had been receptive to this wonder-working, miracle-performing, illness-curing rabbi from Nazareth. His friends, family, and boyhood acquaintances, however, were not amused at his abilities and lessons.

The people were offended that Jesus taught in this way. They did not understand how he got this power and wisdom. All they saw was an illegitimate son of a carpenter, as proven by the comment about his being Mary's son rather than Joseph's. To them, Jesus had no business receiving a rabbi's education and then teaching others about God.

Instead of welcoming Jesus and celebrating his calling, his family accused him of being somewhat mad or in need of mental help, as Mark 3 insinuates. Jesus was the hometown zero rather than the hero. What does this mean for us who are followers of Jesus? Simply put, Jesus does not meet the supposed qualifications of a Savior. Do not be lulled into a false sense of concern over this; rather, rejoice that Jesus, who was mistaken for a possessed madman, is instead God in flesh who is all too aware of the human condition and has experienced many things that you have experienced or may experience in your life. Fear not, for though the image of Christ may fall short of humanity's expectations, Christ is humanity's true hero.

May 4

THE OBEDIENCE
OF THE ONE

For as through the one man's disobedience the many were made sinners, even so through the obedience of the One the many will be made righteous. —Romans 5:19 (NASB)

In following the account of the fall of humanity in Genesis 3, we see that it is through the sin of Adam that all of humanity is doomed to live a life of difficulty and struggle, the most difficult struggle being against the temptations and the resulting sin. It was through the actions, the sins, of this one person that all were made sinners; that is what Paul says to the Roman believers.

It is not the end of the story, though. It is only the beginning. Through the obedience of another single individual, all who believe in this individual as their Savior are made righteous. This one individual is Jesus Christ, and it was Jesus' obedience to God the Father—going to the cross, dying, and being raised to new life again—that lead to the righteousness of all who believe in these events and who cling to Jesus as their Savior and the Son of God.

In this life, we will all disobey at some point. If you have any experience with young children, you know this is the truth. You too have been disobedient, but do not be overcome with the feelings of defeat because of your disobedience; it does not define you if you are a believer in Christ. What truly defines you is your faith in Christ. This makes you righteous because Jesus was obedient on your behalf, knowing that you could not become righteous on your own. Reflect on this truth today and rejoice over Christ's obedience.

May 5

SPIRITUAL EXERCISE: WONDERING IN CREATION

Too often in Western society, people are distracted rather than present in the moment. In the popular movie, *The Empire Strikes Back*, Yoda, the wise teacher of the Jedi in the ways of the Force, reveals that Luke, the protagonist of the film, is not ready to be trained because he never remains in the present. His mind always wanders, drifting, daydreaming, thinking of the future. In this 1980 classic film of pop culture, we are not only made privy to an observation of a brash young hero but are also given an opportunity to gaze into the cultural mirror and see ourselves too.

With this spiritual exercise, you are encouraged to be present in the moment. Use the senses that God has blessed you with and notice the things that often go unnoticed in your daily routine. What do you see, smell, hear, feel, and taste? Take special note of nature. If you can get outside today, do so. If you cannot get outside, take a few moments to look at a pet, a potted plant, the view out the window, or even your reflection in the mirror. As you study whatever you find in the natural, created world, take note of the Divine fingerprints that cover it. How has God revealed God's self to you in that tree, in the bird's song, in the wag of your dog's tail, or in your own face?

The point of this exercise is to be present in the moment. If your mind begins to wander, acknowledge that fact and calmly refocus on what you were studying. Do not beat yourself up for having succumbed to wandering. This exercise takes practice. Calm yourself and focus on something that God created. Take a few minutes to wonder at God's handiwork.

May 6
PAUL'S REALITY OF GRACE

But by the grace of God I am what I am, and his grace to me was not without effect. No, I worked harder than all of them—yet not I, but the grace of God that was with me.
—1 Corinthians 15:10 (NIV)

While he was known as Saul, Paul practiced a legalistic form of Judaism that demanded 100 percent on all tests. A paraphrase of the late, great preacher Fred Craddock from a series on Luke goes like this: "one 99 in a lifetime of 100s never averages 100 percent." Paul knew that he did not average 100 percent, but that was what he believed God demanded. Paul wasn't wrong; that *is* what God demands. However, we cannot give 100 percent all the time. We fail. Thankfully, Christ gave 100 percent, and we have grace.

Paul, when reflecting on his former life, the life of a devout and legalistic Jew, recognized that his work was not enough for the grace of God. Nothing that this pious man could have done was good enough. But he tried. Are you trying too hard to be a "good Christian"? If you rely on the merit system, I have one guarantee for you: you *will* fail. There is no doubt about this reality. However, there is a path of least resistance, a path that is easier and a burden that is lighter to bear: the path and the burden of faith.

Have faith in the grace of God today. Rest in the knowledge that you simply aren't good enough, but do not become burdened as this reality sinks in. No one is good enough, not Paul or Peter, not Moses or Elijah. Only Christ is good enough. And your faith in Christ makes you good enough. Rest today in Paul's understanding of grace from God.

May 7
LUKE'S REALITY OF GRACE

"He replied, 'Your brother has come, and your father has killed
the fatted calf, because he has got him back safe and sound.'
Then he became angry and refused to go in. His father came out
and began to plead with him." —Luke 15:27-28 (NRSV)

Grace is nice when we are the recipients. When someone else receives grace, we often are not such big fans of it. We see their mistakes. We know who they are, and we do not want to see them receive this wonderful gift for whatever reason. In the story of the prodigal son, the elder son, the one who stays at home and works the fields, is angry and jealous when the younger, disobedient son returns from his reckless and sinful living.

When someone we know is living a life that is sinful, someone we believe should be punished for that lifestyle or those committed sins, gets away with those sins, we likely may become enraged at their being forgiven. These feelings are experienced more profoundly when we are the ones who have been wronged and the powers that be forgive the offense.

In the case of our passage, the older brother was mad at the father for offering to forgive the younger son. The Gospel according to Luke paints a picture of undeserved grace. From the human perspective of justice and right and wrong, the elder son was justified in being angry. From the Divine perspective in Luke's Gospel, the father is justified in offering grace to the younger son, though it was undeserved. If you believe in Christ as your Savior, you have received undeserved grace. That is your reality. Reflect on that gift, relish in this grace, and offer your praise and thanks to God for giving you such a wondrous gift.

May 8

CLAWS

Wherever He [Jesus] entered villages, or cities, or countryside, they were laying the sick in the market places, and imploring Him that they might just touch the fringe of His cloak; and as many as touched it were being cured. —Mark 6:56 (NASB)

Jesus' contemporaries saw a wonderful miracle worker, someone who presented a message of hope, someone who had compassion on them when the world around them ignored or mistreated them. The people in this verse were desperate just for the chance to touch the hem of Jesus' cloak and have an opportunity for healing. Jesus had compassion on these people and healed the sick, taught them of the hope of the coming kingdom of heaven, and fed them.

The world has an itch that the church can scratch. Too often, though, we have clawed and mangled those in need of compassion. There are hungry, hurting people that the church ignores or, worse yet, marginalizes because they do not fit into a preconceived mold, seem "too far out there" to be helped because they are actively "living in sin," won't "change themselves," or [insert a further shallow, trite reason for not sharing the gospel here].

Retract your claws and see the people around you for who they are, broken and hurting creations of God in need of compassion and love from a tangible source of Divine care. You are that tangible source. Show someone in your life today the compassion of God. Remember that this compassion was shown to you first so that you might be able to show it to others. The world longs for this compassion. Don't let biases or preconceived notions prevent you from being a compassionate presence in the name of Christ for someone else today.

May 9
CLEANING THE FISH

Jesus said to them again, "Peace be with you. As the Father has sent me, even so I am sending you." —John 20:21 (ESV)

Too many Christians expect that a broken and sinful person must "get right with God" before they come to church or participate in the community of faith. Oh, how backward this is! We must catch the fish before we can clean the fish. If you have ever been fishing, you know this is true. You cannot dive into the lake and clean the fish prior to catching the fish; this is a logical fallacy.

Since this is the truth, how can we expect the opposite in terms of faith and conversion, repentance and spiritual healing? The short answer is that we cannot. If we do, we set the other person up for failure before they've even begun their spiritual journey. We live in a broken and fallen world. This does not excuse our sinfulness but rather explains it. Given this information, we cannot expect anyone new to the faith to be cleansed of their sins before they participate; neither can we expect an instant cleansing and full repentance. All the Christians I know—including myself—continue to wrestle with temptation and sin. Do not impose impossible expectations on others when you do not impose them on yourself. And if you do impose them on yourself, then lighten up—you're a sinner. It isn't righteous, but it's true. Thankfully, Jesus *was* sent to clean the fish. All that you've been tasked to do is catch the fish. That was what Jesus said to his first disciples when he called them. He said he would make them "fishers of men" (Matt 4:19). Just catch the fish with the mercy of God and the love of Christ, and let the Triune God do the hard part in cleaning those fish.

May 10

THE TRUTH IN THE MESSIANIC SECRET

Then he began to teach them that the Son of Man must undergo
great suffering, and be rejected by the elders, the chief priests,
and the scribes, and be killed, and after three days rise again.
—*Mark 8:31 (NRSV)*

Jesus had just asked his disciples who they think he is. Peter spoke up, as he was prone to do, and announced that Jesus is the Messiah or the anointed one of God. Jesus then told the disciples to keep this a secret because it was not yet time to reveal his identity. This is probably because it was the will of God that the Son must first die and be resurrected for the forgiveness of the sins of all who believe.

This did not sit well with Peter. The Jewish idea of the Messiah was that this anointed one of God would lead the Israelites to reclaim the former glory they had under the rule of kings David and Solomon. The one who would lead the people from beneath the oppressive sandal of the Roman Empire could not suffer and die; that would not bring salvation. The idea did not compute with this outspoken apostle. Following our verse for today, Peter will rebuke Jesus.

The truth of the messianic secret is that the Savior of the world does not appear to be what we *want* in a savior, but Jesus is exactly what we *need* in a Savior. If this makes no sense to our minds, that is all right; love often makes no sense, and yet it exists and is beautiful, particularly sacrificial love. The sacrificial love of Christ is the truth behind this secret. That love had to be revealed to the world in Jesus' death on the cross and his subsequent resurrection on that first Easter Sunday morning. Praise be to God today for the truth of this wonderful secret.

May 11

THE MOST POWERFUL COMMAND

A new command I give you: Love one another. As I have loved you, so you must love one another. —John 13:34 (NIV)

In some cases, loving other people is easy. Some people are simply lovable. Because of the way they carry themselves in their interactions with others, we cannot help but love them. Others we love because we genuinely are fond of their presence in our lives. Our spouse or partner, our child(ren), parents, and other family are more easily loved than some others. Or they're supposed to be, anyway. The same is true with good friends.

However, other people are simply unlovable, or they appear so on the surface. The bully at school, the rival at work, the guy who cut you off on the interstate—people both familiar and unfamiliar can be difficult to love. You may also think of historical figures who were guilty of atrocious crimes against humanity; surely they are unlovable.

Jesus, though, gives the command to love others as Christ first loved each of us. Ponder that for a moment as you consider the entire gospel of Jesus Christ. We are commanded to love others sacrificially, without bias. This is not a suggestion or a request. God in flesh is telling us that we need to love others the way God loves us. Consider the reality that you are loved by the Creator of all things. Consider now that all people who have ever lived, are living, and will live are loved by God, no matter how dark their actions may be deemed by human standards. Does that mean all are forgiven? No. But all are loved. Love someone today.

May 12

SPIRITUAL EXERCISE: LECTIO DIVINA
(DIVINE READING)

On this day, you are invited to practice a "divine reading" of a select passage of Scripture. Please follow the guide provided as you meditate on this passage.

- Read the passage twice, pausing between each reading for a moment of silence. Identify key words as you read the passage without elaboration.
- Read the passage again. Pause for silence and answer the following question: Where does the content of the reading touch my life today?
- Read the passage once more, again pausing for silence, and complete this sentence: I believe God wants me to . . .

> When the LORD saw that he had gone over to look, God called to him from within the bush, "Moses! Moses!" And Moses said, "Here I am."
> . . . Then he said, "I am the God of your father, the God of Abraham, the God of Isaac and the God of Jacob." At this, Moses hid his face, because he was afraid to look at God.
> . . . Moses said to God, "Suppose I go to the Israelites and say to them, 'The God of your fathers has sent me to you,' and they ask me, 'What is his name?' Then what shall I tell them?"
> God said to Moses, "I AM WHO I AM. This is what you are to say to the Israelites: 'I AM has sent me to you.'" —Exodus 3:4, 6, 13-14 (NIV)

May 13

THE BREAD OF LIFE

Jesus said to them, "I am the bread of life; he who comes to Me will not hunger, and he who believes in Me will never thirst.
—John 6:35 (NASB)

Provision. Jesus is saying that he is the ultimate provision for those who believe in him as the Messiah. He makes seven pivotal "I am" statements throughout John's account of the gospel. Each of these statements reveals a little more of Jesus' identity as the second person of the Trinity, the Son of God and the Savior of humanity.

In this statement, Jesus assures his listeners that those who believe in him as the Messiah will not be hungry or thirsty. Hunger and thirst are real challenges for many people in this world, both literally and spiritually speaking. In this case, Jesus is speaking of spiritual hunger.

Jesus Christ holds the unique ability to satisfy our spiritual hunger. This statement, like all of the "I am" statements of Jesus, suggests that he is the only source of satisfaction, spiritually speaking. There is a plethora of options for us to sample, but none satisfies our hunger like Jesus. Nothing *can* satisfy our spiritual hunger other than Jesus.

Be encouraged in your spiritual walk on this day to seek the lasting and eternal bread, Jesus Christ. As you commune with Christ, your spiritual hunger will be satisfied.

May 14

THE LIGHT OF THE WORLD

Again Jesus spoke to them, saying, "I am the light of the world. Whoever follows me will not walk in darkness, but will have the light of life." —John 8:12 (ESV)

We often hear that this world is full of darkness and sin. When we turn on the news and hear of murders, wars, starving children, and abuse of all kinds, it is easy to understand why we hear that we live in dark times. It is also easier to understand why some Christians speak of their hope that Jesus will come back soon.

It is true that some cruel, evil, and dark things happen in this life. It is also true that, despite this darkness, there is a light that shines. This light reveals itself in many ways—in the caring of a disaster response team, the compassion of a couple taking in a foster child, and donations to various organizations that provide for needy children, battered women, and other disenfranchised or vulnerable people groups and individuals.

The ultimate light, though, is Jesus Christ. The light is not found in Christ but *is* Christ. Jesus offers himself to us as a spiritual guide in this world, equipping us to shine his light into the darkness, to speak up for those without a voice, to care for those who cannot care for themselves, to work alongside of others who provide for, protect, and lift the weak and helpless.

Seek a way that you might be able to shine the Light that *is* Christ in this world of darkness. Do not be overwhelmed by the dark, but be encouraged by the Light that shines in and around you as a follower of Christ.

May 15

THE SHEEP GATE

Therefore Jesus said again, "Very truly I tell you, I am the gate for the sheep." —John 10:7 (NIV)

Jesus is the only true passageway to the full presence of God. Any other passageway is false and leads to spiritual destruction. In this statement, Jesus makes two things clear. First, we are told that Jesus is the *only* gate for the sheep to enter that leads to the path of eternal life. Second, we learn that all other gates lead to destruction and are opened by liars and cheats.

The truth of Christ's words echoes throughout eternity. Christians believe in Jesus of Nazareth serving as our only access point to God the Father, our only mediator, our only path to salvation.

In this life, there will be those who intentionally or unintentionally try to pull us away from Jesus Christ. Some of these individuals will even come in Jesus' name, presenting a message that appears to be wrapped in Christian theology and steeped in Jesus' teachings. Be mindful. Seek the only true path and passageway: Jesus Christ.

As you journey through life on this day, seek discernment from the Holy Spirit so that you may recognize when it is truly Jesus calling out to you, leading you through the open gate. Find comfort in knowing that your Savior is patient with you, not forcing, not berating, only lovingly calling you to this true gate, to himself and to eternal life and salvation.

May 16

THE GOOD SHEPHERD

"I am the good shepherd. The good shepherd lays down his life for the sheep." —John 10:11 (NRSV)

The good shepherd, the protector and provider. The one who loves and gives sacrificially. This is our God in flesh. The Christian Messiah or Christ is the ultimate caregiver and provider for his followers. The idea of a shepherd conveys the image of one who does all that is necessary to provide for the flock under his care.

Ultimately, this means the shepherd will feed, water, lead, protect, and even be willing to lay his life down for the sheep. This is Christ for Christians. The various "I am" statements of Jesus reveal that this is exactly who Christ claims to be. Christ is the one who feeds, waters, cares for, protects, and even dies for the sheep under his care.

This image is intended to evoke comfort in the hearer. It is wonderful to know that we have one who is willing to go above and beyond to ensure that we are cared for in the ultimate sense, the spiritual and lasting sense of eternal life. This is your encouragement today: to find comfort in this imagery and then share that comfort with someone else.

There is great hope in this verse. Jesus gives his life for us, not so that we might be rescued from one disaster only to meet another disaster later in our journey. Instead, we are rescued from the ultimate disaster of banishment from the full presence of God the Father. Our Savior has put his life down for us and then taken it up again so that we too might live forevermore. Find hope in this Christian truth.

May 17

THE RESURRECTION
AND LIFE

Jesus said to her, "I am the resurrection and the life; he who believes in Me will live even if he dies." —John 11:25 (NASB)

We who believe in Jesus Christ will die. Death is an unavoidable reality for all people. The adage goes something like this: Only two things are certain in this life, death and taxes. In truth, death is the only certainty, and that cold embrace is reserved for all, unless Christ does return in our lifetime. Eschatological discussions aside, we all die.

For Christians, however, death is only a passageway to eternal life. Christ was the first to be resurrected in the truest sense, never to die again. Lazarus may have been raised to life after his funeral, but he surely died again in the physical sense.

Chaplains often deal with situations bathed in the gloom of death. Christian chaplains who are ministering to Christian patients and families have common ground to work with: hope in the resurrection.

Though we all must face death, Christians may face this ultimate destination with the hope that we will be resurrected spiritually to a new and eternal life in the full presence of God the Father.

This message may feel stale because it is touted so often in Christian circles. However, it cannot be a message that has grown stale, for it is the most hope-filled and important message in all of Christianity. We who believe in Jesus as the Christ will follow him in being resurrected to new life. Go with this hope renewed today, and allow it to emanate from your very being as you journey through this life.

May 18

THE WAY, THE TRUTH, AND THE LIFE

Jesus said to him, "I am the way, and the truth, and the life. No one comes to the Father except through me." —John 14:6 (ESV)

The first verses of John 14 are popular to read during Christian funerals. This chapter shows us that Jesus offers comfort to his closest disciples and followers just after telling them that he is preparing to leave them—to die. Naturally, the disciples are afraid.

Then, after assuring his disciples that he will return to retrieve them after he has prepared a place for them in God the Father's full presence, Jesus makes this "I am" statement. Jesus of Nazareth is the Messiah who serves as the only path to true spiritual enlightenment and salvation.

When we talk about getting from point A to point B, there are often different routes to take, some easy and others perilous. Granted, there are certain places even in this life that demand we follow one predetermined path to reach the goal. Those things are few and far between, however, as there are often creative and different paths that may have been overlooked before. But the path to eternal life and spiritual enlightenment goes through Jesus Christ alone.

Yes, there are a plethora of non-Christian spiritualities and paths that one may take. They all may offer some sense of peace and tranquility or some limited fulfillment. Following Jesus Christ, though, leads to everlasting peace and total fulfillment. This is the truth that I encourage you to cling to throughout your daily journey of faith.

May 19

SPIRITUAL EXERCISE: GUIDED PRAYER

This week's devotions have revolved around the various "I am" statements of Jesus throughout the Gospel according to John. Each statement reveals a little more about the identity of Jesus of Nazareth as the promised Messiah or Christ.

What does it mean to us that Jesus is the Messiah or Christ? In short, it means God is faithful to God's promises. It means Jesus is our Savior and our intermediary, the one who defends us in the presence of God the Father, though we are sinners. Take some time today to pray over this revelation. Thank God for our intercessor. Ask to be equipped to share the identity of Christ with others in this world. Thank God for God's faithfulness to send us a Savior.

Suggested Scripture: Isaiah 49:5-6; Daniel 7:13-14; Malachi 3:1

Suggested Prayer:

> *Eternal God,*
> *While there are none like you, there is your Son and our Savior,*
> *Jesus Christ. Thank you for your faithfulness to your promises.*
> *Thank you that you have revealed that Jesus of Nazareth is*
> *indeed your promised Son and our Savior. Your word teaches*
> *that Jesus Christ is our route to you, our provider, our sustainer,*
> *the one who enlightens us and protects us. Oh, that we could*
> *comprehend your love of us! We heap praises upon you, that you*
> *have revealed to us that we have a Savior in and through Jesus*
> *Christ. Help us to share this with others and to relish this blessed*
> *assurance ourselves. In the name of Christ, amen.*

May 20

THE TRUE VINE

"I am the true vine, and my Father is the gardener." —John
15:1 (NIV)

Jesus Christ is the true vine. God the Father is the gardener who prunes and keeps the vine. And we are the branches on the vine. We are the producers of fruit, though it would not be possible without the sustenance of the vine and the pruning of the gardener. What does this mean, specifically the interconnectedness of humanity to the Divine?

We are unable to produce true spiritual fruit when we are not properly grafted onto the true vine that is Jesus Christ. Yes, we may be able to produce a variety of fruit that is not bad, but fruit that is everlasting is produced from the True Vine and the branches that are part of that vine, fed by that vine, sustained by that vine.

This is the final "I am" statement that Jesus makes prior to his crucifixion in the Gospel of John. There is a promise of continued sustenance even after Jesus dies, is resurrected, and is physically absent from his disciples. They will be maintained as they remain grafted onto the True Vine.

The same is true for all Christians throughout history. We continue to be sustained spiritually as we remain grafted onto the True Vine through faith. Jesus Christ is the Vine that gives us the power to produce good spiritual fruit. It is through Christ alone that we can say we have any of the fruit of the Spirit that Paul talks about in his letter to the Galatians.

May 21
KEEP MOVING

And leaving the crowd behind, they took him with them in the boat, just as he was. Other boats were with him. —Mark 4:36 (NRSV)

Jesus had been teaching the crowd in parables and was now leaving them, along with his disciples, and moving on to another region to continue his ministry. It is important to realize that Jesus, throughout the Gospel accounts, continued to move about. His ministry was never stationary for long. Not only did Jesus move about; he also sent his disciples and followers out to spread the message of the coming dominion of God.

What does this mean for you and me? Frankly, it means that we too must keep moving. This is not necessarily a literal interpretation that we ought to move from one town to another. Rather, it means that we ought to continue to minister to new and different people throughout our lives. Maybe that does mean we need to move from one town to the next. It could also mean we ought to move from one place to the next within our own setting and minster to people as we encounter them—at the store, the post office, the bank, our workplace, our school, and so on.

Be encouraged to continue to move as an emissary for Christ in the here and now. Show others the love, mercy, and grace of God. Take every opportunity to have mercy on those who wrong you, to love even your enemies, and to be gracious to all people as God has shown you mercy, loved you, and offers grace to you.

May 22

FREE WATER, FREEING WATER

The Spirit and the bride say, "Come." And let the one who hears say, "Come." And let the one who is thirsty come; let the one who wishes take the water of life without cost. —Revelation 22:17 (NASB)

"Free water" should be an oxymoron, though it is not in most societies. Jesus is speaking through John in the book of Revelation. Here, he is offering a wonderful gift to those who would receive these words. This gift is no different from what he offered in the Gospel accounts; it is himself. Jesus is the free water that frees us from our sin.

Jesus is speaking of an invitation by the Holy Spirit and the church to those who do not yet believe. They are invited to partake in the living water. All are invited to join this communion, though not all will do so. This invitation is open. This invitation promises water that quenches the most powerful of thirsts: a thirst to belong.

This free-to-you water frees you from sin, death, and doom. When you partake, you are not only welcomed into the Body of Christ but are cleansed, made new, and given the assurance that your sins are forgiven, that you are destined to be in the full presence of God forevermore, and that there is hope in your life that cannot be measured.

You are encouraged to reflect on your own experience of partaking in the water of life. You are then encouraged to invite others to drink deeply from this cup of salvation.

May 23

REMEMBER YOUR CALLING

I think it right, as long as I am in this body, to stir you up by way of reminder. —2 Peter 1:13 (ESV)

Peter is the traditional author of this letter that bears his name. In this section of the letter, he encourages his readers to remember the various virtues of the Christian faith: kindness, self-control, perseverance, godliness, etc. These are all qualities that help Christians live in ways that our religious identification, "Christian" or "little Christ," demands of us.

As we carry ourselves as "little Christs," it is important to remember why we do this. Primarily, it is out of devotion to God to live as Christ lived. Doing this also opens the door for chances to share the gospel with others. People see how we behave long before they hear what we have to say. It is important to continue to behave in such a way that shows we have decided to follow Christ in this life.

We are also called to encourage one another in our individual walks of faith. Peter was encouraging his fellow believers in their various challenges. He encouraged them to remain true to their convictions and to stand apart from the crowd around them. Find the encouragement to follow in Christ's steps, to be encouragers of the Christian faith as Peter was, and to walk humbly with God.

May 24

JESUS HAS ALL THE POWER

Jesus knew that the Father had put all things under his power, and that he had come from God and was returning to God; so he got up from the meal, took off his outer clothing, and wrapped a towel around his waist. After that, he poured water into a basin and began to wash his disciples' feet, drying them with the towel that was wrapped around him. —John 13:3-5 (NIV)

Jesus, God in flesh, had and continues to have all the power of God. Yet in this passage we see that God in flesh takes on the role of a servant. The one with the highest social standing in the group would not lower typically lower himself to wash the feet of the others. This is a socially bizarre picture.

No matter how strange it must have been for the disciples to have Jesus wash their feet (and Peter even says so later in the passage), it is a beautiful model for us to follow. Jesus—again, God in flesh, the Creator of all things, and Savior of humanity—is washing the feet of these twelve men. Why? Out of love and service to them.

You do not have to wash the feet of someone else to be a servant and follow Jesus' model. Instead, offer them genuine love and serve them simply because Jesus would do the same and has done the same for you. Service can look like donating time, money, or other resources. Service can be sitting with someone who is hurting, no matter their pain. It can be giving voice to the voiceless and standing in solidarity with the marginalized. Jesus had all the power in the universe, yet he served. Be encouraged to follow in our Savior's footsteps.

May 25

WE DON'T KNOW
WHAT WE'RE DOING

Jesus said, "Father, forgive them, for they do not know what they are doing." And they divided up his clothes by casting lots.
—Luke 23:34 (NIV)

Jesus was beaten, spat upon, and mocked. Then his arms and legs were nailed to the rough wood of the cross. Yet, despite the agony Christ must have been suffering, his heart overflowed with forgiveness.

What a dreadful world we live in at times. Violence, slavery, molestation, rape, racism, sexism, and the list flows *ad nauseam*. Truly, we do not know what we are doing. Even at times, playfully, we harm one another. Which is more egregious, the sin that is committed intentionally or the one committed unintentionally? The answer is a resounding "both." We dare not measure one against the other. Both are equally sinful.

We all do things that are harmful to other people. It doesn't matter whether we realize that we are doing these things, though knowledge helps us prevent the hurtful behavior in the future. Our world is busy teaching us how to point the finger at others, and we fail to see the importance of taking responsibility for our actions and speech.

The truth of the matter is this: your sins and mine nailed Jesus to the cross. Your sins and mine compelled God to act with great decisiveness and overwhelming drama. God in flesh died to forgive you and me of our sins. No one is innocent, whether we know it or not. We do not know what we are doing at times, but rest assured of these two things: we all sin, and everyone who believes in Jesus Christ is forgiven of their sins. Reflect on this truth today.

May 26

SPIRITUAL EXERCISE: PSALM OF PRAISE

This is a day on which you are encouraged to reflect on the following psalm. What does the Spirit tell you through these words? Do you find it easy to offer praises to God today? If not, then commune with God and listen for the Divine voice. Can you identify what is preventing your ability to offer praises?

> Praise the LORD, my soul. LORD my God, you are very great;
>   you are clothed with splendor and majesty. . . .
> All creatures look to you to give them their food at the proper
>   time.
> When you give it to them, they gather it up; when you open your
>   hand, they are satisfied with good things.
> When you hide your face, they are terrified; when you take away
>   their breath, they die and return to the dust.
> When you send your Spirit, they are created, and you renew the
>   face of the ground. . . .
> I will sing to the LORD all my life; I will sing praises to my God
>   as long as I live.
> May my meditation be pleasing to him, as I rejoice in the LORD
>   . . . .
> Praise the LORD, my soul. Praise the LORD. —Psalm 104:1,
>   27-30, 33-34, 35b (NIV)

May 27

PRESENCE

"And surely, I am with you always, to the very end of the age."
—*Matthew 28:20b (NIV)*

In courses that teach pastoral care, one of the most important lessons is to offer what is called a "non-anxious" or "little anxious" presence. This means the pastoral caregiver is taught to sit with the person going through a crisis and be calm, patient, and often quiet while the person in crisis expresses themselves.

That non-anxious presence is often one of the most powerful tools in the pastoral caregiver's backpack, whether they are a pastor, chaplain, counselor, or layperson.

Jesus understood the importance of presence. Often throughout his ministry, Jesus' presence was enough to evoke faith or major changes in the lives of those with whom he communed. Look to Zacchaeus as an example.

In his final moments with his disciples in Matthew's account of the gospel, just before ascending to heaven, Jesus promised his closest followers his continued presence. We too may look to that promise for comfort and peace in our lives. The presence of God in the form of the third person of the Trinity, the Holy Spirit, goes with us always when we believe in Christ.

You are encouraged to find peace in the continued presence of God. There will indeed be untold crises and pain in your life, as well as many joyous occasions. Whatever you face today, cling to the truth that God's presence is with you always.

May 28
NO FEAR FOR PROVISION

They are like trees planted by streams of water, which yield their fruit in its season, and their leaves do not wither. In all that they do, they prosper. —Psalm 1:3 (NRSV)

Financial strain, bare cupboards, bills piling high, seemingly insurmountable debt, children in need of clothes and shoes. At times it seems that the supply of our personal money is dwarfed by the demand on our financial resources. This is terrifying. Financial stress can cause friction in our relationships too, especially when we are sharing the financial burden with others.

This is not a self-help book. I am not one to promise financial blessings in the name of God if only you would do certain things, pray certain prayers, or believe hard enough in the power of God. I am not one to say that you will overcome your financial difficulties by claiming victory over your debt.

Perhaps you do not have any overwhelming financial burdens. Your burdens could be emotional, spiritual, or relational. Perhaps you are overly burdened at work or school. Maybe your stress lies elsewhere.

No matter the case, I can promise you this: when you have faith in God and trust in God, no matter the circumstances, God will provide. I am not promising that God will give you all the money at once to meet your needs and desires. I am not promising that God will make your spouse listen to you when you feel ignored. I am promising that, if you work toward your goals and remain faithful to God as you work, God will be with you and will provide—perhaps not as you desire and suspect, but God will provide.

May 29
WOE TO THE CORRUPT

Woe to those who decree iniquitous decrees, and the writers who keep writing oppression, to turn aside the needy from justice and to rob the poor of my people of their right, that widows may be their spoil, and that they may make the fatherless their prey!
—Isaiah 10:1-2 (ESV)

Corruption is often applied to government or big corporations, essentially entities without a face. The truth is that we are all corrupt. We who are Christians have been forgiven our corruption, but that does not mean we are spared the temptation to exercise corrupt behaviors.

The verses for today, and many of the words of most prophets found in what Christians call the Old Testament, condemn corrupt governments and individuals. Specifically, the prophets target those who use their power to oppress the neediest in society—namely orphans, widows, and foreigners.

Do not fall into the false belief that corruption has nothing to do with you and that you are powerless to stop corruption or prevent the powerless in our society from falling victim to the corruption of our system. Corruption exists within the individual as well. We tweak things in our favor, ask for favors, or give favors to those who may have influence or power to make our lives easier. Avoid doing this because, often, when we make something out to favor ourselves, someone else pays for our mistake because of that corruption that exists.

Seek justice in all things today, not simply for yourself but also for those who struggle and are in genuine need of justice from corruption.

May 30
A TERRIFYING ENCOUNTER

You have not come to a mountain that can be touched and that is burning with fire; to darkness, gloom and storm. —Hebrews 12:18 (NIV)

In the Christian Old Testament, to encounter God meant to flirt with doom and death. At Mount Sinai, the people could not touch the mountain. Even the animals could not touch the mountain without being stoned to death. To encounter God was a serious meeting. When Moses and his cohort ascended the mountain, only Moses could encounter God.

When the temple in Jerusalem was completed, only the high priest could go into the holy of holies, and this occurred only once a year, on the Day of Atonement.

To encounter God was to encounter a being that has no equal and that overwhelms all people. Moses' face shone so brightly after speaking with God that the people demanded that he cover his face with a shawl to dim the light.

We are reminded in our New Testament verse of the stark contrast between the old and new covenants. The old covenant was limiting in our human experience with the Divine. We could not approach God in the same sense that we can now, through Christ. It is a good reminder of the seriousness of these Divine-human encounters.

Reflect today on the seriousness of the nature of meeting God in prayer and worship. To commune with the Divine is an honor for us as human beings. To be able to approach the Divine without the overwhelmingly terrifying storm, fire, and darkness is comforting. Yet knowing that our God is above all things is equally important.

May 31

AN APPROACHABLE GOD

But you have come to Mount Zion and to the city of the
living God, the heavenly Jerusalem, and to myriads of angels.
—Hebrews 12:22 (NASB)

We have no reason to fear being stoned to death because we approach the Divine. Because of our mediator and Savior, we have an opportunity to approach God that our spiritual forebears did not have. Jesus gives us the freedom to access God the Father without fear of God's overwhelming presence.

There is a danger, though. With this free access comes the temptation to get too familiar with God and fail to offer revered awe to our Creator and Redeemer. Do not fall into the temptation to become too familiar with God and thus fail to seek to honor and adore God.

However, with the freedom in Christ to approach God comes a wonderful gift. We can approach God in a familiar way. We walk a delicate line between being familiar with God and losing our awe toward God. Tread lightly and bask in the wonder of the God of the universe who created all things, is mighty and glorious, is loving and merciful. God aims all this glory and love squarely at you to redeem you and save you from death and sin.

Reflect today on the glory of our God, whom we can approach freely and without hesitation. Approach God today and offer your thanks and praise, especially since you need not fear God's might but may rejoice in God's love.

June 1

CARE FOR THE MARGINALIZED

"Thus, says the LORD of hosts, render true judgments, show kindness and mercy to one another, do not oppress the widow, the fatherless, the sojourner, or the poor, and let none of you devise evil against another in your heart." —Zechariah 7:9-10 (ESV)

In the politically heated climate of our world, it is easy to find ourselves on one side of the political aisle or the other. Sometimes we differ from family and friends or even from fellow Christians. Sometimes we agree with those same people on various issues that are deemed "hot button."

In this period in human history, when people groups are used as political ammunition by the two most powerful and divided political parties in the United States, it is important to remember that there are indeed people living in crisis.

I do not claim to have the right political answers to the questions of immigration, asylum, and refugees. I do have the answers from a Christian perspective, though. No matter our political leanings and personal feelings toward these individuals, we must remember God's stance on foreigners, the oppressed, and the marginalized. *Care for them.*

For many, this is a tough pill to swallow. Politicians on both sides of the aisle claim that their party has the right answer and the other party is foolish. The truth is that people in crisis need our compassion, our prayers, and our action. How will we respond to them? Reflect on this today, and reflect on the truth that you too are a refugee, taken in by God. Do not be overcome with fear, be overcome with compassion for your fellow human beings.

June 2

SPIRITUAL EXERCISE: PSALM OF PRAISE

Today you are encouraged to reflect on the following psalm. What does the Spirit tell you through these words? Do you find it easy to offer praises to God today? If not, then commune with God and listen for the Divine voice. Can you identify what is preventing your ability to offer praises?

> O LORD, our Lord, how majestic is your name in all the earth!
>   You have set your glory above the heavens. Out of the mouth
>   of babies and infants, you have established strength because
>   of your foes, to still the enemy and the avenger.
> When I look at your heavens, the work of your fingers, the moon
>   and the stars, which you have set in place,
> what is man that you are mindful of him, and the son of man
>   that you care for him?
> Yet you have made him a little lower than the heavenly beings
>   and crowned him with glory and honor.
> You have given him dominion over the works of your hands; you
>   have put all things under his feet,
> all sheep and oxen, and also the beasts of the field,
> the birds of the heavens, and the fish of the sea, whatever passes
>   along the paths of the seas.
> O LORD, our Lord, how majestic is your name in all the earth!
>   —Psalm 8 (ESV)

June 3

LOOSE LIPS WOUND HEARTS

Without wood a fire goes out; without a gossip a quarrel dies down. —*Proverbs 26:20 (NIV)*

Gossip is one of the most dangerous sins that we may commit. It may not lead to physical pain, but it can certainly lead to much emotional, mental, and spiritual pain. Some gossip may even lead to physical pain too.

The question, *"Did you hear about . . . ?"* often leads to falsehoods, exaggerated information, and hurt feelings. While this is not the only method of gossip, it is the easiest to identify. It is interesting that gossip has become a socially acceptable sin that is alive and well even within the fellowship of the church.

The danger is not simply that the person who gossips might be caught; gossip also harms the one who is being talked about, and it harms those who are sharing in the conversation. We are so adept at this sin that we use tactics to lessen the blow of the sin. We say things like, "I don't want to speak ill of him, but . . . ," or "She's so sweet, but . . . ."

Reflect on your conversations. Be mindful of what you say, and if you begin to stray into the realm of gossip, excuse yourself from the conversation or steer it in another direction. Be proactive in this matter, and remove yourself from the temptation before you even arrive. If you know that someone regularly participates in gossip, encourage them to talk about something else, or begin to decrease the amount of time you spend with them. Do not close yourself off from them, but protect yourself from engaging in the destructive habit of gossip.

June 4

FORGETFUL FOLLOWERS

For if any are hearers of the word and not doers, they are like those who look at themselves in a mirror; for they look at themselves and, on going away, immediately forget what they were like. —*James 1:23-24 (NRSV)*

How often do you look at yourself in the mirror throughout the day? It is likely that you see yourself in the mirror as you start your morning, shaving, brushing teeth, putting on makeup or contact lenses. Whatever you do during your daily routine, you probably look at yourself more than once at the beginning of the day and then a few more times as the day passes. You know what you look like.

Do you know what you look like as a Christian, though? It is easy for us to claim to know or believe something, but then, when confronted with an opportunity to put our beliefs into action, we flounder.

Reflect on your walk with Christ lately. Have you been floundering? Be encouraged to read through the Scriptures, attend Bible study and worship services, and commune with God and fellow believers. This will equip you with the knowledge of how to carry yourself as a believer. Once you accomplish this, go out and put what you have learned into action.

Love other people, exercise patience with others, be at peace with other people, and strive to see others as God sees them—loved, cherished, and covered in grace.

June 5

FAITHFUL STEWARDS

There is precious treasure and oil in the dwelling of the wise, But a foolish man swallows it up. —*Proverbs 21:20 (NASB)*

Being smart with your resources is considered a good idea. Financial advisors, businesspeople, and many others will teach the practice of making good investments, not spending money with wild abandon, and being careful to budget your income and manage your spending.

This is a smart move from a faith standpoint too. Being smart with your spending is a wise practice that is taught within Scripture. When I was young, my father taught me this about my finances: "When you get paid, make sure to do this: give to God ten percent, give to yourself ten percent, and then live off the rest."

The lesson was about tithing, putting some money into a savings account, and then paying my bills and buying things that I wanted with the rest. This lesson came to me when I was not yet old enough to have my own job. Later, I would learn the part about paying bills.

Being a good steward sometimes means that we do not get to spend money on the things we want or think we want right now. Sometimes it means making sure our bills are paid and that we have food and other necessities. Then we must wait before we can buy that shiny, new thing we want.

Be patient in your spending. Reflect on where your money goes, and resolve to pay off any debt first while making sure that your bills are covered. Only then should you buy the new thing. Delayed gratification may not be popular, but often it is best.

June 6
DON'T MINCE WORDS

He said therefore to the crowds that came out to be baptized by him, "You brood of vipers! Who warned you to flee from the wrath to come?" —Luke 3:7 (ESV)

John the Baptist is one of those individuals from Scripture who, like others, did not mince words. He called it like he saw it. As people came to him to hear his preaching and to be baptized in the Jordan River, he called them the children of vipers. John also called out Herod for the sin of taking his brother's wife as his own. John's boldness led to his arrest. His words were often unpopular but true.

When we speak, we must be mindful and careful to speak truthfully, even if it is an unpopular truth. But do not confuse tact with mincing words. We should be tactful most of the time. However, we should not sugarcoat an issue to save face or to avoid a hardship. This is dishonest and may make things more complicated later.

Be encouraged to speak plainly and in truth. Avoid hurting others for the sake of hurting others, but do not withhold the truth to avoid hurting others either. The momentary hurt will pass, but withholding the truth may cause more harm in the long run. Speak plainly and kindly in ways that others will understand and accept. Be encouraged as well to receive the "plain speech" of others who are interested in your growth and development as a follower of Christ and a loved one.

June 7

WHAT DOES IT MEAN THAT GOD IS WITH YOU?

The LORD your God is with you, the Mighty Warrior who saves. He will take great delight in you; in his love he will no longer rebuke you but will rejoice over you with singing. —Zephaniah 3:17 (NIV)

What does it mean to you when you hear the words, "God is with you"? I think this is a fair question to ask but a difficult one to answer. Your answer most likely depends on what is going on in your life when you think about the question.

If you are doing well financially, your relationships are smooth, and there are few challenges or no crises, it probably means you are at peace with God and, hopefully, are thankful that things seem to be going so well.

On the other hand, if life is hard, you are grieving the death of a loved one or the loss of a job, experiencing financial insecurity, or facing a host of other issues, you probably are not at peace with God. Maybe, if you are facing crises, you are shaking your fists at God or "arguing with God," as an elderly pastor friend of mine used to say.

This is an important question to reflect on at different stages throughout your life, especially regarding your spiritual walk. Scripture, as in our verse for today, reminds us that God is with us. What does that mean for you? Does God's presence feel like a blessing? A curse? A distant reality? A close comfort? Maybe you cannot express your feelings. Reflect today on what this means to you. Be honest with yourself and God. God can handle your feelings, and your honesty will go far in helping you cope with hardships.

June 8

EXTREME RESPONSE

They got up, drove him out of the town, and led him to the brow of the hill on which their town was built, so that they might hurl him off the cliff. —Luke 4:29 (NRSV)

Jesus had just declared that he was the Messiah promised by Isaiah, the one who would provide freedom to the captive and preach good news to the poor. Jesus further declared that he would not perform miracles in his hometown of Galilee and that Gentiles would be included in the kingdom of God. These things were inflammatory. While much of Jesus' preaching and teaching was accepted by many of the people who heard him, his messages for his boyhood neighbors and friends were not well received.

The people drove Jesus out of the town, pushing him toward the cliff on which their town had been built with murderous plans to heave him off the precipice. This time, Jesus left the crowd unscathed. The crowd responded this way because they were dealing with failed expectations. They believed that Jesus would do something miraculous for them, and he did not.

What are your expectations for God? Do you long for miracles in the here and now? Most of us do, whether they are miracles of healing, provision, protection, or something else.

You are encouraged to continue praying for miracles in the here and now. Remember, though, that these are minor miracles. The true miracle that Jesus Christ performed was forgiving your sins through his death and resurrection. Cling to this miracle and to the hope that all Christians have in Jesus Christ.

June 9

SPIRITUAL EXERCISE: REFLECTING ON WATER

Throughout Scripture, water is used to express many ideas. In what Christians call the Old Testament, water—particularly the sea—is the place of chaos, the dwelling of the leviathan, an unsafe region that cannot be controlled. In the account of Noah and the flood, water destroys the earth.

Water is also used in purification rites, and in our New Testament water is used to baptize people into the faith. People are cleansed of their sins and birthed into a new life with Christ at the lead. For Christians, water is an important symbol, as baptism plays a huge role in our spiritual journeys.

Reflect on the symbol of water. Think back to your own baptism if you have been baptized and can remember the experience. What thoughts come to your mind? What images? What feelings? Are there any new revelations regarding water and what it means to you as a Christian? Use the remainder of this page to write notes about your experience.

_____

_____

_____

_____

_____

_____

_____

June 10
PRONE TO VIOLENCE

They said, "Lord, look, here are two swords." And He said to them, "It is enough." —Luke 22:38 (NASB)

The martial art of Aikido teaches practitioners to use their partner's momentum against them to pin, throw, or apply pressure through various joint locks. The aim is to cause the partner to yield through the least amount of effort expended and injury caused. It is a more "peaceful" martial art.

The disciples may not have known any martial arts, but according to Luke they were armed with at least two swords on the night when Jesus was betrayed by Judas into the hands of the high priest. To the disciples' credit, they were in Jerusalem, not Galilee, and many people did not look favorably on their rabbi. Jesus was even warning them of the dangers that would befall them after his arrest. But the swords and the violence associated with such weapons are not Jesus' way. They are unnecessary. Jesus responded to this declaration by saying, "It is enough." Jesus was not saying that two swords would be enough against the Roman occupation force or the high priest's guards; rather, he was saying, "This talk of violence is enough."

Jesus recognized that a sword would not help Peter as he denied Jesus three times a few hours after this conversation took place. Jesus knew that a sword would not help his other disciples as they fled into the night when he was taken away. Jesus knew a sword would not bring salvation. While there is nothing wrong with martial arts or weapons when used for sport, or perhaps even defense, violence does not lead to salvation. Reflect on Jesus' example of a nonviolent life and his teachings that include even enemies in the community of faith.

June 11
TRUE COMMUNITY

A friend loves at all times, and a brother is born for adversity.
—Proverbs 17:17 (ESV)

We all long for community. Even the most introverted among us need social interaction to some degree. True community, though, is difficult to find. Acquaintances come and go. Even friendships do not last unless there is some level of interaction between the parties involved. Being vulnerable is part of sharing in true community, but becoming vulnerable with others is difficult and often painful.

Scott Peck, a medical doctor who has studied how strangers enter true community, has observed that there are four predictable stages of entering true community. They are pseudocommunity, chaos, emptiness, and true community.

Pseudocommunity is false community that exists on the surface. Everyone and everything are "fine." Chaos is when everyone in the community begins to discover their differences and, with good or ill intentions, attempts to convert everyone else to their way of thinking. Emptiness is when vulnerability begins to take over and no one is attempting to convert others any longer; everyone is simply being open with their thoughts and feelings. Finally, true community exists when the community in question has accepted everyone else, differences and all, for who they are.

True community comes after adversity and difficulty and exists based on mutual love and respect. The writer of today's verse understood that. True friends and siblings love one another despite differences and allow space for honest communication. Seek this in your relationships with God's help.

June 12

DO NOT BE MASTERED BY THIS WORLD

All things are lawful for me, but not all things are profitable. All things are lawful for me, but I will not be mastered by anything.
—*1 Corinthians 6:12 (NASB)*

Addiction is a terrible disease. Whether it is an addiction to alcohol, drugs, pornography, food, technology, or anything else, it is hazardous to a person's holistic health. It is easy to say, "I'm not addicted. I can stop whenever I want to." It is easy to point our fingers at others who are addicted to things that seem far worse than our own struggles.

There are plenty of things to which we may become addicted in this life, and all of them draw us away from family, friends, healthy environments, and God. When something pleasurable happens to us, our brains get a shot of dopamine that signals that what we experienced was indeed pleasing and fun. However, not all things that gives us the dopamine rush are healthy, and even too much of something healthy without balance can lead to an unhealthy life.

Paul was talking about sexual immorality in this passage. It is easy to make the connection between sex and pleasure and recognize that unhealthy sexual practices can lead to addiction that may alienate you from your loved ones. It has certainly been a concern for more than two thousand years.

At the risk of sounding like a quote from an after-school TV special, if you or someone you love is addicted to something, seek help. Yes, pray about the issue, but God has gifted many people in this world with the talents and knowledge necessary to help people fight addiction. They can offer needed assistance in getting better. Do not be mastered by anything of this world; rather, be mastered by God.

June 13

MISCONCEPTIONS

Blessed are the meek, for they will inherit the earth. —Matthew 5:5 (NIV)

The Oxford English Dictionary defines "meek" as gentle, quiet, submissive. Those who are meek are not generally expected to inherit much of anything aside from what their parents or guardians give to them. Jesus, though, teaches in his Sermon on the Mount that the meek will inherit the earth.

Jesus was known for flipping preconceived notions upside down. That theme runs throughout the Gospels, particularly in Luke's account, which also includes the Beatitudes—the source of our verse for today. The meek are often portrayed in media as easy to take advantage of. Even in real-life experiences, the meek are pushed to the side by the bold.

Jesus teaches that this is not going to be the way of things in the kingdom or dominion of God. The meek shall inherit the earth. The new creation at Jesus' return will be given to the meek, to those who lower themselves to elevate Christ in their lives, to those who are not ashamed to be servants of the kingdom of God.

Be mindful of what it means to be meek in the kingdom of God. It means that you are lowering yourself to praise Christ. It means that you are willing to decrease so that Christ might increase. It means that you are willing to put the spiritual needs of others before yourself and live a life that reflects the transformative goodness of the gospel of Jesus Christ.

June 14

IDEAL FELLOWSHIP

Day by day, as they spent much time together in the temple, they broke bread at home and ate their food with glad and generous hearts. —Acts 2:46 (NRSV)

We certainly do not live in an ideal world. There are hurts, grudges, mistakes, arguments, gossip, lies, and more, and that is even in the community of believers! But this reality is no excuse for not striving to play a role in an ideal fellowship with other Christians.

The first-century Christians gathered together for worship, study of Scripture, prayer, communion, and eating. If you were to put a modern local church next to an early house church in Jerusalem, they would be indistinguishable in terms of their actions and methods.

The challenge for modern Christians, then, is not to look so different from our spiritual forebears. Instead, we must examine the depth of our fellowship, worship, communion, and other faith practices. It is dangerously easy to fall into the trap of complacency or of going through the motions. It may seem that individuals can only have a small impact on their community, but do not be discouraged. Any individual can indeed have a major impact on a larger group with the right motivation and the genuine desire to examine and, if necessary, alter the status quo.

Be encouraged to reflect on your local fellowship of believers. How does it compare to that of our first-century spiritual ancestors? Are you part of a genuine fellowship? Seek to deepen your own spiritual walk, and then encourage your local siblings in faith to do the same for themselves with the goal to strive for the ideal fellowship.

June 15

LOVE FOR ENEMIES

But I say to you who hear, love your enemies, do good to those who hate you . . . . —Luke 6:27 (ESV)

Some of the things Christians are called to do seem terribly hard. One of those difficult things is offering love to our enemies, to those who would harm us, abuse us, rob us, and perhaps even kill us if given the opportunity. Yet Jesus calls us to love these people.

How can we do such a thing? Our flesh would suggest that we return hate for hate, abuse for abuse, cruelty for cruelty. However, Jesus commands us to love these people. Understand that this is not a romantic love; this is a forgiving, merciful love. Jesus even gives us a perfect example to follow at his crucifixion as he prays that God will forgive those committing this terrible act against him.

How, though, are we to love those who have harmed us? If you or a loved one have been victimized or abused in any way by someone else, this is an especially difficult command. It is easy for others to say, "Simply follow Jesus' teachings and love your enemy." But this is not fair, as it seems to dismiss the trauma associated with the crime against you or your loved one.

Find the time to pray today for those who have been victimized by others. Pray that they may begin or continue the healing process and that they have the support they need. If you are one who has been victimized, abused, or otherwise assaulted, seek help if you have not already. Contact a local minister, find a mental health therapist, or get in touch with some other professional helper. God has blessed these individuals with the skills necessary to walk alongside hurting people.

June 16

SPIRITUAL EXERCISE: LECTIO DIVINA
(DIVINE READING)

You are invited to practice a spiritual exercise, a "divine reading" of a select passage of Scripture. Please follow the guide provided as you meditate on this passage.

• Read the passage twice, pausing between each reading for a moment of silence. Identify keywords as you read the passage without elaboration
• Read the passage again, pause for silence, and answer the following question: Where does the content of the reading touch my life today?
• Read the passage once more, again pausing for silence, and complete this sentence: I believe God wants me to . . . .

> *Blessed are the poor in spirit, for theirs is the kingdom of heaven. Blessed are those who mourn, for they will be comforted. Blessed are the meek, for they will inherit the earth. Blessed are those who hunger and thirst for righteousness, for they will be filled. Blessed are the merciful, for they will be shown mercy. Blessed are the pure in heart, for they will see God. Blessed are the peacemakers, for they will be called children of God. Blessed are those who are persecuted because of righteousness, for theirs is the kingdom of heaven. —Matthew 5:3-10 (NIV)*

June 17

THE THIRD WAY

Whoever hits you on the cheek, offer him the other also . . . .
—Luke 6:29a (NASB)

Scripture is full of commands and teachings that fly in the face of typical human reactions, especially reactions to cruelty or meanness. Consider, for instance, when we are attacked. Our biology tells us to do one of two things: take flight or stand and fight. This is a natural, even animalistic response to danger or aggression.

Walter Wink, a now deceased theologian and Christian ethicist, argued for a third way: Jesus' way. This way tells us that when we are struck on the cheek, we should turn to the aggressor and offer the other cheek. It was a social *faux pas* to do this in the day of Jesus. A person would slap someone of lower status with the back of their right hand across the right cheek. To offer the other cheek meant the aggressor either had to hit you with their left hand, a social no-no, or punch you with the right, which would make the two of you equal in the eyes of society, when the intent was to humiliate rather than physically harm because of the backhanded attack.

Jesus' third way, as Wink puts it, is not submitting to aggression. Neither is it responding with further aggression. It is about meeting aggression head on and then responding in such a way that the aggressor is thrown off balance and does not know how to immediately react again, thereby ceasing the hostile action for the moment. You are encouraged to begin implementing this third way, the way of Christ, into your daily routine. If you encounter an aggressive person, no matter how that aggression manifests itself, move toward the third way—not fleeing or fighting but rather reacting out of love.

June 18

VENGEANCE BELONGS TO GOD

Vengeance is mine, and recompense, for the time when their foot shall slip; because the day of their calamity is at hand, their doom comes swiftly. —Deuteronomy 32:35 (NRSV)

Batman is the popular comic hero who has leaped from the pages of comic books and into every other artistic medium. One of the more successful and popular iterations of the character was the animated series from the early 1990s. In one episode, Batman makes the bold declaration, "I am vengeance, I am the night, I am Batman!" In this line, Batman declares himself the spirit of vengeance against all criminals and evildoers.

While this makes for great drama, especially in a children's show, it is not great Christian theology. None of us serve as the spirit of vengeance against anyone else, even those who have harmed us. Christians are called to a greater path, a higher path, and to make room for God to serve as the spirit of vengeance against those whom God judges are the recipients of that vengeance.

The overall passage that contains our verse of the day offers God's declaration of provision and protection over God's people, especially protection from abusers and others who would cause harm. Waiting for God to dole out vengeance may not be the popular thing to do, and it certainly will not sell movie tickets or attract audiences to television shows, but it is the proper thing to do.

Far be it that we should take on the mantle of the spirit of vengeance. Do not take on that burden. Instead, rest in the knowledge that God's justice will prevail.

June 19

MORE THAN BEFORE

The apostles said to the Lord, "Increase our faith!" —Luke 17:5
(ESV)

Increasing something implies that whatever is being increased already exists or is in someone's possession. In the context of today's verse, the apostles have faith in Jesus as Lord, but they are asking that Jesus increase their faith. They are feeling the weight of their future mission, spreading the gospel, and they want to ensure that they are well equipped to fulfill such a daunting task.

Have you ever felt as though you were ill-equipped to accomplish tasks in your life, whether at work, home, school, or elsewhere? Parents may often feel like they are ill-equipped to handle their children during various stages of development. The disciples felt that their faith was not enough to complete the mission before them, though they did not know what to expect.

The apostles want more of something that they already have. Jesus responds to them in verse 6, telling them that they have enough faith to accomplish all that lies before them. Greek, the original language of the New Testament, has an "if clause" that appears in verse 6 and can be translated as "if you had faith, and you do, then . . . ." Jesus affirms that what they have is indeed enough.

The faith you have is indeed enough for you to face the challenges in your life. Will that faith be tested? Perhaps. Will it be stretched? Maybe. Do you need more than what you have now? No. Simply exercise your true and genuine faith in Jesus Christ as Lord and Savior, and you have enough.

June 20
LONG DAY OF THE YEAR

Blessed is the one who trusts in the LORD, whose trust is the LORD. They are like a tree planted by water, that sends out its roots by the stream, and does not fear when heat comes, for its leaves remain green, and is not anxious in the year of drought, for it does not cease to bear fruit. —Jeremiah 17:7-8 (ESV)

Today is the summer solstice, the longest day of the year in terms of daylight. Summertime can often be hot, which may lead to droughts and other difficulties. Often, the word "drought" is used not only to describe a literal lack of water but also to describe a period when something in general is lacking.

Sportscasters may say that a team on a losing streak is in a drought. Or a batter in baseball who hasn't gotten a hit may be going through a drought. The word is also applied to a person's spiritual journey when they go through a time when it feels as though God is absent or distant. A period of great suffering, or consecutive crises, personal or otherwise, is a drought. Any time period that may be difficult can be labeled as a drought.

Droughts are indeed harsh and try the patience of all who live through them. However, as a follower of Christ, you have been secured, even in times of drought. God is not as distant as the situation makes it out to be. You are indeed like the tree mentioned in the verse, and God is like the stream. In droughts, streams tend to shrink, and it feels like God is distant. But we are nearer the Divine than we think, and we may find rest and nourishment even in the seasons of drought in our lives. Be encouraged to rest in this knowledge and reflect on your journey with God, even amid a drought.

June 21

DO NOT FEAR PEOPLE

And you, son of man, do not be afraid of them or their words.
Do not be afraid, though briers and thorns are all around you
and you live among scorpions. Do not be afraid of what they
say or be terrified by them, though they are a rebellious people.
—Ezekiel 2:6 (NIV)

How much of what you do in life is in fear of how others may respond to you? Is your closet full of the latest fashions? Does your garage house the latest model of your favorite vehicle? What about your phone? How recently did you upgrade it, and what motivated you to do that? There is a great temptation to fit in among our peers in this world. Some people may be intentional about going against the grain, but that is difficult to do in a society so heavily bombarded by advertisements.

Ezekiel lived in a time when it was not popular to follow the One True God. He could have easily succumbed to the temptation to follow the crowd and avoid his calling in life. We all have a Divine calling in our lives, a calling to be followers of Christ in word and deed.

Following the latest fashion and technological trends is nothing to be ashamed of. However, following the trends of hatred, cruelty, unfaithfulness, oppression, bigotry, and so on is sinful. Be encouraged to stand out from the crowd, spiritually speaking, making it known that you are a follower of Jesus Christ by showing love and mercy in a world that is sorely lacking in these wonderful gifts.

June 22

WHO IS GOOD?
WHO IS GOD?

And Jesus said to him, "Why do you call Me good? No one is good except God alone." —Mark 10:18 (NASB)

According to Jesus, no one is good except God alone. Something often said at funerals is how good the deceased person was in life. The mindset seems to be that, since they apparently lived a good life, then they must be deserving of eternity in God's full presence. The problem with that is this: none of us is good. Any good thing we do comes from God. Since we are sinners living in a fallen world, we are naturally prone to do bad things. Even the best among us is guilty of wrongdoing.

Jesus is confronted by a young man of high standing in society, one who appears to be faithful according to the Law. The man greets Jesus by calling him "Good Teacher," and Jesus challenges this title. He points out that only God is good, which is true. Further, Jesus turns the title given to him by this young man into a teaching moment about his own identity. If God is indeed the only one who is good, and this young man is calling Jesus "Good Teacher," then Jesus is God in flesh. It is a roundabout way for Jesus to take on the title of "Son of God," a title that is true regarding Jesus.

Beyond that, we are reminded of our lowly state in comparison to God. As God is the only one who is good, we are unworthy of God's gifts, yet, because God loves us, we may receive God's good gifts. Though we are sinful and fallen, we are so loved by our good God that our sins are forgiven, and we have the assurance of eternity with God. Go into the world and bask in God's goodness, and share a glimpse of this goodness with others today.

June 23

SPIRITUAL EXERCISE: THE SPIRITUAL DISCIPLINE OF SIMPLICITY

Practicing simplicity may evoke images of log cabins buried deep in some far-off corner of the wilderness. Yet the spiritual discipline of simplicity does not require such dramatic isolation. Simplicity, in the spiritual sense, is the act of seeking after the kingdom or dominion of God.

You are encouraged to read Matthew 6 today. As you do, take note of the various things Jesus teaches in his Sermon on the Mount: giving to the needy, praying, fasting, storing treasures in heaven, and avoiding worry. Simplicity is turning our attention from outward, tangible, materialistic ideals to the more basic needs of humanity and a deeper relationship with God. Reflect on your life. What do you own, or want to own, based on the current trends? What are your motivations for making certain purchases? Review your bank account. Over the last month, how much of your budget was spent on items that you needed for survival or paying off debt versus what was spent on unnecessary "stuff"?

The spiritual discipline of simplicity requires us to be honest with ourselves and move our focus away from a "me and mine" attitude and toward an attitude of thankfulness to God for what we have. Simplicity liberates the soul as we begin to recognize that our lives in the here and now are only temporary. What we must look forward to, eternity with God, is glorious and wonderful. As Jesus says, "For where your treasure is, there your heart will be also" (Matt 6:21, NIV).

June 24

ONE AND ONLY ONE

Not that there is another gospel, but there are some who are confusing you and want to pervert the gospel of Christ.
—Galatians 1:7 (NRSV)

We live in an age of remakes and reboots. The media, especially Hollywood, seems to be churning out stories that have been slightly tweaked left and right. Originality has gone the way of the dodo bird. There is something comfortable about remakes, though. A level of nostalgia seems to allow for these remakes. We are offered a familiar story with a fresh take on characters, new subplots, or new musical numbers.

The gospel, though, cannot be remade. Sure, there have been numerous movies, documentaries, and specials that tell the story of Jesus, but the good news of Jesus is one story that cannot be retold, remade, or tweaked. There is no other story that even rivals the gospel in terms of importance or truth.

Paul was warning the Galatians of the false gospels spreading throughout the world in response to the gospel of Jesus Christ. He was aiming to comfort the people in Galatia and assure them that he and his companions were sharing the truth and that they could be trusted. This is the same gospel that has been passed down to us today.

Be encouraged to find peace and comfort in the good news of Jesus Christ. There is no other source of salvation or assurance in this life outside of Christ. Be wary of false gospels or messages that sound like the true gospel. Pray for discernment today and every day so that you may continue to remember and recognize the truth of Christ.

June 25

BLESSING INSTEAD

. . . not returning evil for evil or insult for insult but giving a blessing instead; for you were called for the very purpose that you might inherit a blessing. —1 Peter 3:9 (NASB)

When we are caught up in a moment of hostility or anger, when someone provokes us to such feelings, it is easy to forget our identity as redeemed children of God. We would like to return an insult for an insult, evil for evil. We like to "get back" at people or for those who offend us to succumb to some misfortune. But this is not the way of Christ.

Christ gave us a perfect example of how we ought to respond to insult or evil in our lives: by taking the "third way," as Walter Wink says, and throwing the aggressor off balance. This is the goal in the martial art of Aikido, forcing the aggressor off balance and then taking advantage of the situation.

The Christian response, though, is to offer a blessing instead of perpetuating cruelty. This differs from martial arts in that we are not trying to take control of the situation. Instead, we are trying to live our lives as Christ lived his, as tangible examples of God's merciful, forgiving, and loving nature.

When we are attacked, cursed, insulted, or victimized, we must overcome our natural urge to react with similar behavior aimed at the perpetrator of the insults or evil. Prayerfully consider how best you can offer a blessing when you either witness or are on the receiving end of another person's evil or insult. Be mindful throughout your daily walk, especially when others are present, of how you can respond, seeking the guidance of the Holy Spirit in this matter today and every day of your life in the here and now.

June 26
PEOPLE WILL FAIL US

It is better to take refuge in the LORD than to put confidence in mortals. —Psalm 118:8 (NRSV)

No matter how strong our relationships are with other people, they will disappoint us. This hurts, especially when the other person is a loved one. We want to imagine that our spouse, children, parents, siblings, and close friends will never hurt us. Perhaps they would never intentionally harm us, but even those closest to us—perhaps especially those closest to us—have a way of hurting us, often accidentally.

Ideally, we should be able to trust those around us, to lean on them any time we need a shoulder to cry on, a helping hand, or simply a friendly and loving presence. We ought to be able to trust them and not worry that our trust will be broken. This is not always the case. Even our closest loved ones will fail us from time to time. The failure or betrayal of a loved one is a major plot point in many movies, books, plays, and television shows.

When this happens to you, do not be too discouraged. Yes, it will hurt, and the path to forgiveness and reconciliation between you and the one who hurts you will no doubt be long and difficult. Lean on God throughout your life. Do not become cynical toward others for their inevitable failures. Instead, put your hope first in God, and then exercise forgiveness and mercy toward those in your life. Be loving and patient with others, and above all, trust in God.

June 27

REMOVING GUILT

The angel said to those who were standing before him, "Take off his filthy clothes." And to him he said, "See, I have taken your guilt away from you, and I will clothe you with festal apparel."
—Zechariah 3:4 (NRSV)

We all carry baggage around with us wherever we go. This is the invisible stuff that weighs us down. Concerns over financial matters, familial disagreements, fights with friends, and, from the spiritual realm, the sins that we are guilty of complete this unwanted and burdensome set of baggage.

Knowing that we are guilty of sin can be a potentially overwhelming thought, especially if we are aware of the consequences our sins carry with them both now and in the time to come. Our guilt, both in our own eyes and in the eyes of others, can impact us in powerful ways. Often, when others know of our guilt, they begin to behave differently around us. When we are aware of our own guilt, we can carry a great deal of shame on our shoulders, and that may affect how we interact with others around us.

When we enter a relationship with God, we are assured that our guilt is removed. The prophet Zechariah, in a vision associated with his calling to become a prophet, received the assurance that he was cleansed of his sins. His guilt that was associated with those sins was also removed. If you believe in Jesus Christ, you can have your guilt removed as well. Seek to repent of your sins, and turn toward God so that you too can wear "festal apparel" and be free from the guilt that comes with being a sinner in this life. Guilt is a heavy burden to bear. Find release in the arms of God.

June 28

GOD'S MERCY VERSUS HUMAN MERCY

David said to Gad, "I am in deep distress. Let me fall into the hands of the LORD, for his mercy is very great; but do not let me fall into human hands." —1 Chronicles 21:13 (NIV)

All too often, when we are victims of abuse, attack, or simply the cruel behavior of another person, we want to see them "get what they deserve," whatever that may be. We like to see the person who cut us off in heavy traffic either get pulled over or have car trouble a little further down the road. We enjoy when someone who called us out over a mistake is later called out over their own mistakes. We tend to not be as merciful to others as we ought to be.

David knew he was better off throwing himself on the mercy of God than throwing himself on the mercy of other people. There are few people in life who can be trusted with showing much mercy. Typically, the ones who do are our closest loved ones.

While it is certainly better to fall at the feet of God in search of mercy than it is to fall at another person's feet, do not hesitate to offer mercy to others when given the opportunity. Be a tangible representation of God's mercy. Further, when you fall at the Divine feet, remember that you are undeserving of the mercy you receive. It is a wonderful gift that cannot and should not be taken for granted.

Take some time to reflect on the mercy that God has already given you, and offer God thanksgiving for that mercy. Reflect further on instances when other people gave you mercy, and consider thanking them as well. Then take this mercy from God and pay it forward.

June 29
ADVOCATE

My little children, I am writing these things to you so that you may not sin. But if anyone does sin, we have an advocate with the Father, Jesus Christ the righteous. —*1 John 2:1 (ESV)*

An advocate is someone who supports you, not unlike a reference on a job, school, or program application. They are the people whom you know will stand behind you and give someone else a glowing recommendation on your behalf. Sometimes in life, whom you know matters more than what you know.

In the case of our spiritual lives, this is certainly the case. Having an advocate in Jesus Christ is far more beneficial than knowing the rule book front to back and inside and out. In the case of Christ specifically, he is our advocate, speaking on our behalf to God the Creator in our moments of weakness. While the Bible does not give a play-by-play, it may go something like this:

You sin but believe in Jesus Christ as your Savior. God is disappointed in your sin, but Jesus speaks up on your behalf to God and states that you believe Jesus is God's Son who died for the remission of your sins. You are then forgiven of that sin in the eyes of God.

Jesus Christ is your ultimate advocate or defender. Jesus is the one you want on your side at the end of the day. You cannot defend yourself in the eyes of the Divine, and no one else aside from Jesus can adequately defend you either. Remember that you have this powerful, loving, and merciful advocate in your corner, and cling to the hope that surrounds this reality today: your sins are forgiven as you believe in Jesus Christ.

June 30

SPIRITUAL EXERCISE: GUIDED PRAYER

The natural world, everything that is not created by humanity, is a wonder of God. From mighty trees to tiny bees and everything in between, God has brought them all into existence. We may wonder why some things exist, like mosquitoes and wasps, yet all of them are beautiful in their own way. Take some time to enjoy something that occurs in the natural world, whether it is a flower in your yard, a plant in your home, your pet, honey on your biscuit, a hot cup of coffee, a starry night, or something else that interests you or catches your senses. Reflect on the simplicity of that creation or, conversely, its complexity. What is awe inspiring about that bit of nature you are reflecting on? How creative did God seem to get when bringing the object of your reflection into being? Think also about yourself and your own complexities and intricacies.

Suggested Scripture: Genesis 1:1-2:25; Nehemiah 9:6; Isaiah 66:2; John 1:1-18

Suggested Prayer:
> *Wonderful Creator,*
> *Thank you for all that you have brought into existence for me*
> *to appreciate. The sights, smells, sounds, tastes—everything that*
> *dazzles my senses and brings me joy in the natural world—*
> *reminds me of your creativity and fills me with awe. Help me*
> *to be sensitive to your first command in Genesis: to care for the*
> *garden. Equip me to care for this world that you have given as*
> *you care for me. Amen.*

July 1
TRUE SINS

This was the guilt of your sister Sodom: she and her daughters had pride, excess of food, and prosperous ease, but did not aid the poor and needy. —Ezekiel 16:49 (NRSV)

It is easy for most people to see the faults of others before they recognize their own faults. Those who can truly reflect on their lives, ask tough questions of themselves, and answer them honestly are able to see when they are wrong.

Too often we look at someone, see what is on the surface, and have knee-jerk reactions that lead to rash decisions. In the story of Sodom, we see homosexuality and attempted rape, and we react. The point of the story, though, is that the people were lustful, gluttonous, prideful, and selfish. Our society is guilty of this too.

The selfishness that is celebrated and promoted until we accept it as the norm is sinful. We need to be mindful of this sin. In our assurance of forgiveness as Christians, are we too ready to condemn those who are outside the faith, either non-Christians or Christians who do not fit our preconceived notions of what a Christian is supposed to be? Be mindful that you do not condemn others, for that is the work of God. Do not take on the burden of being the judge.

Instead, take on the responsibility of being a little Christ, a Christian. Love others, share mercy with them, offer grace to them. Remember that you are the recipient of these gifts too, despite your sins and shortcomings. Rejoice in this knowledge and share it with others.

July 2

INEXPRESSIBLE JOY

Though you have not seen him, you love him; and even though you do not see him now, you believe in him and are filled with an inexpressible and glorious joy. —1 Peter 1:8 (NIV)

Joy can be found in different things. Depending on our personality, coworkers, classmates, family, friends, and even the weather can impact our joy. Sometimes what happens to us affects our joy, either stealing it away or giving it to us.

But Peter, the author of our verse for today, is not talking about an emotion. He is talking about a state of mind. This joy is not so fickle that a failing car engine or a coworker's snide morning greeting can affect it. Peter is talking about a joy that is not found naturally in this fallen world. It is a resource that is Divine in nature; therefore, people, events, and situations cannot and will not fill our joy account, but neither will they deplete that joy account.

Much like the joy Peter is referring to, Jesus and the Holy Spirit are intangible in this life. We cannot see them, though we can see the result of joy and the result of Jesus and the Holy Spirit as they are present in the lives of genuine believers.

Remember the gift of inexpressible joy that you have been given. Peter explains that there are no words known that can express the joy of being a follower of Jesus Christ. Remember this joy and cling to it this day. You are a beloved and cherished child of God, so remember the joy in your identity.

July 3

DOUBTING

So, the other disciples were saying to him, "We have seen the Lord!" But he [Thomas] said to them, "Unless I see in His hands the imprint of the nails and put my finger into the place of the nails, and put my hand into His side, I will not believe." —John 20:25 (NASB)

Thomas gets a bad rap as the disciple who questioned what the others had seen. He is commonly called "doubting Thomas," a fitting nickname following the episode that contains our verse for today. Thomas reacted in a way that many of us likely react when our friends and relatives share an experience with us. We may not be as vocal as Thomas was in this passage, but we secretly want to share in the experience that the others are describing.

Is it so wrong to doubt? Hardly. It is a natural part of the faith experience. To doubt is not necessarily to fail to believe. Rather, doubt comes from a lack of physical or tangible evidence. That is what Thomas wanted, after all: physical proof that Jesus was indeed alive, resurrected from a gruesome death. Hence the disciple's desire to place his own finger and hand into Jesus' wounds.

Have you ever doubted anything about your faith in Jesus Christ—or perhaps even the entirety of it? Do not be embarrassed if you have; God knows whether you have doubted in the past or perhaps are dealing with some doubts now. Do not fret. My prayer for you during a season of doubt is that you will find peace as you wade through the difficulties of life and your journey of faith.

July 4

OVERWHELMED

When the cares of my heart are many, your consolations cheer my soul. —Psalm 94:19 (ESV)

Being overwhelmed is not fun. It is just that: overwhelming. Often it is difficult to focus. We may become agitated, angry, short-tempered, or otherwise testy with people, especially those closest to us. Sometimes our feeling of being overwhelmed is the result of our loved one's behaviors or actions. Sometimes we are hurt, overworked, or simply underappreciated.

On the other hand, while we can be overwhelmed in the negative sense, we can be overwhelmed in the positive sense too—overwhelmed with feelings of love or joy, excitement or anticipation. Any of these can be brought about by our life circumstances or our loved ones.

God through Jesus Christ is the only sure source of relief from being negatively overwhelmed, of untold anticipation and excitement, and of love and joy unmeasured.

If you are experiencing feelings of being overwhelmed in the negative sense, where things seem to be going badly and you do not know how to escape the stress, turn to God. While this may not solve the crisis that is causing your overwhelming thoughts and feelings, it will help you turn those feelings aside and focus on the task at hand. Seek the peace of God through Christ in your moments of being overwhelmed, and rediscover that you are overwhelmed with love from the Divine today and every day.

July 5

SOMETIMES THERE ARE NO ANSWERS

They sat with him on the ground seven days and seven nights, and no one spoke a word to him, for they saw that his suffering was very great. —Job 2:13 (NRSV)

Sometimes it is easy to find answers to life's situations through our spiritual lens. It feels as though God is clearly guiding us on a specific path. Perhaps Scripture opens our eyes to a truth surrounding a question we are facing. Other moments in life, it feels as though Scripture and God's guidance are like a compass sitting on a magnet, spinning in circles without a clear answer.

Job's three friends, after learning of the catastrophes that had befallen him, decided to go to him. When they saw him, they wept aloud, tore their clothes, and sprinkled dust and ash on their heads in solidarity with their friend. Then they sat quietly with him for an entire week.

They did not have any answers for their friend. They did not know what to say, and neither did Job. There are moments in life when Scripture quotes and one-liners from our spiritual friends hurt more than they help. They lead to more questions than answers. In moments like this, our hearts ache, our spirits are weak, and we may feel lost in this world and in our spiritual journey.

When you face answerless questions, do not flee from them and do not seek to answer them simply to offer yourself false comfort. Sit with the question and reflect on it for a while. Pray for God's peace even if there is no answer available, for there are times in life when no one and no source has an answer for our question.

July 6
REPENTANCE IN ACTION

Wash and make yourselves clean. Take your evil deeds out of my sight; stop doing wrong. Learn to do right; seek justice. Defend the oppressed. Take up the cause of the fatherless; plead the case of the widow. —Isaiah 1:16-17 (NIV)

Repentance—moving away from sin and back toward God—is more than simply confessing our sins to God and saying, "I'm sorry for what I did." It is about putting those thoughts and words into action. God was challenging the people of Israel over their unfaithfulness and lip service to the Divine. They were not putting their faith into action in their lives. God wanted them to repent, to genuinely turn back to God.

This is something we must continue to do in our own lives. We cannot assume that once we confess our faith in Jesus Christ, all of our confessing and repenting is over and done with, that we can check it off our list and move forward in our lives. If only it were that simple and easy, but it is not.

Repentance looks like putting our faith into action, not simply going through the motions of our faith. Christ has called his followers to action in loving our neighbors and our enemies, providing for the needy and most vulnerable in our society, living out an active faith every day. We must strive to do these things as a part of our repentance. Do not confuse this as a "works-righteous" stance. Our works do not earn us a place in the presence of God; only our faith in Jesus' work on the cross does that. However, our faith leads us to do the work of Christ in the here and now as a part of turning from the sinfulness of this world. In place of our sins ought to be our faith working in our lives.

July 7

SPIRITUAL EXERCISE: LECTIO DIVINA
(DIVINE READING)

Today you are invited to practice a spiritual exercise: a "divine reading" of a select passage of Scripture. Please follow the guide provided as you meditate on this passage.

- Read the passage twice, pausing between each reading for a moment of silence. Identify keywords as you read the passage without elaboration.
- Read the passage again, pause for silence, and answer the following question: Where does the content of the reading touch my life today?
- Read the passage once more, again pausing for silence, and complete this sentence: I believe God wants me to . . . .

> *O LORD, do not rebuke me in your anger, or discipline me in your wrath. Be gracious to me, O LORD, for I am languishing; O LORD, heal me, for my bones are shaking with terror. My soul also is struck with terror, while you, O LORD—how long? Turn, O LORD, save my life; deliver me for the sake of your steadfast love.... I am weary with my moaning; every night I flood my bed with tears; I drench my couch with my weeping. My eyes waste away because of grief; they grow weak because of all my foes. Depart from me, all you workers of evil, for the LORD has heard the sound of my weeping. The LORD has heard my supplication; the LORD accepts my prayer. —Psalm 6:1-4, 6-9 (NRSV)*

July 8
LIVE AT PEACE

If it is possible, so far as it depends on you, live peaceably with all. —Romans 12:18 (NRSV)

Living at peace with others is often a difficult task. Too often in life we tend to allow minor differences between ourselves and others to drive wedges that seem irreparable or impassable. Part of the problem seems to stem from control. Many people like to be in control of their lives and the surrounding situations. We enjoy being able to ensure that we have peace through our own means. However, when other people are introduced into the equation of life, our control of the situation slips away.

There are moments in life when we must relinquish control, allowing our superiors at work, our spouses at home, our children, parents, friends, or whomever to take the reins—for whatever reason.

We are called to live peaceably with others when it comes to how we behave and carry ourselves. This, again, is about control. We cannot control other people and how they behave, what they say, or how they carry themselves. We may fundamentally disagree with them on certain issues. However, for the sake of our faith, our relationship to God through Jesus Christ, and our relationship with the other person (no matter who they are), we must strive to control ourselves in such a way that we are at peace with the individual(s) in question. Be encouraged to put this into practice today. Try to live peaceably with someone who gets under your skin. You cannot control them, but you can certainly control how you react to them.

July 9

PROMISES TO A REPENTANT PEOPLE

Therefore, having these promises, beloved, let us cleanse ourselves from all defilement of flesh and spirit, perfecting holiness in the fear of God. —2 Corinthians 7:1 (NASB)

God promises to cleanse and save those who come to God in true faith. A part of that faith is repenting of our sins, essentially laying those sins down and turning our backs on them without picking them back up. This is easier said than done. However, the promises that we have from God after we set those sins to the side are great. This is not an endorsement of the idea that our deeds make us pure or lead us to salvation; only our faith in Jesus' life, death, and resurrection does that.

As we enter a relationship with the Divine, though, we are called to purify ourselves from the temptations and sins of this world and life. Full purification can only come through Christ, but we can begin the process through faith and an active avoidance of the sins that tempt us.

We strive to avoid sin because of our relationship with God. We love, respect, and are in awe of God and therefore strive to live a life that is honoring and pleasing to God. Instead of hatred toward others, we have love. Instead of violence or cruelty, we exhibit peace. Instead of greed and selfishness, we are generous and gracious. All these things are tangible, albeit broad, examples of living a repentant life. Busy yourself with tangible examples of God's grace, love, and mercy today when you feel tempted to fall into sin. This is the life of a repentant sinner who is promised eternal life through Christ Jesus.

July 10
THE GIFT OF THE SPIRIT

In him you also, when you heard the word of truth, the gospel of your salvation, and believed in him, were sealed with the promised Holy Spirit . . . . —Ephesians 1:13 (ESV)

The Holy Spirit, the third person of the Divine Trinity, is a gift from God the Father through God the Son. The Spirit is also called the Comforter and offers us guidance, peace, and reminders of God's presence in our lives.

Before Jesus was crucified, he promised his disciples that a Comforter would come to offer them peace and guidance in the work they were to do: the spread of the gospel. The spirit continues to work in and among the people of God in Christ, equipping, guiding, and comforting.

This is a blessed gift that we have all received as we believe in Jesus, the very presence of God in our lives. Yes, admittedly, a tangible presence would be nice for us, since we are creatures who rely on our senses to understand the world in which we live.

Do not be fooled, however, into believing that we do not have tangible reminders of God's presence in our lives. Those who believe and are sensitive to the Holy Spirit's work can serve, and often do, as those tangible reminders of God's presence. Further, as we encounter the natural world and become increasingly sensitive to the idea that God is all around us in nature, we can see the gift of the Holy Spirit dwelling in creation and our fellow believers. Be encouraged to seek the Holy Spirit in your walk today, and be a vessel for this gift that others may draw from.

July 11

YOU HAVEN'T SEEN
ANYTHING YET

*"If you have raced with men on foot and they have worn you
out, how can you compete with horses? If you stumble in safe
country, how will you manage in the thickets by the Jordan?"*
—Jeremiah 12:5 (NIV)

If you are someone who stumbles over your own two feet on smooth, flat
surfaces, you may have more trouble navigating a child's bedroom after
they have played with their LEGO collection. Take heart, though: the child
hasn't even played with their cars, dolls, or books. You only have the sharp,
tiny blocks to contend with at this point! You can still navigate better now
than when the child has pulled everything from the toy box or closet.

Today's verse comes from a passage in which Jeremiah is pleading a case
with God, explaining that the unfaithful and unrighteous prosper while the
faithful struggle. God responds in this verse with a word of warning and
lamentation, essentially telling Jeremiah to cheer up now because it is only
going to get worse.

While our situation may not be the same as that of the ancient Israelites, we do need to take time to focus on the moment we are living in right
now. "Be in the moment," as the saying goes. Do not look to the future
or to other people and their apparent prospering or struggles. Focus on
yourself right now because in the next minute it could get worse or it could
improve. Only God knows.

July 12

GOOD OVER EVIL

Seek good, not evil, that you may live. Then the LORD God Almighty will be with you, just as you say he is. Hate evil, love good; maintain justice in the courts. Perhaps the LORD God Almighty will have mercy on the remnant of Joseph. —Amos 5:14-15 (NRSV)

Even though this message was originally for the Israelites after they were conquered by foreign nations, it is still important for us today. As we live under the new covenant between God and humanity in and through Jesus Christ, we are called to live a life that is above reproach and that avoids evil.

In the Christian journey, maintaining a life that actively practices good over evil is important. It is important because it mirrors Jesus own life, it adheres to Jesus' teachings, it serves as a tangible reminder and example of discipleship for our siblings in faith, and it opens the door for evangelism so we may introduce other people to the saving knowledge of Jesus Christ.

God, through the prophet Amos, gives us examples of living a life that is dedicated to good over evil: maintaining justice in the courts, loving good, and hating evil. Justice is a constant theme throughout the prophetic literature in the Christian Old Testament. Many of the prophets were concerned with maintaining true justice among the Israelite people. Too often the Israelites were not practicing true justice, and the guilty were set free without punishment while the innocent suffered at the hands of the corrupt. Seek justice today. If you cannot identify a need, pray that the Spirit will lead you to one and that you will have the courage and wisdom to fight for justice as a follower of Christ.

July 13

GOD'S PROMISE TO GOD'S SERVANT

I am the LORD, I have called You in righteousness, I will also hold You by the hand and watch over You, and I will appoint You as a covenant to the people, as a light to the nations.
—Isaiah 42:6 (NASB)

Isaiah is known as the messianic prophet, largely because his book holds more prophecies directly dealing with the Messiah than any other prophetic book in the Christian Old Testament. The verse for today is concerning the coming Messiah. The people of God needed a Light, a Savior, one to lead them from their sin and unfaithfulness and to give them hope.

God promised the people that this Savior, God's Servant, would come and fulfill the promise. Before that happened, though, God promised the Servant that God the Father would be with this Servant. This promise followed Jesus throughout his earthly ministry, even to the cross and the grave.

It should give us hope to know that God the Father was with God the Son throughout the trials and ordeals of his ministry. To know that we, too, are priceless in the eyes of God. To know that nothing stands in the way of God's love of us, not even God the Son.

Armed with this knowledge and faith, be encouraged today to face the challenges that lie before you, knowing that the God who makes promises will not fail you, will not abandon you, and will not turn away from you. Does this mean that life will be made easier? No. Look to Jesus' experience in the garden the night of his betrayal. Does this mean we can find some peace amid our chaos? Yes. Rest in that peace and in the promises of our faithful God.

July 14

SPIRITUAL EXERCISE: GUIDED PRAYER

Stewardship is caring for and looking after things that are important to us, whether those things are objects, other people in our lives, nature itself, or something else. We are all called to care for something or someone else in this life, whether we know it yet or not. The first command God gives to humans in the Bible is to care for the garden of Eden.

What are you called to care for? What gives you a great passion to protect and preserve? Pray about this today. First, ask for clarity in identifying what God has called you to care for in this life. Once you have identified whatever it is, pray that God will equip you to fulfill your specific calling. Pray that God will further equip you to be a good steward of the resources, relationships, and all the other blessings you have in this life.

Suggested Scripture: Leviticus 27:30; 1 Chronicles 29:14; Matthew 6:19-21; Romans 12:6-8; 1 Peter 4:10

Suggested Prayer:

Blessed God,

Giver of all good gifts, thank you for the innumerable blessings that you have poured into my life. Grant me the wisdom to know how to manage all the gifts you have given. Remind me that all these gifts truly belong to you, and help me treat them as yours. Help me know how best to care for the things you have given to me and to care for the world that I call home in the here and now. Amen.

July 15
HOPE IN THE UNSEEN

Now faith is confidence in what we hope for and assurance about what we do not see. —Hebrews 11:1 (NIV)

"Seeing is believing." This line is quoted in the children's movie *Polar Express* in reference to Santa Claus. The idiom has indeed been quoted innumerable times by people in reference to any number of topics, events, things, or people both fictional and true to life. It was even true about the disciples of Jesus after his resurrection. Do not let Thomas take all the credit for failing to believe. The Gospel accounts tell us that all the disciples who heard the women declare the resurrection thought it was a tall tale.

The author of Hebrews, though, teaches that faith is believing in something that we do not see and having the assurance that what we believe is indeed true. It is not having to plunge our hand into Jesus' pierced side in order to believe that he is resurrected. This is faith.

But faith is a burden. Believing in the unseen is difficult. We are physical beings who rely on our senses to understand the world. However, putting faith in something that is unseen, while illogical and sometimes odd, is the ultimate show of trust, which in turn gives to us the ultimate hope.

As you continue your spiritual journey, reflect on having faith in the unseen God. What does that mean to you? Do you find it easy to have faith in the unseen, or does that stretch you? When do you find it easiest to put your hope in the unseen? When do you find it most difficult?

July 16

THE SHADOW THAT LASTED A DAY

*It was now about noon, and darkness came over the whole land
until three in the afternoon, while the sun's light failed; and
the curtain of the temple was torn in two. —Luke 23:44-45
(NRSV)*

The cross is central to Christianity. Depending on your denominational
background, the image of the cross will potentially look a little different
than it does in other Christian denominations. However, the core of the
image, two lines intersecting, remains the same.

On the day Christians call Good Friday, Jesus was crucified on a cross.
That is why this image is so important to Christianity. On that first Good
Friday, the cross cast a dark and ominous shadow across the world: the Son
of God was dead. The hope of humanity had, seemingly to the first disciples and followers of Christ, been extinguished, destroyed by sin and death.

There is hope, though. This shadow, cast by a cruel and ugly thing,
would last only a single day. This shadow would be gobbled up by the
darkness of the tomb, and that darkness would give way to the Light of the
World, to the first Easter Sunday, to the resurrection of Jesus Christ.

The promise of the gospel of Jesus Christ is not that his followers will
be spared the shadows of this life but that our Savior has experienced many
of those shadows and has made a way for us to finally escape them and fall
into the Divine arms of God the Father. Fear not the temporary shadows of
this life, and instead look to the inbreaking Light of the World for comfort
amid the shadows.

July 17

DISCERNING THE WILL
OF GOD

*And do not be conformed to this world, but be transformed by
the renewing of your mind, so that you may prove what the
will of God is, that which is good and acceptable and perfect.*
—*Romans 12:2 (NASB)*

God has a will for each believer's life. It is up to the individual to discern or understand what that will for their lives may be. Often this can be discovered through spiritual meditation, contemplative prayer, seeking the Divine in your life, and, sometimes, asking for the helping guidance of more mature believers.

Be challenged to seek God's will for your life today. If you already have an inkling about the calling God has placed in your life, reexamine that calling. It is never wrong to continue to seek God's calling, even if you have discerned and then answered that call.

Be challenged to serve as a spiritual guide, an assistant, for another believer as they seek to discern their calling. Be open to any opportunity to join someone along their path of discovering the Divine calling in their life.

Today, pray intentionally and contemplatively, slowly and meditatively about your calling. Have you discerned what God is calling you to do? Are you struggling to identify that calling? Have you learned what you are called to do but avoided answering the call? Commune with God today about this topic, your call, and reflect on what you discover.

July 18

A TOUGH CALL

And I heard the voice of the Lord saying, "Whom shall I send,
and who will go for us?" Then I said, "Here I am! Send me."
And he said, "Go, and say to this people: 'Keep on hearing,
but do not understand; keep on seeing, but do not perceive.'"
—Isaiah 6:8-9 (ESV)

Isaiah's call is one of the most familiar in all of Scripture and is often read when a candidate announces that they have been called into some form of ministry. It is a delight to read verse 8 of Isaiah 6. Who among us would not want to say that we answer in the affirmative to God's calling in our lives?

Too often we skip the following few verses. What exactly is Isaiah called to do for God? Isaiah is called to issue a grim word of warning against the people of Israel for their lack of faith in the One True God. This could not have been, and indeed was not, an easy calling for Isaiah to fulfill. Tradition tells us that Isaiah was sawn in two because of his prophecies against Israel in the name of God.

As you continue to wrestle with your call, to examine your call, or to live into your call, remember that it will not always be easy. You may already know that well. Take heart amid any challenges associated with your calling. God will continue to equip you for whatever God has called you to do. During the stress of your calling, find a moment to breath intentionally and contemplatively while communing with God. Slow down and seek to encounter God for the strength and endurance you need as you follow God's calling in your life.

July 19
CHRIST'S PEOPLE

*He it is who gave himself for us that he might redeem us from
all iniquity and purify for himself a people of his own who are
zealous for good deeds. —Titus 2:14 (NRSV)*

We who are believers in Jesus of Nazareth as the Christ of God, as Luke's
Gospel puts it, are set apart. Beyond being set apart, we are also called to be
zealous for good deeds. There is a lot going on in our verse for today. We
have a call-and-response situation. Jesus calls us as his people through our
faith in his identity as the Christ. We are then to respond in faith, being
zealous for good deeds as Christ's people.

Christ's people, Christians, ought to play a special role in the world,
especially as they are armed with the knowledge that they are indeed set
apart by God through Christ. Our role is to serve God in true faith by
also serving humanity and the world at large. From the first command in
Genesis, through the Ten Commandments the people received at Mount
Sinai, to Jesus' teachings, Scripture is filled with teachings on how we ought
to care for humanity and nature.

As a follower of Christ, be zealous for, excited about, and devoted to
doing good deeds. Do not stretch yourself too thin, however. Instead, find
one or two ministry projects and devote yourself to them, whether it is
collecting funds and goods for a local shelter or crisis ministry, starting a
free pantry at your local church or community, mentoring a youth or child
in a nearby school, joining a nature conservation group, or simply picking
up trash on the side of your road. Commit to being a follower of Christ
in more than just word. Prayerfully consider where your passion lies in
helping humanity or the world, and find out how to get involved.

July 20

EVERYTHING THROUGH CHRIST

For by Him all things were created, both in the heavens and on earth, visible and invisible, whether thrones or dominions or rulers or authorities—all things have been created through Him and for Him. He is before all things, and in Him all things hold together. —Colossians 1:16-17 (NASB)

Everything is in and through Christ, from the beginning of time to the end and beyond. Everything known and unknown, seen and unseen, is through Christ. The ability to comprehend this is beyond human minds; we cannot fathom infinity because we are finite. There is something overwhelming in thinking about everything being created through Christ. It can also be comforting to reflect on everything being created through Christ.

Hopefully this thought—that everything came into being in and through Jesus Christ—brings you a level of comfort and peace, even knowing that there is evil and cruelty in life. All of this, at the end, is subject to Christ.

In a world that seems to continue to prove chaotic and painful, it is comforting to know that, no matter the chaos and pain, Christ is above all things. As you face the day and the various events that will occur, whether they are perceived as good or bad, remember that they are all through Christ, and therefore they are subject to Christ. What does it mean to you to believe that everything is from Christ? How does it impact the way you look at other people in your life when you know that they are beloved by Christ, just as you are?

July 21

SPIRITUAL EXERCISE: MEDITATION

Christian meditation is a practice of deep prayer. Specifically, it is prayer without all the words. Carmelite Brother Lawrence of the Resurrection said that meditation is "the pure loving gaze that finds God everywhere." This idea is at the heart of the stillness, silence, and attentiveness of meditation.

Christian meditation is an intentional practice of silence and stillness, following God's calling throughout Scripture. As you seek to encounter the Divine, you are encouraged to practice the spiritual exercise of meditation: deep, intentional, silent prayer.

To begin, sit comfortably upright and lightly close your eyes. Breathe intentionally as you sit, and clear your mind of distractions. Repeating a word if you become distracted may be helpful as you strive to silently encounter God. Distractions come in all forms—a sound, a thought, a feeling, or a body sensation. Use a word that is sacred to you, something like Sacred, Jesus, God, Mercy, Abba, or another word that holds spiritual significance. Use the word to center your mind on God and invite the holy Presence of God to commune with you. Do this for fifteen or twenty minutes without elaborating or reflecting on your experience during the meditation.

As you conclude the meditative discipline, remain silent and keep your eyes closed for another couple of minutes as you reenter the busyness of your life. Remember that Christian meditation is a deep and silent prayer, a communion with God that does not require you to come up with anything to say. Simply seek to be with God in the moment.

July 22

CRUCIFYING THE INNOCENT FOR THE GUILTY

Now when the centurion saw what had happened, he began praising God, saying, "Certainly this man was innocent."
—Luke 23:47 (NASB)

The innocent was killed so that the guilty may be made free and forgiven. Christ was essentially the scapegoat for humanity. We who believe in Jesus as the Christ have had our sins removed from us. We no longer bear the guilt and shame of the things we have done against ourselves, against others, and, most importantly, against God.

When we stop to think about this, it may be difficult to process. If we learn of an innocent individual being punished for another's wrongdoing, we may feel sympathetic toward that individual. We may even wish to intervene on behalf of that individual. Sometimes our hearts break for those who suffer wrongdoing when they are innocent.

In the case of Jesus, we have the ultimate example of the innocent suffering in place of the guilty. Our hearts may indeed break over Jesus' suffering, humiliation, anxiety, and crucifixion; however, we ought to breathe a sigh of relief and, paradoxically, rejoice that we have someone who did indeed step into our shoes and bear the burden of our punishment so that we might survive.

Reflect today on what it means that Jesus took your sins to the cross and, though he was innocent of all sin, died for the forgiveness of the sins of all humanity. Breathe in the freedom that this innocent has given to you, and rest in the gift of salvation.

July 23
WHEN YOU'RE TIRED

Come to me, all you who are weary and burdened, and I will give you rest. —Matthew 11:28 (NIV)

To be tired is an overwhelming experience, especially when there are other burdens laying upon your heart and mind. We often are more susceptible to lashing out in a cruel way when we are hungry, angry, lonely, and/or tired. Whether you are weary now, have been in the past, or will be in the future, remember that Christ will bear your burdens as you place them at his feet.

Granted, it can be one of the most difficult things in this life to release our own wearisomeness and burdens. For some reason, we seem to be drawn to these things. Sometimes taking a nap, resting in our favorite chair or hammock, or getting a good night's rest is all we need to shake off the weariness of life. Sometimes, though, that weariness cannot be defeated through typical means of recharging our energy reserves.

The next time you find yourself truly tired because life has piled heavy burdens on your shoulders, seek the easier burden of Christ. Take your load to God and commune with the Divine over the burden(s). Breathe slowly and intentionally, sit comfortably, and close your eyes. Begin a meditative prayer. If you happen to fall asleep during the meditative prayer, so be it; such rest may be a gift from God. Seek to recharge your spiritual batteries as well as your physical, mental, and emotional ones. Holistic health is important for maintaining the energy we need to function in the here and now. As you commune with God, it may be helpful to imagine yourself laying a heavy burden at Jesus' feet and then taking a seat near Jesus and away from the burden.

July 24

THE IMPORTANCE OF SELF-CARE

Then he [Elijah] lay down under the broom tree and fell asleep. Suddenly an angel touched him and said to him, "Get up and eat." He looked, and there at his head was a cake baked on hot stones, and a jar of water. He ate and drank, and lay down again. —1 Kings 19:5-6 (NRSV)

The great prophet of the Christian Old Testament, Elijah, had just dismantled the pagan religious structure that had become the most prominent religion in Israel. He had defeated the priests of the false god Baal and was on the run from a corrupt queen, Jezebel, who sought to kill him.

Elijah had fled into the wilderness to escape Jezebel's wrath. As Elijah fell asleep in the wilderness, without food and water, he was stirred by an angel who provided for his physical needs. This is repeated in the following verses, and we learn that Elijah can continue forty days with the food and water God gives him through the angelic visits.

While God gave Elijah the necessary provisions, we cannot lose sight of the lesson: Elijah needed to take care of himself so he could continue his journey, and that meant he needed to eat and rest. At times in our lives—during crises, when we are overworked, when we are stretched too thin by our responsibilities at home, work, church, or elsewhere—we can neglect our self-care.

Take some time today to reflect on your own self-care. Are you eating enough, and is it healthy? Are you getting enough restful sleep? Are you active? Are you drinking enough water? Are you spending time with God? Are you spending time with creation? Are you doing something for yourself amid the busyness of your daily responsibilities? Be sure to take care of yourself.

July 25

COMMUNAL SALVATION

For God so loved the world, that he gave his only Son, that
whoever believes in him should not perish but have eternal life.
—John 3:16 (ESV)

Christians often focus too much attention on their personal salvation and not enough on the communal salvation of the entire church or Body of Christ. Many Protestants say things like, "Jesus is my personal Savior." While there is nothing intrinsically wrong with this statement, such language does lend itself to an individualistic relationship with Christ that may dismiss the image of the Body of Christ.

The fact is that Christ came for the salvation of all people. The opportunity for salvation is open to everyone, and it behooves Christians to remember this truth. To make our relationship all about personal salvation is to open the door for the privileged mindset that only those like us may be open to receive salvation in and through Christ. This is a real danger, and it is untrue.

Reflect today on whether you take your personal relationship with Christ too personally. Do you hold biases when it comes to salvation? Are there those who, in your opinion, are unworthy of this personal relationship because of some outward classification or other societal divider? Be honest in your self-reflection. Remember that Christ did indeed come to give you salvation, but Christ came for all so that no one would be without the opportunity to have salvation through him.

July 26

THE REAL PLAN

Indeed, God did not send the Son into the world to condemn the world, but in order that the world might be saved through him.
—John 3:17 (NRSV)

There is much confusion about God when reading the Scriptures, especially the books and passages that fall into the literary genre of apocalyptic. It is easy to read these Scripture passages and think that God is going to annihilate anyone and everyone who stands in God's way, to think that God will have a smile on the Divine face while passing judgment. That is not the case. The gospel is about God's love and intention to save humanity from God's wrath that is aimed at humanity's sins.

Often, as children reared in the church we memorize John 3:16, but too often the next verse is omitted from this memorization. Yes, God loves all the world and sent Jesus, but why? To bring salvation, not condemnation. Christians are often identified by non-Christians as judgmental; this stereotype harms our witness and our ability to offer love and mercy. Sometimes others do not want to accept it from us—and understandably so.

Remember the real plan of God today, and allow that plan to be visible through your life in both word and deed. You do not need to be the world's greatest evangelist to ensure that others know the Divine plan of salvation, the true plan of Scripture. You simply need to be a tangible representation of God's loving mercy that others may witness. Reflect on God's real plan and how you are a pivotal part of that real plan today.

July 27

THE SHEMA

Hear, O Israel: The LORD our God, the LORD is one.
—Deuteronomy 6:4 (NIV)

The Shema is a Jewish prayer that begins with our Scripture verse for today. It is typically recited during the morning and evening prayers and is of high importance for devout Jews in their prayer lives. The key to the importance of this verse rests in the monotheistic confession that our God is the only God. The prayer in its entirety encompasses Deuteronomy 6:4-9.

Christianity finds its roots in Judaism; the earliest Christians were considered a Jewish cult in the first century after Jesus' crucifixion and resurrection. As members of the two of the Abrahamic faiths, Jews and Christians share the theological idea that God is one God, that there are none like our God, and that there will never be any like our God.

You are encouraged to reflect on the shared theological truth that Christianity and Judaism are monotheistic religions, meaning we worship one God. What does this mean to you? What does it mean that this one God, who created everything, has a personal relationship with you through God's Son, Jesus Christ? What does it mean that you are a part of the Body of Christ, or the Bride of Christ in the form of the church, whether you attend regularly or not? Consider praying our verse for today and reflect on the prayer.

July 28

SPIRITUAL EXERCISE: PSALM OF PRAISE

Today you are encouraged to reflect on the following psalm. What does the Spirit tell you through these words? Do you find it easy to offer praises to God today? If not, then commune with God and listen for the Divine voice. Can you identify what is preventing your ability to offer praises?

> *Out of the depths I cry to you, O LORD. Lord, hear my voice! Let your ears be attentive to the voice of my supplications! If you, O LORD, should mark iniquities, Lord, who could stand? But there is forgiveness with you, so that you may be revered. I wait for the LORD, my soul waits, and in his word I hope; my soul waits for the Lord more than those who watch for the morning, more than those who watch for the morning. O Israel, hope in the LORD! For with the LORD there is steadfast love, and with him is great power to redeem. It is he who will redeem Israel from all its iniquities. —Psalm 130 (NRSV)*

July 29

THE TENDERNESS
OF GOD

I led them with cords of human kindness, with bands of love.
I was to them like those who lift infants to their cheeks. I bent
down to them and fed them. —Hosea 11:4 (NRSV)

The eleventh chapter of Hosea is all about God's love for the chosen people, the Israelites. The tenderness throughout this chapter is akin to the love a mother has for her children. This motherly figure sees the burden of her children and removes the chore. She then lifts her children into her arms and feeds them. The imagery is intimate, gentle, and loving. It also extends into the new covenant through Jesus Christ. God remains as one who tenderly loves the chosen people, members of the new covenant, Christians.

God's tenderness is also extended to you. While life is indeed filled with both sorrow and joy, remember that God's tenderness is a constant companion through both the highs and lows of life. The people of Israel, during the time of the prophets, needed the tenderness of God as they faced their foes, all of which were brought about as a result of their unfaithfulness. However, God knew that the people still needed mercy; this is evident in Christ's life, death, and resurrection.

The same tenderness that God showed to the Israelites, described in an almost motherly way, has been and is being shown to you. If you fall today, do not hesitate to run to God as a loved child might run to their parents. God will pick you up, though perhaps not in the traditional sense, and will care for you and tend to your needs as you seek the face of the Divine.

July 30

BLESSINGS TO YOU

The LORD bless you and keep you; the LORD make his face shine on you and be gracious to you; the LORD turn his face toward you and give you peace. —Numbers 6:24-26 (NIV)

This is an often-quoted benediction in Christian worship settings, a blessing to leave the people with before they depart to become the church scattered throughout their corner of the world. What a wonderful reminder to receive: that God is with you, that God may bless you in your journey throughout this life, that God may watch over you and protect you, that you may receive Divine peace.

It is true that there are moments in this life that feel void of these blessings. Strive not to allow those moments to overwhelm you. Yes, acknowledge them, but do not give them power over you or your relationship with God. Instead, cling to the blessings that God has promised you and the community of faith.

The next time you gather in a communal worship setting, pay closer attention to the benediction that is offered, either through music or the spoken word. How does it bless you? It need not mirror the above benediction, but does it contain the same elements of blessing and promise that God is with you as you depart from the gathered church?

Bask in the blessings of God, and reflect on what those blessings look like in the here and now, in your life: Strength through a crisis, close and meaningful relationships with others, a roof over your head, food in your pantry. Think of these blessings, both small and large by your estimation, and offer thanks to God for each of them.

July 31

SUFFERING IS A PART OF FAITH

And He was saying to them all, "If anyone wishes to come after Me, he must deny himself, and take up his cross daily and follow Me." —Luke 9:23 (NASB)

No one likes to suffer. By its definition, suffering is unpleasant. Yet Jesus teaches that his followers must suffer at times as they remain faithful to him. What that looks like will vary from person to person. Since this is inevitable, should we go looking for suffering? No, do not look for something that will find you in due time. Instead, seek the patience, endurance, and peace to face suffering in life.

As we read today's verse, we might ask, "Must it be this way? Is suffering necessary?" The answer is elusive. What can be determined is that, since Christ suffered and since Christ tells us to take up our own cross, we must trust that suffering is a part of the path of all Christians, indeed all people. The difference is that Christians have a source of strength and peace to draw from: Christ. Tangibly, that strength and peace is realized in our fellow believers.

There is suffering in this life—it is inevitable, and it comes in a variety of forms. Do not seek it, and do not flee from it when it rears its ugly head. Instead, take up this cross of suffering and walk alongside of Jesus, trusting that Jesus walks alongside you. You are not alone in your suffering. If you are not facing suffering at this stage in your life, seek to be a tangible representation of Christ for another person as they suffer.

August 1

ADDICTION

"All things are lawful for me," but not all things are beneficial.
"All things are lawful for me," but I will not be dominated by
anything. —1 Corinthians 6:12 (NRSV)

Paul was dealing with an unruly crowd in Corinth. He quotes some of the Corinthian believers in our verse for today: "all things are lawful for me." They were making the argument that they could indulge in just about anything their hearts desired. Paul, though, warns that this indulgence may lead to addiction.

Addictions are destructive not only to the person wrestling with the addiction but to all their loved ones too. Whether it is an addiction to games, social media, pornography, drugs, alcohol, gambling, or something else, it is imperative that the person struggling seek help as soon as possible.

The loved ones of the person addicted should surround the person with firm love and support them as they strive to come clean. If you are addicted to something in this life, please seek the help you need. If you are close to someone who is addicted, please journey with them and be supportive of them as they strive to come clean. Do not walk this journey alone; there are resources that can be of help. Seek local addiction assistance, counselors, and programs that can be helpful.

The hotline and web address for the Substance Abuse and Mental Health Services Administration is: 1-800-662-HELP (4357). The website is https://www.samhsa.gov/. The website for the American Addiction Center is https://americanaddictioncenters.org/.

August 2

THE DANGER OF TRADITION

Because this people draw near with their words and honor Me
with their lip service, but they remove their hearts far from Me,
and their reverence for Me consists of tradition learned by rote
. . . . —Isaiah 29:13 (NASB)

During the life of Isaiah, the people of God were unfaithful. They were best known for their shallow faith and their ability to worship by muscle memory as opposed to genuine worship of God. It is a dangerous thing to attend worship or practice religious ceremonies without genuine intentions of worshiping and honoring God.

In situations such as these, we must reflect on why we attend worship, why we pray, why we do anything that we have been taught to do from a religious or spiritual perspective. Put everything under scrutiny, examine all motivations, and weigh every intent. The Israelites failed to do this, and their worship became offensive to God. God would no longer hear their prayers or accept their worshipful efforts. God warned them to stop coming into the temple to worship and told them no longer to congregate with the intent to worship because it was all a lie. None of the efforts were for God; instead, the people were driven by vanity and tradition.

"Because Mom and Dad or Grandma and Grandpa took me to church" is not reason enough to continue attending. That does not mean forgoing worship attendance is preferred. What it does mean is that when we gather for worship, we examine our hearts and minds, asking the tough questions and answering them honestly. Why am I here? What keeps drawing me to this place, to this group? If the answers are not God centered, consider why.

August 3

IMAGO DEI
(IMAGE OF GOD)

Then God said, "Let us make humankind in our image,
according to our likeness; and let them have dominion over
the fish of the sea, and over the birds of the air, and over the
cattle, and over all the wild animals of the earth, and over every
creeping thing that creeps upon the earth." —Genesis 1:26
(NRSV)

You have within you, as your essence, the image of God. Every person you meet, indeed every person in this world, has been created in the image of God and carries that image within them everywhere they go, whether they believe it or not.

There is a twofold lesson in this theological truth: you are a beloved child and creation of God, and so is everyone else. This is a truth that I often shared in theory at Christian gatherings, in sermons, in Bible studies, in mission and outreach planning, and at fellowship gatherings. However, the practice of recognizing the image of God in all people often stumbles out of the gate, especially when there is a difference between ourselves and another person. Sometimes that difference is only on the surface; they look, sound, or behave differently. Sometimes it involves a sin that they or we wrestle with. Sometimes the difference is theological, political, philosophical, or another guiding principle in our or their lives.

Consider this truth again today: all people are created in the image of God and ought to have access to the same dignity and respect that you feel you are owed by others. Commune with God, seeking clear guidance on not only recognizing God's image in others but also accepting that shared image and living into that image with others.

August 4
SPIRITUAL EXERCISE: PSALM OF PRAISE

You are encouraged to reflect on the following psalm. What does the Spirit tell you through these words? Do you find it easy to offer praises to God today? If not, then commune with God and listen for the Divine voice. Can you identify what is preventing your ability to offer praises?

> *Praise the LORD. Praise God in his sanctuary; praise him in his mighty heavens.*
> *Praise him for his acts of power; praise him for his surpassing greatness.*
> *Praise him with the sounding of the trumpet, praise him with the harp and lyre,*
> *praise him with tambourine and dancing, praise him with the strings and pipe,*
> *praise him with the clash of cymbals, praise him with resounding cymbals.*
> *Let everything that has breath praise the LORD.*
> *Praise the LORD. —Psalm 150 (NIV)*

August 5

GO ABOUT YOUR LIFE

"Go therefore and make disciples of all nations, baptizing them in the name of the Father and of the Son and of the Holy Spirit." —Matthew 28:19 (ESV)

This command from Jesus to his disciples, and by default to all Christians throughout history, is often called the Great Commission. It is usually cited as an important calling for all Christians to fulfill in their lives. The truth is that the command is not an imperative in the Greek. That means it is not something that will necessarily be a vocation or something that will make or break you as a Christian.

According to the original language of the New Testament, it appears that, instead of saying that all Christians ought to busy themselves constantly with making disciples of others, Jesus said to simply go about your life and live in such a way that others know you are a Christian. A big turnoff for non-Christians and Christians alike is being asked where we would spend eternity if we were to die by the close of the day. The "turn or burn" attitude is not effective in disciple-making.

Rather than being overly aggressive in evangelism, seek to live your life in such a way that others will know you are a follower of Jesus Christ by what you say and do on a regular basis. That is what Jesus was commanding: a lifelong commitment to evangelism and sharing the gospel, not sporadic, ill-conceived, even well-meaning street preaching or tracts. Consider what you would respond to most. Consider how Jesus ministered to people throughout the Gospel accounts. Commune with God through prayer, and seek to be equipped to offer the gospel message to those in your life in a way that will lead them to respond in the affirmative.

August 6

FORGIVENESS FOR ALL

He is the one whom God exalted to His right hand as a Prince and a Savior, to grant repentance to Israel, and forgiveness of sins. —Acts 5:31 (NASB)

Peter and John were taken to the religious leaders to answer for their crime of not obeying the prohibition against teaching in Jesus' name. In response to this charge, Peter declared that they were obeying God by disobeying the prohibitions given by the Sanhedrin, the Jewish religious leaders in Jerusalem.

These leaders were offended when Peter made the claim that they had killed an innocent man in Jesus. However, even though Peter was making this claim, he was opening the door to salvation for these leaders who had indeed pushed for Jesus' execution on the cross.

This is an important lesson that all of Jesus' followers ought to take seriously: even those guilty of pushing for Jesus' death are eligible to receive forgiveness if they respond in the affirmative to the gospel of Christ. What a potent message—that no one is so sinful that they cannot receive salvation if they repent and turn to God through Jesus Christ. No sin that you commit could ever remove you totally from the presence of God. It may feel like it after the sin comes to light, but that is a falsehood, an unfounded lie. Just as the members of the Sanhedrin were given an opportunity to repent and turn to God through Christ, all people have this same opportunity. It needs only to be given them. Resolve to repent, live in your repentance, and give others the opportunity to know Christ as you know Christ, the Savior.

August 7

THE WEAKER AND
THE STRONGER

We who are strong have an obligation to bear with the failings of the weak, and not to please ourselves. —Romans 15:1 (ESV)

Paul encouraged the believers in Rome to avoid causing their fellow Christians to stumble in their faith. When someone is less mature in their walk with God, they may have certain restrictions that either they or someone else has imposed on them. We who are more mature in our walk with God may not have these same restrictions imposed on ourselves.

It is fine to have certain restrictions in life, and it is also fine to forgo some restrictions that other Christians may hold to strongly, particularly when it comes to diet or other temporal things of that nature. However, because of our shared faith with the weaker sibling in faith, we cannot partake of or pursue something that we find acceptable when someone in our company finds it unacceptable.

As you journey in this life, particularly focusing on your spiritual walk, there should be some growth, maturing, and depth added to your current level of faith and spirituality. As you journey, you will encounter individuals who share your faith yet are either more mature than or not as mature as you. Be patient with each of these individuals. Hopefully those who are more mature will help you in your journey so that you may help those who are not as mature as yourself. Pray that God will send a more mature sibling in faith to equip you to one day help someone who is young in faith. If you are more mature than others, be patient and live out your spiritual maturity so that others may learn from you.

August 8

THE PURPOSE OF
SCRIPTURE

All scripture is inspired by God and is useful for teaching, for reproof, for correction, and for training in righteousness, so that everyone who belongs to God may be proficient, equipped for every good work. —2 Timothy 3:16-17 (NRSV)

Scripture is a tool used for learning, growing, teaching, correcting, and equipping believers in their walk with God. We have the story of God encountering God's people. We have the gospel of Christ, God in flesh, and we have the early church forming and responding to God in flesh.

Scripture helps maintain some level of uniformity among believers. Granted, there are more Christian denominations than one may care to count; however, no matter our various stances on baptism, leadership, or whatever else divides us, we learn our most sacred truths from Scripture: that God is Creator, that Christ is Savior, and that the Holy Spirit is our Comforter.

Be encouraged to take a more active approach to reading Scripture. If you have yet to read the Bible all the way through, attempt that soon. If you have read the Bible from cover to cover, consider a new way to read it beyond starting in Genesis and ending in Revelation. Perhaps begin in Luke and then move into Acts. Or start in Isaiah and then read Matthew. Or find another method, another reading guide, that piques your interest. Perhaps reading a section at a time and reflecting more deeply on what each section reveals is a new method of reading a familiar text. No matter your chosen method, set your mind to reading the Scriptures with greater intentionality, reflecting a little longer on what is being said throughout this book that we call the Bible.

August 9

NO ONE HAS SEEN

*No one has ever seen God; but if we love one another, God lives
in us and his love is made complete in us. —1 John 4:12 (NIV)*

No one has ever seen God. Yes, some of the figures throughout our Old
Testament indeed encountered the Divine in such a way that it was like
seeing God. However, no one has ever fully laid eyes on God.

For some, it is a challenge to faith that we are not able to see God.
Do not be discouraged that you cannot see God in the here and now;
instead, be encouraged to be a tangible representation of who God is in the
here and now. John, in his first letter that he wrote, describes God as love.
Throughout the letter, we see that John maintains this understanding and
repeats the point that God is love, reassuring the first readers and all readers
since of this truth.

Though we have never seen God, we have opportunities to see the love
of God in our lives and the lives of other believers. The next best thing to
seeing God face to face is seeing the love of God manifest in fellow believers.
While you cannot gaze on the face of the Divine in this life, seek to allow
others to experience the love of the Divine through your words and deeds.

Be encouraged to be intentional about your words and deeds today.
Allow others to see the love of God in you. Seek also to see the love of God
in the words and deeds of others. Do not be discouraged if at first that is
difficult to identify. Keep searching and keep loving.

August 10
THE WAY TO PRAY

In the same way the Spirit also helps our weakness; for we do not know how to pray as we should, but the Spirit Himself intercedes for us with groanings too deep for words. —Romans 8:26 (NASB)

As we grow in spiritual maturity and intentionality, it is common that when we pray individually, we begin to say less and less. We offer praise and lift petitions to God, but we may catch ourselves simply existing in a moment of pure communion with God, not uttering a word, spoken or thought, and enjoying the presence of the Divine.

As we grow in our spiritual maturity, this is ideal, for often there are moments in life when words fail us. We do not know what to say. We are speechless. This may be out of fear or joy, confusion or awe, or some other reason. Be encouraged to be silent in your personal prayers more often. You need not hold your tongue all the time; simply make room for more silence between "Dear God" and "Amen."

As you journey on your walk with God, allow the Spirit to guide your prayers. Remember that God knows your requests, concerns, and praises before you utter one of them. Do not hesitate in sharing them, though, for as a loving parent listens to their child, even when it is old news, God listens to God's children. Be intentional to avoid vain repetitions and babblings; instead, allow silence to rule in moments of your prayer, and lean on the guidance of the Spirit to show you what to pray for in that moment.

August 11

SPIRITUAL EXERCISE: SILENCE AND SOLITUDE

In a society that is constantly moving, encountering, entertaining, and engaging all our senses, silence and solitude are intimidating and anxiety-inducing for many. However, silence and solitude are often great opportunities for encountering the still, small voice of the Divine. It takes great intentionality to be in silence and solitude.

Immediately following his baptism, Jesus went into the wilderness for a period of forty days of solitude prior to his temptation and ministry. Further, Jesus often went off to be by himself after miracles or teaching or before beginning a day. His intention was to pray and experience silent solitude.

You are encouraged to unplug from all electronic devices, remove yourself from the company of others, and simply be in silent solitude. Introduce yourself to this practice slowly at first. You may even set a timer for five minutes. Those first few sessions of silent solitude, even five minutes at a time, will seem to drag because our brains are increasingly overstimulated by our world, and the quiet will seem to overwhelm us in the other extreme. Do not fret. Instead, focus on God during this time. Commune with God. Pray intentionally and silently, waiting for God to encounter you. Reflect on your experience, and use the remainder of the page to write about your experience as you were in silent solitude.

_____

_____

_____

_____

August 12

WOMEN IN OFFICE

I commend to you our sister Phoebe, a deacon of the church at Cenchreae, so that you may welcome her in the Lord as is fitting for the saints, and help her in whatever she may require from you, for she has been a benefactor of many and of myself as well.
—Romans 16:1-2 (NRSV)

Women can lead in the church, too. Paul may have discouraged this in some portions of his letters, but those instances were likely circumstantial and limited to the specific churches to which he wrote in those cities. In other letters, Paul commended and praised the women in leadership of the churches. Phoebe is one such woman, a deaconess of the church.

Phoebe served as a deacon, a servant leader, one who was set apart and recognized for her gifts in the Spirit and her abilities to serve the church and act as an example of Christ. She was further commended as such by Paul, and others were encouraged to assist her, and the other leaders, as necessary.

Leadership in the church is open to those who have been called, who have answered that call, and who recognize that leadership in the church is exemplified in servant leadership, doing for others as Jesus did. Commend your spiritual leaders, encourage them, and, if you see someone with the spiritual gifts of church leadership, encourage them to seek training and perhaps ordination, following a vocation of service to Christ and Christ's church. Avoid putting limitations on the opportunities of others, regardless of their gender, who are willing and able to serve Christ and the church.

August 13

JESUS ABANDONED

All of them deserted him and fled. —Mark 14:50 (NRSV)

What a powerful statement. Jesus had been betrayed by Judas, and the crowd, armed with swords and clubs, was taking him away. The disciples, those who had followed Jesus for the last three years of his life, his closest friends, fled into the darkness of the night. One of them was so afraid that he ran away, slipping out of the grip of the guards and tearing through his clothes to flee, naked (Mark 14:52). The fear is poignant.

There is a stark contrast between the human response to stress and fear and the Divine response. Indeed, there is no reference to God fearing anything; however, throughout both Scripture and personal experience, there are plethora of examples of things that bring about fear or anxiety in the hearts of human beings.

Despite the disciples' abandonment of Jesus, Jesus does not return the favor in kind. Instead, Jesus had just promised his followers that their grief would soon become joy and that one, the Holy Spirit, would come and serve as Comforter to them, and to us, in the here and now.

Hope in the Comforter, the promise of Jesus, when you are anxious or afraid. Do not lose sight, though, of the fact that Jesus was left totally alone by his followers. Reflect on Jesus' night in the garden. What does it mean that God in flesh would suffer such experiences for the forgiveness of the sins of all who believe? For the forgiveness of your sins?

August 14

VERTICAL RECONCILIATION

All this is from God, who through Christ reconciled us to himself
and gave us the ministry of reconciliation; that is, in Christ God
was reconciling the world to himself, not counting their trespasses
against them, and entrusting to us the message of reconciliation.
—2 Corinthians 5:18-19 (ESV)

Reconciliation between God and humanity is the central theme of the gospel of Jesus Christ. Every person who believes that Jesus is the Son of God, who was crucified for the forgiveness of sins, has entered a newly reconciled relationship with the Divine. The wrongs have been made right, the sins are forgiven, and love eternal is poured out into the lives of those who believe.

There is a great hope in the idea that we have been reconciled with God. The great wedge that is sin has been removed, and we are free to enter the full presence of God beyond the here and now. Meanwhile, we have access to peace, hope, love, and assurance that God is with us in all things in this life.

To reconcile means to restore something to harmony, specifically a relationship. Our relationship with the Divine has been restored through the work of Jesus Christ. Celebrate this wondrous correction today. As you pray, thank God that your relationship with God has been restored and made right. Praise God for making this possible in and through Jesus Christ, and reflect on what it means to be in a reconciled relationship with God.

August 15

HORIZONTAL RECONCILIATION

. . . bearing with one another, and forgiving each other, whoever has a complaint against anyone; just as the Lord forgave you, so also should you. —*Colossians 3:13 (NASB)*

Reconciliation is not something that is limited to the Divine-human relationship. Reconciliation is something that needs to be practiced within our human relationships as well. When something goes awry in our relationship with another person, we must seek to restore that relationship in some way.

Reconciling our relationships with others is more difficult than having our relationship with God reconciled. God did the work for us in Jesus Christ; we only need to believe, and it is done. When it comes to our relationships with others, we must put in more effort and consciously attempt to make things right and restore what is damaged or broken.

Our model for doing this is Jesus Christ, who reconciled humanity with the Divine in his work on the cross and through the resurrection. More than that, though, we see in various teachings and parables that Jesus understood the importance of reconciliation between human beings. We must right what is wrong and seek to be the Christ followers that we strive to be.

You are encouraged to reflect on your relationships with others today. Do you need to reconcile with another person? If you do, it may be difficult to begin the process. Strive to avoid shrinking away from the act of reconciliation. No amount of distance or time should keep you from trying to reconcile with someone with whom you have had a falling out. Pray for peace and guidance in this effort, and take the first step.

August 16
YOUTHFUL LEADERSHIP

Let no one look down on your youthfulness, but rather in speech, conduct, love, faith and purity, show yourself an example of those who believe. —1 Timothy 4:12 (NASB)

Each of us has worth in the kingdom of God in both that which is to come and the here and now, no matter our age. Timothy was a young man who was following the teachings of Christ through Paul. He was serving the early church as a pastor and leader. His youth was a stumbling block for those with more experience and years under their belts, but he was equipped to fulfill his calling.

Paul encouraged Timothy to serve Christ and Christ's church faithfully, conducting himself in such a way that no one could attack him or put him down or make an excuse because of his youthfulness. This was to aid the less mature believers to grow spiritually. Age is simply a number by which we measure how many years we have lived; it has no reflection on our spiritual, emotional, or mental maturity.

Reflect on your spiritual age. Approximately how long have you been a believer in Jesus Christ? Reflect on your spiritual maturity in comparison to that age. Reflect further on taking a more active leadership role in your local church or Christian gathering. If you still need more spiritual seasoning, seek a Timothy who may help you to grow into the person God has called you to be.

August 17

THE SEASONED VETERAN

So, Abram went, as the LORD had told him; and Lot went with him. Abram was seventy-five years old when he set out from Harran. —Genesis 12:4 (NIV)

It bears repeating: each of us has worth in the kingdom of God in both that which is to come and the here and now, no matter our age. Abram, later known as Abraham, was seventy-five years old when God called him to leave his pagan family and go to what would later become the nation of Israel's promised land. This is more than coming to a certain point in life and making a career change. This is coming out of retirement and making a huge change in career.

Abram was called to go and begin a family when he and his wife, Sarah, had been unable to do so thus far in their marriage. Yet, without missing a beat, according to Scripture, Abram set off on this journey to begin not only a new chapter in his life but also to start writing a new book. He would eventually become the paterfamilias of the people of Israel and the spiritual ancestor of three major world religions of today.

This seasoned veteran would go on to do many wondrous things, all in the name of following God. Granted, this obedience to God forced Abram to change gears in his life. Undoubtedly, he had become comfortable with some form of routine, yet he was willing to shake it up and go.

Are we that willing? Once we have established ourselves somewhere and are no longer the rookie or the new employee, friend, neighbor, or whatever, are we willing to uproot ourselves and follow God's calling? Reflect on this question today.

August 18

SPIRITUAL EXERCISE: LECTIO DIVINA

(DIVINE READING)

Today you are invited to practice a spiritual exercise, a "divine reading" of a select passage of Scripture. Please follow the guide provided as you meditate on this passage.

- Read the passage twice, pausing between each reading for a moment of silence. Identify keywords as you read the passage without elaboration.
- Read the passage again, pause for silence, and answer the following question: Where does the content of the reading touch my life today?
- Read the passage once more, again pausing for silence, and complete this sentence: I believe God wants me to . . . .

> *Now I appeal to you, brothers and sisters, by the name of our Lord Jesus Christ, that all of you be in agreement and that there be no divisions among you, but that you be united in the same mind and the same purpose. For it has been reported to me by Chloe's people that there are quarrels among you, my brothers and sisters. What I mean is that each of you says, "I belong to Paul," or "I belong to Apollos," or "I belong to Cephas," or "I belong to Christ." Has Christ been divided? Was Paul crucified for you? Or were you baptized in the name of Paul? For Christ did not send me to baptize but to proclaim the gospel, and not with eloquent wisdom, so that the cross of Christ might not be emptied of its power.—1 Corinthians 1:10-13, 17 (NRSV)*

August 19
FAITHFULNESS IN FAITH

*"His master said to him, 'Well done, good and faithful servant.
You have been faithful over a little; I will set you over much.
Enter into the joy of your master.'" —Matthew 25:23 (ESV)*

Most people like to be encouraged on a job well done. The recognition is nice, and the pat on the back makes us feel good about what we have accomplished. Beyond the feeling of satisfaction and encouragement, though, is the need to complete a task that needs finishing.

The people of God through Christ have been called to various tasks in this life. We each have our own gifts and talents and can use those gifts and talents to complete the tasks God has put in our lives. Some of those tasks include discipling younger believers and working as a member of the church at some level.

Participating in such a community and working alongside our fellow Christians is an important part of being a follower of Christ. We were not called to follow Christ in a vacuum or as a private practice. The act of following Christ is to be done as part of a community. Look to the first-century Christians in the New Testament after the Gospel accounts. These people lived, learned, struggled, and grew in faith together.

Seek to be part of a community of faith, whatever that looks like in your walk with Christ, and be a productive member as well. Work with your siblings in faith to grow in spiritual depth and to experience the Divine together. That may look like the more traditional church experience, meeting beneath a steeple, or it may look like an early house church, or it may look like something totally different.

August 20

DIVINE PLANS

*"So in the present case, I say to you, stay away from these men
and let them alone, for if this plan or action is of men, it will be
overthrown; but if it is of God, you will not be able to overthrow
them; or else you may even be found fighting against God."*
—Acts 5:38-39 (NASB)

When God plans something, that plan will work out according to God's
intended end. In the case of our passage today, this was recognized by the
religious leaders in Jerusalem as they bore witness to the burgeoning church
known as the Way.

Too often in life, we make plans without consulting or considering
God. We want to do certain things, go certain places, accomplish certain
goals, and we do not pray, seek Divine guidance, or ask for the input of our
Christian siblings. In cases such as these, we are prone to failure because we
are not following a plan that aligns with what God has in store for us. Be
encouraged to commune with the Divine about the plans you have for your
life, whatever they may be. Be humble enough to follow the plans God has
revealed to you for your life.

What Divine plans have you discerned for your life or the lives of
those near to you? Have you discerned any Divine plans? If you have yet to
discern a plan of God for your life, continue to pray about this. Seek God's
guidance, and seek to move aside and allow the Divine to guide you along
a path to complete the plan in store for you.

August 21
GOD LOVES YOUR ENEMIES

"If you love those who love you, what reward will you get? Are not even the tax collectors doing that?" —Matthew 5:46 (NIV)

Jesus was teaching in what has become known as the Sermon on the Mount. His topic in this case was love. Jesus points out that it is well and good that we love those who love us, but even the people who do not follow the Law, the first five books of our Old Testament, do that. It is indeed easy to love those who already love us.

To love those who already love you is no challenge. It is expected by society and God. It is a norm in this world. On the other hand, to love someone who does not love you in return is a challenge.

Looking to God as an example, we see that it is possible, even necessary, to love our enemies in order for the gift of salvation to continue to spread throughout the world. Paul says, "But God demonstrates his own love for us in this: While we were still sinners, Christ died for us" (Rom 5:8). God loved you even when you were an unforgiven sinner; that is the central message of the gospel.

This love extends even to those whom you may consider your enemies. That is what our verse for today is about—loving those whom we may not consider worthy of our love for whatever reason. This is a tough reality. There are people in this life who are difficult to love, even impossible to love by human standards. Those who harm children come to mind as some of the worst offenders, though they are loved by God, so we ought to love them, too. They should pay for their crimes, yes, but they should be loved and given opportunity to reform as well.

August 22

BEHAVING AS A BODY BEHAVES

Now you are the body of Christ and individually members of it.
—1 Corinthians 12:27 (NRSV)

We are all a part of the Body of Christ. This imagery carries a double meaning. First, we are united as a single body, moving, engaging, and functioning as Christ's body. Second, we are individual members of the same body, which means that we all have specific duties to perform so that this one united body may be most effective in the here and now.

Elsewhere in the New Testament, Paul teaches that we cannot all be feet or eyes or the same body part. We all have specific roles to play in this life that we call the Christian journey. You are encouraged to find your role. Are you called into vocational ministry? To volunteer? To teach your own family of Christ? To go into the mission field? Or perhaps simply to live your life in such a way that everyone will know you are a Christ follower?

No matter your calling, remember that you do have a place in the Body of Christ. Do not be discouraged if you have difficulty identifying that place immediately. Do not let the ignorance of others hinder you. Some cannot discern what your calling may be and may not serve as helpful guides for you. Seek people with humble hearts, those you trust as spiritually mature, and ask for their wisdom and assistance in identifying your calling, your role as a part of the body. Indeed, that is what a body does: it depends on all the individual parts to function normally and continue to grow. Seek to continue to grow in your spiritual walk today by functioning as an active part of the Body of Christ.

August 23
GROWING UP

When I was a child, I spoke like a child, I thought like a child, I reasoned like a child. When I became a man, I gave up childish ways. —1 Corinthians 13:11 (ESV)

When we were younger, our way of understanding the world in which we live was limited. We made sense of things differently than we do at later stages of development. Theoretically, as we grow, our understanding of the world deepens. Noises in the middle of the night are not as creepy, thunder is no longer understood as angelic beings bowling in heaven, and so on.

The same is true with our spirituality. Hopefully, your spiritual life has developed as you have grown. We begin by nursing, drinking spiritual milk as Paul says, and we, in theory, ought to be looking forward to eventually sinking our teeth into something with spiritual substance.

That doesn't mean we need a divinity degree or seminary training. We don't all need to know how to parse the Greek New Testament or understand what the words *eschatology* or *pneumatology* mean, though it is good to learn if you are interested.

Instead, we need to continue to grow in fellowship with God and our fellow believers. Apply the teachings of Christ to your daily life so that others may know that you are his follower. Seek to be an agent of justice, mercy, and grace, all the while loving and serving God in the here and now. Be encouraged to continue to grow in your spiritual life, and grow closer to God, to your fellow Christians, and to other people in general.

August 24

WE BREATHE
THE NAME OF GOD

Let everything that breathes praise the LORD! Praise the LORD!
—Psalm 150:6 (NRSV)

This is the final verse of the final psalm in the book of Psalms in the Bible. The Psalter ends with praises to God. Not only praises but also the message that everything that has breath ought to praise the Lord. The Hebrew understanding of the name of God is *Yahweh*. In the mind of the people of the Old Testament, it was considered taboo, irreverent, and sinful to verbalize the name of God, the idea being that the sinful lips of humanity profane the name of God when it is uttered.

The Hebrew pronunciation of the name of God, Yahweh, is impossible. It sounds like a breath of air because there are no vowels added to the name in the Hebrew. To pronounce the name is to inhale "*yah*" and exhale "*weh*." Truly saying the name of God is breathing normally.

As you breathe today, be conscious of the sound you make and remember that one day everything that has breath will praise the Lord. What an awesome thought! As you breathe today, take some time to meditate, concentrating on your breathing, and offer to God praise and thanksgiving for giving you yet another day of life to live and breathe. Reflect on what it means that everything with breath will praise the Lord. Consider how you might praise the Lord in everything you do today. What might that look like? How might others respond to you as you praise the Lord in all things, even the necessary task of breathing?

August 25
SPIRITUAL EXERCISE: GUIDED PRAYER

You are encouraged today to enter a time of prayer and meditation. Peace seems fleeting in this life, here one moment and gone the next. Whether it is peace throughout this world or in our individual lives, it is a fragile thing that can be shattered by any number of crises or events.

Peace is an important theme throughout Scripture, particularly in the Gospels. In the Gospel according to John, Jesus speaks to his disciples about the coming peace, a gift that they would need and cherish in this life. We too have been given the promise of Divine peace in our lives, through both the calm and the storm. Pray for a reminder of that Divine peace today for yourself, for your loved ones, and for the world at large.

Suggested Scripture: Psalm 119:165; John 14:27; Colossians 3:15

Suggested Prayer:
Prince of Peace,
Thank you for your promise of peace that will calm all fears and remove all anxieties. This world is temporal and tangible and often overwhelms your people with burdens and strife. Cause your peace to overwhelm these burdens, not necessarily removing them but removing their disruptive nature, disallowing them from robbing me of your peace. Grant that I would be an agent of your peace in this life, equipping me to share this blessing with others whom I encounter, calming me even in moments of high stress in encounters with others. This world aches for your peace. Grant us all this gift today. Amen.

August 26

KNOWING WHEN TO STAND AND WHEN TO HIDE

The prudent sees the evil and hides himself, But the naive go on, and are punished for it. —Proverbs 22:3 (NASB)

There is plethora of examples throughout Scripture of individuals standing in the face of injustice, sin, and evil. Any number of our Old Testament prophets comes to mind. What about when it is not beneficial to stand in the face of evil, though? Are there times when we ought to hide away?

The short answer is "yes." There are indeed moments in life when we ought to hide away from injustice, evil, and sin. This may seem counter to the teachings of Jesus and the prophets mentioned above, but take into consideration the importance of planning and biding one's time before making a decisive stand. Consider also your methods of standing against sin and evil in the world.

Remember that, as a Christian, you are an agent of peace and love. Consider carefully how you might react to injustice, sin, and evil. Pray, seeking discernment from God and godly people in your life. Hide if you must, if the situation merits that course of action, and prepare yourself for facing the wrong later.

There is nothing wrong with hiding from evil in this life. Sometimes hiding from sin and evil prevents us from committing another sin or evil in response. Hide from sin and evil, and consider your next move. How has Christ taught us to respond to the injustice, sin, or evil that you face?

August 27
GOD'S KNOWLEDGE OF YOU

For it was you who formed my inward parts; you knit me together in my mother's womb. —Psalm 139:13 (NRSV)

The 139th Psalm describes the great intimacy of God's knowledge of the psalmist. God is aware of the writer's comings and goings, thoughts, and so on. The idea is that God is with the psalmist in all things and everywhere. Not only that, but God was the creator of the psalmist, knitting him together in his mother's womb and forming him in a secret and unseen place.

The Creator of all things knows you in this way too. You were knit together by the Master Craftsman. Every nook and cranny of your being is known by God—the individual hairs on your body, the freckles, and the wrinkles. The Lord set in motion the creative process that eventually grew into the person you are today.

God is intimately aware of who you are—your thoughts, routines, and actions. This should not be something that is intimidating to you; on the contrary, this should offer you a level of peace. God is not "big brother" out to watch your every move and bully, blackmail, or extort you. Instead, God is aware of who you are and everything about you like a loving parent is aware of their children's actions, yet even more intimately so.

Take comfort in the knowledge that God is with you today and that God was the one who created you in your mother's womb. Allow God's intimate knowledge of you to be a comfort, reminding you that God cares for you and is drawn to you.

August 28

ABOVE ALL, SEEK GOD

"But strive first for the kingdom of God and his righteousness, and all these things will be given to you as well." —Matthew 6:33 (NRSV)

In life, there are many things that desire our attention—like people, possessions, hobbies, and entertainment, just to name a few umbrellas under which people and things vie for our attention. There is nothing wrong with seeking relationships with others, obtaining money, holding a job, finding some worth or value in a hobby or interest. However, above all of these things, strive for the kingdom of God.

What does that mean? Look to have a firm, stable, and healthy relationship with God above having personal relationships with other people, pursuing a career or interest, or filling your bank account. These things are not inherently evil or wrong and can be great and meaningful, but they are ultimately not as important as a relationship with God, the Creator and Savior of humanity.

What does striving for the kingdom of God look like? The Sunday school answers are praying, reading your Bible, and fellowshipping with other believers. Deeper than that, though, prayer is listening as much as it is talking to God. Reading the Bible is more than skimming the text; it is wrestling with the word of God. What is it saying? What does that saying mean to you? Is it a difficult or easy word to digest at this season of your life? Fellowshipping with others looks more like living your life in the good *and* the bad with other believers; welcoming others into your struggles and sitting with them as they struggle; and celebrating with them over their joys and weeping with them over their losses.

August 29
SIMPLE INSTRUCTIONS

And Elisha sent a messenger to him, saying, "Go and wash in the Jordan seven times, and your flesh shall be restored, and you shall be clean." —2 Kings 5:10 (ESV)

Elisha was the bald apprentice to Elijah who witnessed his teacher being taken up into heaven aboard a fiery chariot and who asked for a double portion of the Spirit from his teacher. All of that aside, following Elijah's ascension, Elisha went to work as the prophet of God.

One of the miracles Elisha performed was the healing of a leper named Naaman, a general of the army of Aram. The instructions were simple: go and wash in the Jordan River seven times. The simplicity of the instructions insulted the military leader, and he initially refused.

When we reflect on the simplicity of our faith and the way that we receive salvation, it can be underwhelming. We are simply to believe that Jesus is the Son of God who died for the forgiveness of our sins and is now resurrected, living forever. Just believe—that is the basic understanding or prerequisite for receiving salvation from God.

It is almost insultingly easy! Do not be fooled or insulted by the simple instructions of our faith. Remember that the disciples, not just Thomas, had difficulty believing even though they saw Christ risen. The Christian faith is paradoxical in that it is both easy and yet difficult to believe. Be encouraged to reflect on your faith. Has it ever been difficult for you to believe? If so, how did you work through those feelings and thoughts?

August 30
FOLLOW YOUR CALLING

*Then Amos replied to Amaziah, "I am not a prophet, nor am
I the son of a prophet; for I am a herdsman and a grower of
sycamore figs. But the LORD took me from following the flock
and the LORD said to me, 'Go prophesy to My people Israel.'"*
—Amos 7:14-15 (NASB)

Amos was a shepherd and farmer before he was called to be a prophet for
God. It was not until later in his life, after he had established himself as
a field worker, that he was called to be a prophet. Abraham was similarly
called from the life of a herdsman in the land of a pagan people to go and
establish a people of his own who would be dedicated to God through a
covenant.

Looking to each of the disciples in the Gospel accounts, we see fish-
ermen, a tax collector, and others who had established themselves in other
vocations, yet they were called by Christ to follow him and then establish
the church in this world.

No matter where you are in life, whether beginning or continuing
your education, just beginning your career, contemplating a second career
choice, nearing retirement, or enjoying your golden years, be encouraged
to continue to reflect on the call that God has placed on your life. To what
have you been called? How have you been equipped to follow that calling?
Has something caused you to go "off track" and pursue another vocation
or career? Remember that God called all kinds of people: young people,
senior citizens, poorly equipped by human standards, small, meek, and the
list continues. Reflect on your calling, and strive to follow the calling that
God has placed on your life.

August 31
ROOTED IN CHRIST

As you therefore have received Christ Jesus the Lord, continue to live your lives in him, rooted and built up in him and established in the faith, just as you were taught, abounding in thanksgiving. —Colossians 2:6-7 (NRSV)

Being rooted in something means that we are deeply impacted by it. When we root ourselves in something, we find support, nutrition, meaning, and life in it. As Christians, we should be rooted in Christ, receiving spiritual nutrition, ethical guidance, mercy, grace, forgiveness for our sins, and unconditional love for simply existing.

As we find our roots in Christ, we are then equipped to go and follow our calling, to share what we experience in Christ, to apply Christ's lessons to our lives, and to engage the world around us for the kingdom of God.

In what are you rooted? Theoretically it should be Christ, but often we find that we have roots in many different areas of our lives. Sometimes those things are sinful and unhealthy like an addiction. Other times those things involve our relationships with others or our careers. While it is not wrong to find meaning in our vocations, and it is indeed healthy to find nourishment from our spouses or significant others, we cannot rely on these other sources to nourish us in the way that Christ can nourish us. Reflect on where your roots lie. Are they implanted in Christ or another source? Following your reflection, seek to strengthen your roots in Christ.

September 1

SPIRITUAL EXERCISE: PSALM OF PRAISE

Today, you are encouraged to reflect on the following psalm. What does the Spirit tell you through these words? Do you find it easy to offer praises to God today? If not, then commune with God and listen for the Divine voice. Can you identify what is preventing your ability to offer praises?

> *Shout for joy to the LORD, all the earth.*
> *Worship the LORD with gladness; come before him with joyful songs.*
> *Know that the LORD is God. It is he who made us, and we are his; we are his people, the sheep of his pasture.*
> *Enter his gates with thanksgiving and his courts with praise; give thanks to him and praise his name.*
> *For the LORD is good and his love endures forever; his faithfulness continues through all generations. —Psalm 100 (NIV)*

September 2
HAVING VS. WANTING

Make sure that your character is free from the love of money, being content with what you have; for He Himself has said, " I will never desert you, nor will I ever forsake you." —Hebrews 13:5 (NASB)

Mr. Spock, the half-Vulcan/half-human science officer from *Star Trek* was quoted as saying in one episode, "You may find that having is not so pleasing a thing as wanting. This is not logical, but it is often true."

The fictional character was speaking about contentment. Often, when we find something we think we want to have, our anticipation builds and we create a fantasy of what it will be like to finally have it. Then, as Spock has reminded us, when we do have what we desire, the luster diminishes. The anticipation, we find, was greater than the reward.

Rather than seeking to satisfy the desires of this life that ebb and flow with trends in fashion, technology, and the other things that influencers of modern society often deem of utmost importance, we should seek contentment.

The author of our verse for today spoke specifically of avoiding love of money, though this lesson may be applied to all material possessions. Spock was speaking in the context of having a spouse and the various aspects of that relationship. Be encouraged to find contentment in your life today, and then carry that contentment throughout your life. Chasing possessions wearies the body and mind and depletes the soul. Instead, chase a meaningful relationship with God and your fellow believers.

September 3
SPIRITUAL PRIORITIES

You have looked for much, and, lo, it came to little; and when you brought it home, I blew it away. Why? says the LORD of hosts. Because my house lies in ruins, while all of you hurry off to your own houses. —Haggai 1:9 (NRSV)

What comes first for you in life? Many people will answer that their spouse or significant other comes first. Or maybe their children. Their parents. Their career, education, hobbies, etc. What about your spiritual life? Your relationship with God? Where does that fall on the list of important things?

Truth be told, you are at the top of God's priority list. That is clearly spelled out in the gospel of Jesus Christ. At the time of Haggai, the Israelites had returned to Jerusalem after their exile and fell back into their old habits as a people. They did not have their priorities in the right order. They built their own homes and then began moving about as normal without building a place to worship and honor God. For the Israelites of the Christian Old Testament, the temple was the dwelling place of God on earth. Effectively, then, God no longer had a dwelling among God's people, and that was troubling.

Where is God in your list of priorities? Yes, we have bills to pay and we must tend to our families. However, God must still take precedence on our priority lists, even above our immediate families and careers. This is not divine vanity; it is human devotion. Be encouraged to examine your priority list today. Where does God fall on that list? Make an effort to be more intentional about including time with God every day and in everything that you do.

September 4

RESTORING A RELATIONSHIP

All this is from God, who through Christ reconciled us to himself
and gave us the ministry of reconciliation; that is, in Christ God
was reconciling the world to himself, not counting their trespasses
against them, and entrusting to us the message of reconciliation.
—*2 Corinthians 5:18-19 (ESV)*

Since the beginning of all things, God has been working to have a relationship with humanity. The thing is, a relationship is a two-way street that takes work on the part of both parties. Further, both parties must want that relationship to work in order for it to be healthy and true.

Though God has done everything to ensure a healthy relationship with humanity, humanity has broken the relationship. But this brokenness is not the end of the story. Through Jesus Christ, God has worked, is working, and will work to reconcile or restore this broken relationship between Godself and humanity.

The good news of the coming kingdom of God is that humanity is reconciled; our relationship with God is restored and made new. Our relationship with God is made new, even though all any of us have contributed to that relationship is pain and separation. God has not given up and will not give up. God desires nothing more than having a relationship with you and will do all that God can, except force you, to have that relationship. This is so important to God that God sent Jesus Christ to the cross to ensure that you and God are reconciled and your relationship repaired. Reflect on this truth today.

September 5

GOD SEEKS
THE SINNERS

Then the man and his wife heard the sound of the LORD God as he was walking in the garden in the cool of the day, and they hid from the LORD God among the trees of the garden. —Genesis 3:8 (NIV)

God knew what had happened: Adam and Eve had sinned, partaking of the forbidden fruit and becoming aware and ashamed of their nakedness. God sought these sinners, knowing that they had done exactly what God had told them not to do.

Take a moment to reflect on what is happening in the verse for today. God, in full knowledge of the sin that Adam and Eve had committed, still wanted a relationship with them. God's desire is to commune with us, though we are sinners. That is the grace of God: that though we are sinners, we are still loved by the Divine.

What does it mean to you that you are loved by the Creator of all things, even though you have done nothing to earn that love and can do nothing to earn that love? What does it mean to you to know that God seeks a relationship with you and has gone to such great lengths as to send God's Son to the cross for you?

Reflect on this today: that you are sought by God and that God wants to commune with you and have a relationship with you, though there is so much that stands between you and God. Dismiss those things and seek God as God has sought you.

September 6

TEMPORARY VS. ETERNAL

Therefore, we do not lose heart, but though our outer man is decaying, yet our inner man is being renewed day by day. For momentary, light affliction is producing for us an eternal weight of glory far beyond all comparison, while we look not at the things which are seen, but at the things which are not seen; for the things which are seen are temporal, but the things which are not seen are eternal. —2 Corinthians 4:16-18 (NASB)

The passage above can be difficult to understand. It is full of "churchy" language that is fluffy yet weighty, confusing yet imperative for us to understand. Paul is teaching that there are challenges in this life, things that weigh heavily on us and make it feel as though God is distant. However, while it may feel that God is distant, that things are hard and may never get easier, we cannot lose sight of our real goal.

One day, perhaps in the distant future or perhaps in the next few minutes—we cannot know—we will leave this life and experience rest from all that is weighing us down.

It is difficult to think of the things that are to come. The eternal is not tangible for us. Right now, we have bills to pay, families to care for, jobs to do, education to complete, chores waiting for us, and the list continues. Be encouraged to take a few minutes today to reflect on what it means to look forward to the unseen. Reflect also on what it means to deal with "light affliction." Finally, reflect on what it means that our outer self is decaying while our inner self is being renewed every day.

September 7
THE MYSTERY OF GOD

As for me, I would seek God, and to God I would commit my cause. He does great things and unsearchable, marvelous things without number. —Job 5:8-9 (NRSV)

Too often within Christianity, there have been errant attempts to explain away, answer, or otherwise remove mystery from God. Protestants are particularly guilty of this. Humanity naturally seems to want to answer mysteries. Many people confess that they do not like mysteries. We like to know the answers to how things are done, how tasks are performed, or how the illusionist causes the assistant to disappear.

Smoke and mirrors that confound us are offensive. The truth, however, is that there is indeed much mystery surrounding the Divine. When we ponder the Divine, we attempt to wrap our finite and limited minds around what is limitless. It cannot be done. Yes, there are answers within Scripture or through the work of the Holy Spirit, but not all our questions about God have answers that we can know in this lifetime. And frankly, when we encounter God in the fullness of the Divine presence, we probably will not care to ask the questions that plague us now.

Our verses for today reveal that Job understood that God was and is capable of many great things that cannot be numbered or fully understood. If there is a being who can do such things, then it stands to reason that the same being cannot be fully known or understood by human efforts. Reflect on how it feels to know that God is not fully knowable.

September 8

SPIRITUAL EXERCISE: LECTIO DIVINA
(DIVINE READING)

Today you are invited to practice a spiritual exercise, a "divine reading" of a select passage of Scripture. Please follow the guide provided as you meditate on this passage.

- Read the passage twice, pausing between each reading for a moment of silence. Identify keywords as you read the passage without elaboration
- Read the passage again, pause for silence, and answer the following question: Where does the content of the reading touch my life today?
- Read the passage once more, again pausing for silence, and complete this sentence: I believe God wants me to . . . .

> *Pray like this: Our Father who is in heaven, uphold the holiness of your name.*
> *Bring in your kingdom so that your will is done on earth as it's done in heaven.*
> *Give us the bread we need for today.*
> *Forgive us for the ways we have wronged you, just as we also forgive those who have wronged us.*
> *And don't lead us into temptation but rescue us from the evil one. —Matthew 6:9-13 (CEB)*

September 9
MAJOR CHANGES

And all who heard him were amazed and said, "Is not this the man who made havoc in Jerusalem of those who called upon this name? And has he not come here for this purpose, to bring them bound before the chief priests?" —Acts 9:21 (ESV)

Often a conversion to Christianity brings about major changes. Sometimes those changes occur suddenly, while others are more gradual. For Saul, who would later go by Paul, the changes were immediate and drastic. He had set out on a mission to arrest followers of Jesus Christ in Damascus and bring them back to Jerusalem for trial and punishment. However, his encounter with Jesus Christ on the road led to a major change. It was so drastic that the followers of Christ did not initially believe the reports they heard about Saul.

When we hear that someone who is vocal about certain subjects or topics, and is sometimes argumentative, changes their minds, it is difficult to believe them—particularly in our modern context when everyone is strongly opinionated and often the group that disagrees is vilified.

But a change of heart is not uncommon. When it comes to encountering others who may have had a change of heart, either moving toward agreeing with you or away from agreeing with you, it is imperative to maintain peace if possible. No matter the issue, argumentative, combative, or forceful opinions and voices rarely if ever change another person's mind. Besides, if the change is to move toward Jesus Christ, who are we to disbelieve a person's conversion? In those cases, rally to that person and lift them up in prayer, Christ-like love, and support, and come alongside them in the journey as they seek to encounter God more deeply, just as you seek to encounter God.

September 10
GOD'S GOOD PURPOSE

For it is God who works in you to will and to act in order to fulfill his good purpose. —Philippians 2:13 (NIV)

It is the will of God that all who follow Jesus Christ act out of love for God and other people. We are called to live out this ideal in our own walk during life in the here and now.

This is hard for humanity, even the faithful, to accept and follow. People are notoriously strong willed and independent, and this is lauded in Western society. We enjoy believing that we know and understand the right things. We hold to the idea that we have our "stuff" together and in order, or at least we pretend to for the sake of others.

The verse for today is somewhat vague on what good purpose God wills for you. Do not misunderstand the verse as saying that God wants to bless you with wealth, health, or prosperity of some kind. Instead, understand that God is calling you to do some good thing in the name of God in this world. Is that to feed the poor? Help the sick? Care for those in prison? Engage in activism on behalf of a marginalized people group?

Encounter the Divine today and begin searching for the good purpose that God is willing for your life. Do not be afraid or shrink away from that calling as God reveals it to you. Find the courage and encouragement to fulfill it, knowing that God will equip you along the way, no matter the challenges.

September 11
BEAR WITH ME

[Love] bears all things, believes all things, hopes all things, endures all things. —1 Corinthians 13:7 (NASB)

The love chapter in the first letter to the Corinthian church, chapter 13, is often read at weddings. The truth, though, is that the love Paul describes is the ideal love between God and humanity. In the case of the verse today, love bears, believes, hopes, and endures all things. This is a stout love.

For most human relationships, it seems that if a certain line were crossed, it would take Divine intervention to ensure that the relationship survived. In truth, the Divine intervention has already occurred through the life, ministry, death, and resurrection of Jesus Christ.

This ideal love between God and humanity is the model for human relationships with one another. God loves us perfectly, bearing with our sinfulness and enduring our faithlessness. In looking to this model and trusting that this is how God loves us, we are better equipped to understand that it is indeed possible to love others as we are called to love them.

Ponder God's love for you today. Consider that God's love for you bears with all the things you do that go against God's calling in your life, God's commands throughout Scripture, and the perfect model of love that is Jesus Christ. As you consider this, allow your love for others to bear with their failings as God's love for you bears with your failings.

September 12

BELIEF IN THE ANOINTED ONE

Do not let your hearts be troubled. Believe in God, believe also in me. —John 14:1 (NRSV)

Jesus was comforting his disciples on the night of his betrayal. Part of his method of comforting them was to encourage their faith in him as the Anointed One of God or the Messiah or Christ. Peter had already identified Jesus as the Christ earlier in Jesus' ministry, so it was not a foreign concept for these closest followers to ponder and consider.

This concept, belief in Jesus as the Christ, is central to Christianity. It is what makes Christians who we are. While this is a central belief in Christianity, it is an odd belief. God became flesh and then died to forgive humanity of our sins. What a bizarre concept indeed.

Yet it is belief in this concept that assures us salvation and promises us that we will, one day, be in the full presence of God for all eternity.

Take some time today to reflect on what belief in Jesus as the Christ of God means. What promises do you hold on to considering this belief? How does your life reflect belief in this concept? How might you want to grow in your spiritual life as it is based on this belief? Do you find peace in the belief that Jesus of Nazareth is indeed the Christ? If not, reflect on why peace eludes you.

A DAILY WALK WITH GOD

September 13

HUMOR

Recognizing Peter's voice, in her [Rhoda's] joy she did not open the gate but ran in and reported that Peter was standing at the gate. —Acts 12:14 (ESV)

In the overall passage in which our verse is found, Peter has been freed from prison and has shown up, in the middle of the night, at a home where many followers of Christ are staying. Peter knocks and is not given entry because the young woman who answers the door is so overjoyed that she cannot believe her ears.

It is comical to imagine Peter standing at the door and the young woman being so excited that she forgets to open it. Instead, she rouses everyone else in the house first.

While Scripture never mentions Jesus laughing, it is hard to imagine that God in flesh who experienced all the highs and lows of being human did not laugh on occasion. Scripture and Christianity may be a serious thing, something to take seriously as followers of Christ, for they give us direction, hope, and a sense of belonging in this life. However, to live seriously all the time is to miss the blessed gift of humor.

Look for the humor in life. Share some humor with others. Try to find the joy in everyday life when you can, and laugh, giggle, or chuckle at the silliness that occurs. Laughing is surely a gift from God. Enjoy it as such this day.

September 14
GOD'S POWER AT WORK IN YOU

Now to him who is able to do immeasurably more than all we
ask or imagine, according to his power that is at work within us
. . . . —Ephesians 3:20 (NIV)

This is an interesting thought: that the power of God is at work in *you*. It is a thought that can easily be misunderstood or, more likely, overlooked, as Christians are often too busy to pay attention to the power of God at work in our lives. In the busyness of Western society, it is easy to become numb to the subtlety of the Holy Spirit working in our lives, even for Christians who are active in their faith. Sometimes activity can be misunderstood or mislabeled for spiritual works or faithfulness.

The power of God, though—the same power that split the Red Sea, stopped the sun in the sky, prevented rain, healed the sick, raised people from sickness, and resurrected Jesus Christ—is at work in your life. What a marvelous reality.

Ponder this declaration from the Scripture reading for today. What does it truly mean to have the power of God working in your life? How does that power manifest itself in your life? How are you being used as a conduit for the power of God in the lives of others around you? As a Christian, you have the ability to submit yourself to the power of God and not only become more aware of the power working in you but also serve as a conduit through which that power flows, specifically the love, mercy, grace, and forgiveness of God. How will you allow this Divine power to flow through you today?

September 15

SPIRITUAL EXERCISE: CONFESSION

Confession, as the old saying goes, is good for the soul. It is good to confess our wrongs, whether actions or thoughts. Doing so lifts a burden from our hearts and shoulders, though it can be a painful process. Many people in Western society are private, especially when it comes to our shortcomings, failures, and sins. We do not like to have the magnifying glass hover over our lives for extended periods of time because we fear being "found out."

In Protestant circles, the word "confession" feels Catholic. Though most Protestants do not view confession as a sacrament and do not regularly confess our sins to others, it is still a good practice. There are numerous scriptural examples of confession both to God and to others that may be cited as examples for the importance of confession in our spiritual lives. The model prayer, or the Lord's prayer, that Jesus offers as an example for us to follow shows that prayers of confession are appropriate. James, in the letter that bears his name, teaches that we ought to confess our sins to one another and pray for one another that we might be healed (Jas 5:16).

You are encouraged to offer a prayer of confession to God on this day. Confess your sins to God, remembering that God already knows your sins, both those you remember and confess and those you do not. When you confess to God, reflect on the reality that these sins that you confess are forgiven. Reflect on what it means that these sins cannot damn you and have been removed from you through God's immense love for you revealed in and through Jesus Christ. Consider also confessing to a trusted confidant today, and use them as an accountability and prayer partner for your spiritual journey.

September 16

NEVER-ENDING SUPPORT

And the LORD will continually guide you, and satisfy your desire in scorched places, and give strength to your bones; and you will be like a watered garden, and like a spring of water whose waters do not fail. —Isaiah 58:11 (NASB)

Often in life there are times of struggle, seasons of crisis. Christians often use this language, borrowing from Psalms, to describe hardship or difficulty. There is nothing wrong with admitting that sometimes we are overwhelmed or are facing a particularly difficult time in our lives.

Whatever that difficulty or difficulties may be, it is important to remember that we have someone who is with us in those challenging times. Specifically, God is with us. When we decide to open ourselves to the truth that God is with us, God's presence can be refreshing in our weakness.

The challenges or difficulties in life can leave us feeling like we are wandering through a parched desert, a dark valley, with no respite. However, God can and indeed does offer respite in the form of divine peace and restoration. When we face spiritual dryness, financial crisis, the loss of a dearly loved person, a job, or some other difficulty, let us remember God.

This does not mean that everything will magically be better once we turn to God during seasons of hurt or crisis. However, we will be better equipped to face the challenges ahead as we lean on God through our time of chaos. Remember this when the days of weakness and wandering in lonesome places arrive in your life.

September 17

DEEPLY CHERISHED

Are not five sparrows sold for two pennies? Yet not one of them is forgotten in God's sight. But even the hairs of your head are all counted. Do not be afraid; you are of more value than many sparrows. —Luke 12:6-7 (NRSV)

No matter how we read the creation accounts in Genesis, one thing we can learn from them, besides the fact that God is the creator of all things, is that God cares deeply for creation, specifically for humanity, the most favored creation.

Since humans are the favored creation of the Divine, it stands to reason that God would care most of all about people, above plants and animals. As we observe creation around us, we may take note that the flora and fauna native to the region of the world in which we live survive and thrive without aid from an outside source. Each of these things also has an earthly value. This value depends on the person measuring the plant or animal life.

What is beyond value, though, is you and every other human being on this planet. You are so valuable to God that every hair on your head is known to God. This phrase simply means that God knows every detail about you. Nothing is small or insignificant enough that it can be overlooked or ignored. Is there someone or something in this life that is so meaningful to you that you know every minute detail about them? This is how God cares for you and for every individual person in this world. Reflect on the truth that God cherishes you so deeply that God invests time in knowing all there is to know about you. What does this mean to you?

September 18
THE INVISIBLE, VISIBLE

He is the image of the invisible God, the firstborn of all creation.
—Colossians 1:15 (ESV)

Christians worship a God who is invisible to the five senses we have at our disposal. Granted, if we are in tune to God and sensitive to how God moves and functions in the here and now, we can experience God. However, this experience is still limited. God is invisible to us; further, we cannot experience God in all the Divine essence in this life.

The gospel of Jesus Christ teaches us of God in flesh, a central Christian theological understanding that gives us an image of the invisible God. Sometimes, worshiping an invisible God is difficult. Even within the Christian Old Testament, the invisible God was never fully visible. God revealed God's self through miracles of nature and theophanies, but never did human eyes gaze at the Divine being except for Moses himself.

Jesus' arrival changed all of that. With Jesus' dual nature of being fully both human and Divine, human eyes could finally see God plainly. What a blessing it must have been for those followers who saw Jesus the Christ in flesh once they realized who he was. Further, Christ is above even the angelic beings in heaven, which gives Christ unparalleled authority.

The invisible God has been made visible. We do not live in first-century Judea and are not privy to the visible God, but this does not make our faith moot. Instead, that is what we must have faith in: that the invisible God was made visible in and through Jesus the Christ, that the invisible God encountered humanity on our own terms. Reflect on this today.

September 19

MINDFULNESS VS. MIND FULLNESS

Let the words of my mouth and the meditation of my heart be
acceptable in Your sight, O LORD, my rock and my Redeemer.
—Psalm 19:14 (NASB)

There is a distinct difference between being mindful and having our minds filled. Mindfulness is being aware, whether of your surroundings, your thoughts or feelings, the people you are around, and so on. But having a mind full of thoughts, dreams, feelings, and more can be distracting and can even slow our progress in various projects or goals. Sometimes we may even be so focused on an end goal, something in the future, that we are not mindful of the present and the path to that goal.

Some moments should be dedicated to focusing on the future, but that cannot happen all the time because it leads to mind fullness. We cannot worry about everything, though there is a time and a place to focus on our problems.

Be encouraged today to meditate on Scripture and actively commune with God. If something comes to mind, acknowledge it and then refocus on the task at hand. Calm your mind today and strive to focus only on the task immediately before you. If you have some downtime, meditate on a favorite verse of Scripture, or reflect on a part of God's creation that you do not normally pay much attention to, like a plant or singing birds. Strive to declutter your mind and relax your thoughts, centering yourself on one thing at a time.

September 20

MEETING OUR TRUE NEEDS

And my God will meet all your needs according to the riches of his glory in Christ Jesus. —Philippians 4:19 (NIV)

There are several individuals who preach and teach that God wants to bless us with happiness, wealth, and health. This comes from the "Word of Faith" movement or the name-it-claim-it thought process. The idea is that if you name something you want in faith and in the name of Jesus, then you will receive whatever you ask for. This is a false gospel, a prosperity gospel that distorts the true gospel of Christ for the benefit of those who teach such falsehoods.

While our physical needs are important, and it is nice to have a little more than we need, these are not as important as our spiritual needs. The prosperity gospel fails in different ways because it focuses too much on our physical needs and not enough on our spiritual needs.

All of our spiritual needs have been met in and through Jesus Christ. We have been given forgiveness and love, and as we believe in Christ we begin to see our true worth in the eyes of God, value that far exceeds the health, wealth, and prosperity that a false teacher can hope for or proclaim. It is difficult to appreciate or understand the intangible gifts and promises from God when we live in a world that demands tangible results at work, tangible food for our bellies, tangible money for our purchases or debts, and more. However, rest assured that your spiritual needs are met by Christ, and seek to enjoy this promise and blessing today. Reflect on what it means to have your needs met through Christ.

September 21
DOING GOOD

Therefore, as we have opportunity, let us do good to all people, especially to those who belong to the family of believers.
—*Galatians 6:10 (NIV)*

Doing good seems to be a basic and even simple idea of Christianity. We are called to do good in this world, for this world, and to those who live in this world. God wants us to care for nature and for our fellow human beings. Christians, in theory, have a great place to practice this goodness within the church, among our fellow believers. However, many Christians seem to struggle with doing good, particularly when we get heated or passionate about something.

There are countless local churches and denominations around the world, particularly in the southern United States, that reveal that we cannot get along and often go our separate ways before striving to resolve the issues that come between us and our fellow believers. There are over forty denominations of Baptists within the United States alone!

The good that Christians can do though far outweighs the bad. Many hospitals, schools, shelters, orphanages, and other centers intended to aid humanity have Christian roots. We can do much good in the world. You, too, can do much good. Consider how you might do good within your local church family. How can you mend broken relationships? How can you organize a group to aid those who are suffering? Go and do good with and for others, and it will do you much good as well.

September 22

SPIRITUAL EXERCISE: GUIDED PRAYER

Today you are encouraged to spend time communing with God in prayer. Praying for those who are considered the "other" in society is an important step in moving toward interaction and love. The word "other" indicates that these individuals or groups within society are viewed as outcasts. The identity of the "others" may vary from person to person. It may be that the "other" for you looks different from you, practices a different faith, has a different sexual orientation, or is otherwise different from you. Pray for these people and for yourself in interacting with them. As Christians, we accept that all people are made in the image of God and hold great value, no matter how different they may be from ourselves.

Suggested Scripture: Genesis 1:26-27; John 3:16; Romans 3:23-24

Suggested Prayer:
> Holy God,
> Thank you that I have worth and value in your eyes. Open my own eyes to see the value and worth in all people, even if I disagree with them in some fundamental way. Give me a humble and loving heart for all of humanity. Amen.

September 23

THINKING AHEAD

I have decided what to do so that, when I am dismissed as manager, people may welcome me into their homes. —Luke 16:4 (NRSV)

The parable of the shrewd manager stands out among Jesus' teachings for one reason: Jesus applauds this manager's actions. This may seem odd because his actions, lowering the amounts owed to his soon-to-be former employer, were ethically and morally wrong. However, his motivation was to secure his future.

The manager was soon to be out of work and, as a result, would be homeless and without any income. Thus, he would need some assistance in meeting his needs. In response to this looming change to his employment status, the manager ingratiated himself to those who owed his boss great quantities of olive oil and wheat, which were valuable commodities in the first-century Judean culture.

Jesus praises the forethinking of the manager. The positive aspect of his behavior was that he was planning for his future. We too must plan for our future, and not only our future in the here and now. Making financial plans and preparing for children's college funds, retirement, and what will happen to our belongings once we die are important. However, these plans have an expiration date, even though we do not know exactly when that date will be. Be encouraged to make plans for your eternal future. Trust in Christ in the here and now so that you will have a secured eternity. Then encourage others through your witness to plan accordingly as well.

September 24
HARD RESET

Therefore, if anyone is in Christ, he is a new creation. The old has passed away; behold, the new has come. —2 Corinthians 5:17 (ESV)

"Hard reset" is a phrase that refers to bringing a piece of technology back to its factory cleanliness. For instance, performing a hard reset on a smartphone clears it of all the photos, apps, and other information added to it since it was first purchased. A hard reset effectively wipes out all the clutter on a device and makes it like new again.

Originally, God called creation "good" and humanity "very good" (see the creation account in Genesis 1). After the introduction of sin into the world, things needed a renewal. Laws were put into place; purification rites and methods of cleansing were enacted. But none of these things fully brought humanity and creation back to the goodness of the beginning. A hard reset was required.

Jesus brought about that reset, making everyone who believed in Jesus as the Christ a new creation and doing away with the old. Once again, we are "very good," or so we will be once we are in the full presence of God the Father through faith in God the Son and the work of God the Spirit.

Take some time today to reflect on being made new in Christ. Having gone through a spiritual hard reset, what does it mean to you that you are renewed and cleansed of the clutter of your personal sins?

September 25

A HARD REMINDER

Concerning him we have much to say, and it is hard to explain, since you have become dull of hearing. —Hebrews 5:11 (NASB)

Growth is an essential part of the Christian life. Without growth there is stagnation and complacency. Neither of those states are healthy for the called people of God. Keep in mind that you do not have to pursue a vocational ministry position like pastor, missionary, or music minister in order to be called by God.

Look to the Scriptures, and you will see that a life of complacency and stagnation does not mesh with being called by God. From Abraham through the first-century church as described in the New Testament letters, the people of God are constantly moving, growing, failing, and then repenting and moving forward again. When they are not in motion, God calls them out on their complacency and challenges them to move.

Whether through an Old Testament prophet or through individuals like Paul, Peter, and John, the people of God are reminded to follow their calling in faith. Sometimes that reminder difficult to process. The writer of our verse today did not hold back and challenged the early Christians, who had become "dull of hearing," to grow in their faith. As Paul said in another letter, they needed to move from spiritual milk to spiritual solid food (1 Cor 3:2).

Be encouraged to grow in your walk with God daily. As you do, you will move from milk to solid food eventually. This may look like going from singing "Jesus Loves Me" to asking "Where are you, God?" to finally sitting quietly as you encounter God in the moment. Keep growing in faith and in relationship to the Divine.

September 26
A WELL-BALANCED DIET

Jesus answered, "It is written: 'Man shall not live on bread alone, but on every word that comes from the mouth of God.'"
—Matthew 4:4 (NIV)

Do you recall the cereal commercials from your childhood? A colorful character would snag your attention and encourage you to eat a sugary cereal, and a voiceover at the close of the commercial would say something like, ". . . part of a balanced breakfast." The advertisers knew that their product alone was not a balanced and nutritious meal.

A balanced diet includes protein, dairy, grain, fruit, vegetables, healthy fats, and an occasional sweet treat. Similarly, a spiritual diet consists of communing with God in prayer, both speaking and listening, fellowship with other believers, worship, individual devotional time, giving, scriptural study, learning, and working for the kingdom of God.

In the context of our verse for today, Jesus was tempted by the devil in the wilderness prior to his earthly ministry. Jesus knew that God, through our various spiritual disciplines or exercises and activities, feeds and nourishes us so that we may continue to grow and develop into well-balanced and healthy followers Christ.

It is true that, physically, we need a well-balanced diet to remain healthy and so our bodies may function at their best. Spiritually, this is true as well, though the diet is somewhat different. To remain at our healthiest spiritually, we must feast on the word of God. That is, we must read our Bibles and share our thoughts and questions in study, and we must also seek the guidance of the Holy Spirit. Follow the Spirit's guidance today.

September 27

FELLOWSHIP IS CRUCIAL

And let us consider how to provoke one another to love and good deeds, not neglecting to meet together, as is the habit of some, but encouraging one another, and all the more as you see the Day approaching. —Hebrews 10:24-25 (NRSV)

Even introverts need companionship. All people need to interact, at least some, with others who share their faith. It is true that we may not be able to discuss our religious affiliation at work because of various reasons, or we may not have an opportunity to do so as we run errands, but we must come together and share in being the gathered people of God on a regular basis. This is healthy and good for us.

Whether it means attending church services on Sunday morning, participating in a Bible study group, or meeting with fellow believers for a short time at a favorite restaurant or other public place, we are to gather with others who believe in Christ as we believe.

Part of participating in a fellowship of gathered believers is finding encouragement in faith. Often, circumstances in life may threaten our sense of peace, cause hatred or unrighteous anger to rise within us, or even lead to existential crises that threaten to tear us asunder spiritually.

Being part of a regular meeting of the faithful may not prevent these things from happening, but it certainly helps when we have a group of trusted siblings in Christ to lean on when these things occur. Nourish yourself in the fellowship of other followers of Christ. Lean on them, allow them to lean on you, and learn from one another.

September 28
VICTORY IN JESUS

I am writing to you, little children, because your sins are forgiven for his name's sake. —1 John 2:12 (ESV)

Victory in Jesus is not just the refrain of an old hymn; it is the truth of the Christian faith. But what is this victory, and if we are victors, who is the loser? Our victory in Jesus is the forgiveness of our sins. We no longer bear the burden of our lies, anger, hatred, misdeeds, careless words, idolatrous behavior, and faithlessness. We are cleansed and made whole in Christ.

Whom did Christ vanquish for us? Our sins and the evil one, the ruler of this world, the devil or Satan, the spirit of evil that exists and threatens to tear us away from God, though it cannot. This one whom Christ has overcome is identified with various terms.

You have won when you believe in Jesus as the Christ of God. Do not let that truth escape your mind. On the other hand, do not become complacent in your victory. While you may be secure in the hands of God from all alarms and threats, there are others who do not know Christ as you do: as Lord and Savior. Seek to be an example of light and love in the lives of others today, ensuring that Christ can be seen in your actions and heard in your words. Your victory is assured as you have faith; help to introduce others to this same victory today and throughout your life. This is the greatest thing we can do for other people.

September 29

SPIRITUAL EXERCISE: REFLECTING ON LIGHT

Throughout Scripture, light is used to express knowledge, truth, and righteousness, among other generally more positive ideals. The first thing God creates in the first creation account in Genesis is light. Jesus declares in the eighth chapter of the Gospel of John, "I am the light of the world"; this is one of Jesus' famous "I am" statements. God traveled with the Israelites, leading them in the wilderness as a pillar of fire in the night, lighting their way. Paul saw a great light when he encountered the risen Christ on the road to Damascus. These are just a few examples of light in Scripture. Light is generally thought of as a good thing. With light, we can see clearly what was previously hidden by darkness and shadow.

When you ponder the idea of light in its scriptural context, what further thoughts come to your mind? What hopes? What fears? Take some time to reflect on light within the Christian context, and use the remainder of this page to jot down your reflections.

_____

_____

_____

_____

_____

_____

September 30
HEAVENLY PROCESSION

Then we who are alive and remain will be caught up together with them in the clouds to meet the Lord in the air, and so we shall always be with the Lord. —1 Thessalonians 4:17 (NASB)

The Greek language, which is the language of the majority of the New Testament, suggests that Jesus' return will play out like a gatekeep or watchman who sees someone important coming and alerts the town. Once alerted, the townsfolk will go out and meet this individual and then return to the town with them, celebrating their arrival.

When Jesus returns, whenever that will be, the church will celebrate and meet the victorious Christ. According to the author of 1 Thessalonians, the church will meet Jesus in the air and escort him back to the earth as he begins his reign, whatever that looks like.

It is a dangerous pastime to predict exactly what will happen when Christ returns, or when it will happen. Rather than occupy your mind with these answerless questions, focus on the truth that whenever and however Christ returns, it will be a time of great celebration for Christ's people. Further, as we wait for the return, let us busy ourselves by ensuring that more and more people will have reason to celebrate Christ's return by sharing his love, mercy, grace, and forgiveness with them in the here and now.

Rest assured in the knowledge and faith that, whenever Christ does return, as a believer you will not be left out of the celebration. Instead, strive to commune with God and serve as the salt and light of Christ in practical ways in this life.

October 1

DEPRESSION

But he [Elijah] himself went a day's journey into the wilderness and came and sat down under a solitary broom tree. He asked that he might die: "It is enough; now, O LORD, take away my life, for I am no better than my ancestors." —1 Kings 19:4 (NRSV)

Depression is a tough condition to overcome. It is interesting to note that many individuals from the Christian Scriptures dealt with depression. Elijah was one of them. Despite what many would call successful events in his life—defeating prophets of false gods because he worshiped the One True God, outrunning a horse on foot, praying for rain after a seven-year drought, and encouraging the people to come back to God—Elijah still wanted to die because of a threat from Queen Jezebel.

Depression often manifests itself even after a person's high achievements. It is an overwhelming disease that cannot be beaten by a single hero. While prayer is a great place to start, seeking support from loved ones is a healthy second step. Searching for local counselors, support groups, and other options with your healthcare provider are important too. If you are depressed, do not walk this path alone. God has equipped professionals in this world to help you through difficult challenges. Call someone today if you or someone you love are experiencing feelings of depression. Do not wait.

The hotline for the Substance Abuse and Mental Health Services Administration is: 1-800-662-HELP (4357). The website is https://www.samhsa.gov/.

October 2

AWE

The LORD is in his holy temple; let all the earth be silent before him. —Habakkuk 2:20 (NIV)

As the writer of Ecclesiastes says, "there is a time for everything." Throughout Scripture, in both the Old and New Testaments of the Christian Bible, there are examples of how people behave in the presence of God. In some instances, there is singing and shouting for joy. In others, there is great fear and trepidation. In yet still others, there is silence and awe. Each is appropriate, and so too are other examples of behavior in the presence of God. It is indeed overwhelming for mortals to encounter God.

The context of today's verse from Habakkuk is a comparison of the God of the Bible to false gods who were introduced to the Israelites. The false gods and idols were breathless and lifeless. The conclusion of God's speech is our verse for today. It is a declaration that God is above all, and all people who enter the temple, coming into God's presence, ought to be silent; indeed, they will fall silent in awe of the Creator of all things and the Savior of all who believe.

Seek to enter God's presence this day, and do so silently. Prayer is often misunderstood as only speaking to God. That is just one part of praying. Commune with the Divine silently today, and reflect on your experience. Strive to repeat this type of prayer more regularly, communing with God in silence.

October 3

OVERWHELMED BY CIRCUMSTANCES OF OUR CREATION

The waters closed in over me to take my life; the deep surrounded me; weeds were wrapped about my head. —Jonah 2:5 (ESV)

The story of Jonah is about a prophet who did not want to answer his call. He was called to give a message of potential mercy to a sinful people group in Nineveh. Jonah felt that these people did not deserve the opportunity to repent and receive mercy. He wanted to withhold mercy from them. He knew that God would give mercy to sinners, but he felt that they were unworthy of that mercy, so he ran in the opposite direction.

He then found himself on a boat in the middle of a vicious storm at sea. The hyper-superstitious sailors listened to Jonah and threw him overboard when he said the storm was his fault. He was then swallowed by a giant whale or fish.

The reluctant prophet ended up in a situation of his own creation. Overwhelmed by this situation, he prayed. Jonah was at fault for his situation; he had no one to blame but himself. We too find ourselves in overwhelming situations of our own creation. Thankfully, God is not so petty that our prayers are unheard when we find ourselves in the belly of our own situations. If you are facing an overwhelming situation, or simply a frustrating or troubling situation of your own creation, seek God's presence and guidance today. Know that you are not abandoned to your fate and that God loves you and wants to be with you in the belly of your own fish. Allow God's Spirit to guide you through this situation, and be patient as God is patient with you. After all, Jonah waited three days!

October 4
WALKING IN LOVE

And this is love, that we walk according to His commandments.
This is the commandment, just as you have heard from the
beginning, that you should walk in it. —2 John 1:6 (NASB)

Christianity is not a religion of rules and regulations, though some people would attempt to sway us into that line of thinking. In truth, there are only two rules, or commands, that Christians ought to follow. Those are to love God with your holistic, entire being and to love others as you love yourself. That's it! No more, no less. These are not easy to follow, but thankfully, Christians are granted grace and forgiveness.

There is a great deal of "love talk" in the letters attributed to John. God is identified as being love itself, and followers are called to abide in this love and find comfort in it, as there is no fear in God.

Be encouraged to walk in love today with everyone you encounter. Walk also with God in love today. Reflect on what it means to love God with your entire being. What does it mean to love others as you love yourself? Do you ever struggle with self-love? This is not a conceited, arrogant, or selfish love but a genuine love and concern for your holistic well-being. Do you take care of yourself? That is an integral part of self-love. Walk in love today, and seek to allow others to see that love in your life. What are some ways that you can make God's love more evident in your daily walk?

October 5

INTERPERSONAL PEACE

May the God of steadfastness and encouragement grant you to live in harmony with one another, in accordance with Christ Jesus. —Romans 15:5 (NRSV)

Living in harmony with other people is difficult. Sometimes it is even difficult to live in harmony with oneself. However, this is what a genuine Christian community ought to strive for. Harmony with others does not mean there is no room for disagreement or differing opinions. It does not mean allowing others to take advantage of us. That is not harmonious.

Seeking to come to terms with others through honest communication, genuine love, and a shared desire to exist within a community leads to harmony. Existing in harmony through Jesus Christ means sharing in loving, genuine community. This is not a romantic love, and neither is it an easy love. The love of Christ is sacrificial and difficult, though it is well worth the cost as it assures those who share in this love a deep, meaningful, and rich relationship—a harmonious relationship built on love of and faith in Jesus Christ and a love of one another.

Seek to live in harmony with others in your life. Attempt to strike that harmonious balance in the relationships closest to you: your spouse, parents, children, in-laws, and closest friends. These are the most difficult to bring into harmony through Christ. Sometimes the help of a professional counselor is required to help find this balance. Do what you must to live in harmony with those close to you. If you can live in harmony with them, then you can live in harmony with anyone.

October 6

SPIRITUAL EXERCISE: GUIDED PRAYER

Spiritual renewal is an important aspect of any spiritual life. Holistic health requires physical and mental exercise and emotional cleansing, whatever that looks like for each individual, and it also requires spiritual renewal. Regular fellowship with like-minded believers, reading and meditating on the word of God, and wondering at the created world in which God has placed humanity can all be parts of renewing ourselves spiritually.

Do not neglect your spiritual well-being, as this leads to spiritual weariness, burnout, or dryness. All these things are potentially depressing and can lead to other problems in life.

Suggested Scripture: Psalm 16:8-11; Jeremiah 31:25; 1 Corinthians 16:16-18: 1 John 1:9

Suggested Prayer:
Merciful God,
No doubt there are seasons of spiritual dryness or hardship no
matter what my devotional, meditative, communal, and prayer
life look like. Please refresh and renew me every day in seasons
of plenty and seasons of wanting. Help me to long for you as the
thirsty long for a refreshing drink of cool water. Remind me of
your ever-present love and mercy, and do not let my senses grow
dull to your grace and love as you dwell so near to me. Help me
seek you daily and always with a renewed sense of awe. Amen.

October 7
NO FEAR IN GOD

There is no fear in love. But perfect love drives out fear, because fear has to do with punishment. The one who fears is not made perfect in love. —1 John 4:18 (NIV)

Fear is a terrible motivator, at least when it comes to relationships. Too often, though, we may react to others out of fear—fear of losing a relationship, benefits of some kind, perhaps even our jobs. However, living in fear of something means living an unfulfilled life. Relationships led by fear are not centered in Christ.

Further, too many Christian leaders have encouraged others to have faith in God out of fear of hell or separation from God. Scaring individuals into heaven is not the way to encourage a life-changing and life-fulfilling relationship with God through Christ.

Do not let anyone fool you into thinking that you need to fear God in order to have a relationship with the Divine. That is not love. It is fair to say that a life apart from God is unfulfilled and leads to destruction. It is better for Christians to come to faith in God through a genuine love of the Divine as opposed to fear of punishment.

Be encouraged to rest in your relationship with God today. Nothing can separate you from the love of God once you come to God in faith through Christ. Further, seek to overcome your fears in this life, trusting that God is with you always.

October 8

GOD DOES NOT FORGET GOD'S PEOPLE

And the exiles of this host of the sons of Israel, who are among the Canaanites as far as Zarephath, and the exiles of Jerusalem who are in Sepharad will possess the cities of the Negev. —Obadiah 1:20 (NASB)

Much of the Christian Old Testament, especially the Prophets, deals with the people of God, the Israelites, as they are going into, living in, and coming out of exile. Obadiah is no different. One of the common themes throughout these prophetic books is the promise that God's people will be restored to the promised land. God did not forget God's people. God does not forget God's people today. God will never forget God's people.

Christians are a part of God's people through the new covenant sealed in Jesus' blood. This means we will not be forgotten, just as the ancient Israelites, our spiritual forebears, were not forgotten. The Israelites must have felt overwhelmed in their exile. Being uprooted from their homes, jobs, and perhaps even families was certainly a traumatic event. Facing this trauma, it would have been easy to assume that God had abandoned them. However, this was not the case.

Life is filled with traumatic events, both large and small. Many of these events can lead even the most faithful followers of Christ down a road of uncertainty and questioning about God. This is normal and even natural. Be encouraged to cling to the truth that God has not abandoned you in the past, is not currently abandoning you, and will not in the future abandon you during the crises of life. This does not mean that the crises will be any easier; it means that the love and peace of God will attend you during these crises.

October 9

STRONG AND COURAGEOUS FOLLOWERS

"Have I not commanded you? Be strong and courageous. Do not be frightened, and do not be dismayed, for the LORD your God is with you wherever you go." —Joshua 1:9 (ESV)

Moses had died, and the people of Israel were poised to enter the promised land. The next leader would have huge sandals to fill and face a challenge for even the most faithful and seasoned of God's people. Joshua, though, was no slouch. He had followed Moses and been on Moses' side since the people were led from captivity in Egypt. However, this was a huge undertaking for the younger man, and he needed encouragement to follow his calling in life.

Sometimes there are moments in life when we must take over for someone else. Perhaps someone at work retires and you are given some of their workload. When a teammate is injured, you may have to go in for them. When someone is sick and cannot help on a project, their role must be delegated to the rest of the group. There are even moments when you might take a job that once belonged to someone else who was beloved and proficient, and that can be intimidating.

If you are facing such a challenge or know someone who is—or in the case that you may face such a challenge later in life—be encouraged and be an encourager. Do not lose sight of the goal of your position. Resist the urge to be overwhelmed by the responsibilities, and seek comfort in knowing that God equips us for the tasks to which we are called. Slow down today. Consider practice a breathing exercise using a focal word or prayer. Seek to find God's guidance, strength, and courage as you face your next challenges.

October 10

REMARKABLE RESOLVE

But Ruth said, "Do not press me to leave you or to turn back from following you! Where you go, I will go; where you lodge, I will lodge; your people shall be my people, and your God my God." —Ruth 1:16 (NRSV)

Ruth was a woman of remarkable resolve. She married into the people of Israel, which meant that she was not originally a part of the people of God. When her husband died, she had the opportunity to return to her people, but she decided to stay with her mother-in-law, Naomi. This takes remarkable resolve in and of itself!

This woman also decided to travel to a land that was not her own, with a family that was not her own by blood, and adopt a faith that was not her own and a God that she had not known from childhood. Even taken one at a time, the changes Ruth was willing to undergo would be overwhelming, but add to them that she was mourning the death of her husband and brother-in-law as well, and it would be easy to say that Ruth made the wrong decision to travel to a foreign land and not return to her own blood kin. This was not what God intended, though. Ruth is one of the five women mentioned by name in the genealogy of Jesus. Her role after the death of her husband was important, and it started with her willingness to remain in a foreign land and worship a God who was foreign to her: the God of Abraham, Isaac, and Jacob.

There are moments in our lives when we are faced with difficult decisions. Sometimes we decide on the easier path for obvious reasons. Consider carefully the next decision that you must make. How much resolve do you need to carry on with the more difficult choice? Where is God leading you?

October 11

A WORSHIPING COMMUNITY

Any of his people among you may go up to Jerusalem in Judah and build the temple of the LORD, the God of Israel, the God who is in Jerusalem, and may their God be with them. —*Ezra 1:3 (NIV)*

The Israelites were finally permitted to return to the promised land after being in exile or paying tribute to a foreign king for nearly a century. Cyrus, the Persian king who had defeated the kingdom of Babylon, permitted this return from exile and gave a command that the Israelites return to their homeland and rebuild the temple in Jerusalem.

The temple held great significance for the people of God, serving as a tangible reminder that God dwelt with them as well as a place of worship of God. One of the first collective projects that the returning Israelites were charged with was the reconstruction of the temple, or the building of the second temple. The significance of this project may be lost on modern Christians, as there is a collective belief that we may encounter God anywhere in the world, whether in a church building, fellowshipping with others, or in solitude.

For the people of God of the Christian Old Testament, however, a central place of worship was extremely important. The people of God, throughout our collective history, have always been a people of worship. Whether through prayer, songs, proclamation of the word, acts of service, or some other form, we worship God in our lives. Encountering the Divine in and through worship is central to our beliefs. Reflect on your communal worship involvement. Humans are social creatures, and it is especially meaningful to worship God with like-minded believers.

October 12

CHRISTIAN SUBMISSION

Be subject to one another out of reverence for Christ.
—*Ephesians 5:1 (NRSV)*

Submitting to others is often seen as weakness and an undesirable trait by most in Western society. It may even be an offensive thought to have to submit oneself to another. The societal idea of submission does not necessarily align with the teachings of the early church.

Christians are called to live in submission to one another. This does not mean we are slaves to one another. Neither does it mean we are robbed of our dignity when we serve others. The idea is that we are called to follow Christ's own example of serving other people in this life at the expense of societal norms, expectations, or demands. Jesus himself washed the disciples' feet at the last supper according to John's Gospel account. It was an image of service and humility that can teach us all.

Submitting to one another in a Christlike manner is a form of love and service to both our fellow humans and to God. Paul expresses that for Christians, this submission to one another ought to flow out of reverence to Christ as we remember Christ's own service and submission to others for the sake of the gospel concerning himself.

If God can lower Godself to be wrapped in flesh and then further lower Godself to be a servant to those first disciples, then we can submit ourselves to others for the sake of sharing the gospel of Jesus Christ and serving as tangible representations of that gospel. This is the ultimate goal of Christians submitting to each other.

October 13

SPIRITUAL EXERCISE: EXAMEN

We live in an age of distraction, and being a people who are saturated with distraction, we can easily drift through life on autopilot. This is a poor way to encounter God or others in any meaningful way. Today we will explore the ancient practice of the daily examen. Saint Ignatius of Loyola introduced the five steps of this spiritual discipline. The point is to reexamine the mundane activities of the day and seek to find where God appears in our experience. The steps are a guide and not intended to be followed too strictly.

The steps are gratitude, petition to the Holy Spirit, review, forgiveness, and renewal. Begin this exercise by reflecting on your day and offering thanks to God for any blessings, gifts, or graces that you have received.

Second, pray that the Holy Spirit would open your mind and heart as you review the events of your day. Doing this helps to center your mind on the Holy Spirit.

Third, review your day. Where did God speak to you? How did the Spirit invite you to be more Christlike? When and in what circumstances was God bestowing gifts, graces, and blessings upon you? How was the Spirit asking you to be lovingly present in various situations? How was God asking you to humbly serve those around you?

Ask for forgiveness for living on autopilot and being unaware of God's presence in the mundane. Avoid scolding yourself in this step; rather, encounter the merciful God of Christianity. Finally, renew yourself for the rest of your day or the following day, and prepare yourself to encounter God in the mundane.

October 14

DIVINE HOST

*But Daniel made up his mind that he would not defile himself
with the king's choice food or with the wine which he drank; so,
he sought permission from the commander of the officials that he
might not defile himself. "Please test your servants for ten days
and let us be given some vegetables to eat and water to drink."*
—Daniel 1:8, 12 (NASB)

Daniel and his companions were living in exile but had found favor with
the foreign king. As such, they were hosted by the king and given meat and
choice wine to consume daily. Daniel though did not want to defile himself
with the food given him by the foreign king who refused to worship God.
Instead, Daniel suggested that he and his companions be given vegetables
and water and then a test performed to see who looked healthier among
the young men selected to be educated by the king's courts—he and his
companions or the ones who consumed the meat and wine.

The point is that the host holds power over the individuals they are
hosting. The host provides food and protection. Daniel was essentially
stating that he and his companions did not need the provisions of the
earthly king but instead would rely on God for their needs. God would be
their host.

Who hosts you? Does your job? Your human relationships? Your
hobbies? Even your sins? Some of these things are good. We need human
interaction, hobbies, and jobs. However, we would be foolish to rely on
these things alone or to place them at a higher level in our lives than God.
Reflect on your life. Who or what is given the highest place? On whom do
you rely as your host?

October 15

HUMAN LOVE

Let him kiss me with the kisses of his mouth! For your love is better than wine. . . . Ah, you are beautiful, my beloved, truly lovely. —Song of Songs 1:2, 16 (NRSV)

Christian Scripture focuses almost exclusively on the relationship between God and humanity. However, one book filled with love poetry focuses on the romantic relationship between a man and a woman. Throughout Christian and Jewish history, this book has been viewed as an allegory reflecting the relationship between God and Israel or Christ and the church.

But one cannot escape the romantic language throughout this poem. While it may be an allegory, it is still a wonderful opportunity to reflect on the intended relationships between romantic partners in this life. The life of a Christian is not intended to be lived alone. Indeed, marriage and the romantic love that is associated with this coupling is a gift from God. To love another person so intimately is akin to the relationship we ought to have with God: a deep, meaningful, and multifaceted relationship.

Reflect on your own human relationships, especially those defined by a deep love of another, whether romantic or not. These relationships are important and meaningful, and we ought to cherish them. Give thanks to God for the people in your life who hold a special place in your heart, and seek to let those people know how important they are to you today.

October 16

DEFEND THE POWERLESS

"Now our flesh is as the flesh of our brothers, our children are as their children. Yet we are forcing our sons and our daughters to be slaves, and some of our daughters have already been enslaved, but it is not in our power to help it, for other men have our fields and our vineyards." —Nehemiah 5:5 (ESV)

One of the most prevalent themes throughout the prophetic books of the Christian Old Testament is justice for the poor or defense of the powerless. The rich, haughty, and powerful are condemned on nearly every page of the prophetic books, while the poor are promised justice from God.

While the original audiences of these messages are dead and gone, the messages are still just as important today as they were when first uttered. There are people all over this world who live in poverty, who live at the mercy of others, who are crushed under foot by the powerful.

You need not go overseas to witness this sort of injustice. It is likely that you only need to go a few miles from your own home, depending on where you live. It is easy to rattle off reasons that we should not help others or seek justice for the oppressed. None of these reasons hold up against Scripture. Excuses like "They should pick themselves up by their own bootstraps," "They are making poor decisions," "It's because they have no familial support," or "Someone else will help" come from a calloused heart.

Reflect on how you might help to defend the powerless in your own town. Research local food banks, shelters, and other forms of aid and consider getting involved so that you may live as Christ lived, serving others in genuine love and faith.

October 17
DON'T BE USED

But when the attendants delivered the king's command, Queen Vashti refused to come. Then the king became furious and burned with anger. —Esther 1:12 (NIV)

King Xerxes of Persia ruled over the land in which the exiled Jews lived. He held a banquet and demanded that his lovely wife, Vashti, make an appearance before his guests. The queen refused to be paraded about as a trophy for the king and his guests. Vashti risked everything when she refused the king. In response to her refusal, King Xerxes exiled his wife and later married Esther.

Vashti refused to be used for the amusement of others, to be ogled, taken advantage of, or objectified even by her husband, though he was behaving less like a husband and more like an immature fool.

The book of Esther is one of only two within Christian Scripture that does not mention God. Song of Songs is the other. However, this does not mean that this book is not important to the formation of God's people, both Jews and Christians. Vashti gives us a beautiful image of an individual who does not back down when others try to use her for their own amusement and to the detriment of her personal dignity. She pays the price in being exiled, though it could have been worse.

Be encouraged to stand up for yourself and for your dignity, recognizing that as a human being you are a favored creation of God. As such, you have immeasurable value and are worthy of love, respect, and dignity no matter what anyone else says. God loves you, and that is enough reason to hold on to your personal dignity.

October 18

EXTERNAL STRENGTH AND INTERNAL WEAKNESS

Finally, after she [Delilah] had nagged him [Samson] with her words day after day, and pestered him, he was tired to death. . . . She let him fall asleep on her lap; and she called a man and had him shave off the seven locks of his head. He began to weaken, and his strength left him. —Judges 16:16, 19 (NRSV)

Samson is the strongest individual within Christian Scripture, at least physically. Emotionally, he is a reed in the wind, blown about at the whim of others, and this eventually leads to his downfall. Samson's story is the longest in the book of Judges, and it is the most tragic. Granted, Samson was a womanizer, a bully, and a shortsighted leader. However, God selected him to lead the people of Israel as a judge before the installation of the first king.

Perhaps it is best to look at Samson as an individual chosen by God despite his character flaws rather than because of his excellent character. We see that God can indeed use anyone, though this may be a difficult idea to accept.

Looking to Samson's story, we can find encouragement to exercise not only our physical bodies but also our mental and emotional selves. To be a physically domineering force is good for some things. But having the emotional intelligence, mental aptitude, and patience to deal with various challenges is just as important as being to physically dominate everything or everyone who comes against you.

Be encouraged to train yourself holistically. Hit the gym, crack open a book, commune with God, and rest. Work to balance yourself as a follower of Christ. Use your gifts, but use all your gifts rather than focus on one.

October 19

WHOM WILL YOU SERVE?

If it is disagreeable in your sight to serve the LORD, choose for yourselves today whom you will serve: whether the gods which your fathers served which were beyond the River, or the gods of the Amorites in whose land you are living; but as for me and my house, we will serve the LORD. —Joshua 24:15 (NASB)

The closing portion of today's verse is familiar and may even be hanging on a wall in your home or the home of someone you know. Whom will you serve? The Hebrew people had finally settled in the promised land, and Joshua was challenging them on their faithfulness and giving them an example to follow in himself and his family. They committed to remain faithful to God in front of the assembled people.

This is a fair question to ask of anyone: whom will you serve? It has been said that if you were to peruse someone's checkbook, you could identify whom they worship. That is a rather narrow definition, though it holds a level of truth.

Whom do you serve? Do you serve the God of the New Testament? Do you serve another god in your life? Your actions, your speech, what occupies the most room in your mind, what takes up the most of your time and, yes, your checkbook all reveal a lot about whom you idolize. Be mindful to worship God. Pay your bills and seek out entertainment, but do nothing at the expense of serving the One True God, for that is a dangerous and costly mistake that we ought to avoid. Reflect on your life today, and consider whom or what you worship.

October 20

SPIRITUAL EXERCISE: PSALM OF PRAISE

Today you are encouraged to reflect on the following psalm. What does the Spirit tell you through these words? Do you find it easy to offer praises to God today? If not, then commune with God and listen for the Divine voice. Can you identify what is preventing your ability to offer praises?

> *Hear my prayer, O LORD; give ear to my supplications in your faithfulness; answer me in your righteousness. Do not enter into judgment with your servant, for no one living is righteous before you. . . .*
> *I remember the days of old, I think about all your deeds, I meditate on the works of your hands. I stretch out my hands to you; my soul thirsts for you like a parched land.*
> *Answer me quickly, O LORD; my spirit fails. Do not hide your face from me or I shall be like those who go down to the Pit.*
> *Let me hear of your steadfast love in the morning, for in you I put my trust. Teach me the way I should go, for to you I lift up my soul. —Psalm 143:1-2, 5-8 (NRSV)*

October 21

REFRESHED

He turns a desert into pools of water, a parched land into springs of water. —Psalm 107:35 (ESV)

There are so many things in this world, in our lives, that can wear us down. Even good things can be too much sometimes: jobs or careers, education, ministry or church involvement, family and friend functions and gatherings. All of these things are good and important for a well-rounded individual. However, they can all lead to a feeling of emptiness, a feeling akin to dipping your hand into a well and expecting cool water only to find warm, dry dust.

Even being involved in a local church, Bible study, or some other Christian fellowship gathering where worship of and communion with God are acknowledged and practiced can lead to a feeling of being empty, especially if you lead the event(s) in some fashion.

Be on guard against feeling empty. Lean on God to find restoration and refreshment. Be encouraged to commune with God today, and ask for refreshment or the endurance you need. Seek to refresh yourself daily. This is difficult to do given the nature of our society that demands so much of our time and offers so many distractions. Spiritual refreshment in God requires discipline, sometimes being disciplined to practice intentional prayer, silence, or reflection. Find the time to be refreshed today.

October 22

PROTECTION

The LORD is my rock and my fortress and my deliverer, my God, my rock, in whom I take refuge; my shield and the horn of my salvation, my stronghold. —Psalm 18:2 (NASB)

The Psalms are filled with praises to God, many with specific mention of God being a refuge, a fortress, or some other form of protection during chaos or a crisis in life. The psalmists of old knew that there would be moments when they needed to find refuge and safety. Whether they carried an emotional burden, faced physical danger, felt mentally overwhelmed or spiritually dry, they knew God could and would serve as their protection.

Much like when a child is hurt or afraid and they call out to their mother, people of any age bracket will at times seek refuge. There have been instances of spouses calling out to one another and friends reaching out to other friends. No one is immune to needing the protection of another at some point in their lives.

The protection that God has to offer is the ultimate protection. It does not come in the form of a literal bastion or defensive tower that springs up in our front yards. However, when we feel most lost, confused, downtrodden, or otherwise exposed and open to danger or hurt, we should look to God. God offers us a safe place to simply exist in moments of turmoil, amid the tempests of life. Are you facing some hardship in life? Seek to find protection in the presence of God. Be thankful to God that the Divine presence is never out of sight or unreachable.

October 23

REVERSAL OF FORTUNE

The LORD upholds all who fall and lifts up all who are bowed down. —Psalm 145:14 (NIV)

Throughout Scripture are instances of individuals and indeed entire people groups who are lowly and oppressed being lifted out of their predicaments. The Israelites are freed from slavery, they are again and again led from oppression by the judges, and they are allowed to return to Jerusalem following the exile into Babylon.

In the New Testament, the Gospel according to Luke is saturated with instances of individuals being lifted out of their societal low points and being exalted. Mary, the poor, tax collectors and other sinners, the sick, women in general, and others are lifted up.

Once again, we are reminded in the Psalms of God's faithfulness to those who believe and are oppressed or pushed down by circumstance, other people, or some other burden in life. Sometimes we are the one who is suffering from oppression, and sometimes we are not. In the moments when you find that you are being pushed down by a circumstance, seek God's strength and endurance. In the moments when you are not being oppressed, seek to find a person or people group who is suffering and be an advocate for them during their strife. Our thoughts and prayers are important, but Christians are called to action, too. Follow the example of Christ and care for those who suffer. Pray that God would lead someone to you to serve as your advocate when you suffer as well.

October 24

THERE'S A TIME
FOR THAT

For everything there is a season, and a time for every matter
under heaven. —Ecclesiastes 3:1 (NRSV)

The writer of Ecclesiastes offers a long list of things that are to be done during specific times in life, though the time is not specified. There is a time to build and destroy, a time to make peace and a time to make war, and so on.

Sometimes we are tempted to do something at a time that is inappropriate. A good gardener knows that you do not plant tomatoes in the fall. The plants will die, and you will lose the investment you made in those seeds or seedlings. We cannot always accomplish our goals within our own timeline. Sometimes we must wait to go back for a degree; other times we must seize the opportunity as it presents itself. Sometimes we must wait to have children, make plans, and prepare. Other times we must move toward starting our own family, either biologically or through adoption.

Whatever decisions you are facing, take time to pray. Seek the guidance of God to determine whether it is the time to act or to wait patiently. Recognize that there are seasons in our own lives just as there are in nature. These seasons change and offer opportunities to accomplish goals, plan for the future, or wait patiently, biding our time for the next season to begin with its renewed opportunities.

What season are you in right now? What decisions must you make? Should you wait or act? Whatever you do, do it after you have communed with God and sought Divine guidance. Be encouraged to find patience while you wait and to be emboldened to act when the time is right.

October 25

THE JOY OF EVANGELISM

I have no greater joy than to hear that my children are walking in the truth. —3 John 4 (ESV)

It is a wonderful thing to come to know Jesus the Christ of God as Savior of your life. It is another great joy to witness the conversion and growing in faith of another person as they come to know Christ the way you know Christ.

John was excited to witness the spiritual growth of others who had come to know Jesus the Christ as their Savior after John ministered to them. These people were not John's literal children, but the familial language is appropriate as he strives to connect with these believers who are newer to the faith than he is.

There is something sweet about following the spiritual journey of another who is coming into the faith. Be thankful to God today for those who helped guide you to a life of faith in Jesus Christ, those wonderful saints who encouraged you, taught you by both word and deed, and lived as examples of Jesus Christ's love, mercy, and grace in your life.

Be encouraged to live in a way that you too might be blessed to witness the spiritual rebirth and growth of another person. Seek to serve as a living example of Jesus' love, mercy, and grace in the life of someone else, and show them the way to eternal life through faith in Jesus Christ. The easiest and most effective way to evangelize someone else is to embody the teachings of Jesus in the here and now. Strive to love others, to be merciful to others, and to forgive, even when the other person has not sought reconciliation.

October 26

KEEP YOURSELF IN THE LOVE OF GOD

But you, beloved, building yourselves up on your most holy faith, praying in the Holy Spirit, keep yourselves in the love of God, waiting anxiously for the mercy of our Lord Jesus Christ to eternal life. —Jude 20-21 (NASB)

Coming to faith in Jesus Christ is the first step in situating oneself in the arms of God forever. This is a place of love, mercy, grace, and forgiveness. The world around us is often an unforgiving place. People are impatient, unkind, lacking empathy, and failing to show forgiveness to others who slight them. Sadly, Christians are often included in that list.

This is not the ideal, and neither is it the way things should be. Christians have a wonderful example to follow when it comes to being forgiving, loving, and gracious. The example is Jesus Christ and God the Creator, in whose arms we now rest.

Keeping ourselves in the love of God helps us remain faithful to God, and it helps us live as Christ-like examples in the here and now. When we are feeling tempted to scream and shout at the person who cut us off on the highway, or ignore the fact that we did the same thing to someone else only a mile back, we must remember that this is not what it means to follow Christ. Further, when others rob us, lie to us or about us, or otherwise truly harm us in some fashion, it is important to keep ourselves in the love of God, remembering the forgiveness that we have received for all of our sins and slights against God and other people. Pray for patience, peace, and the endurance to forgive when others slight you, and rest in the arms of God today, knowing that you are forgiven.

October 27

SPIRITUAL EXERCISE:
LECTIO DIVINA
(DIVINE READING)

On this day you are invited to practice a spiritual exercise, a "divine reading" of a select passage of Scripture. Please follow the guide provided as you meditate on this passage.

- Read the passage twice, pausing between each reading for a moment of silence. Identify keywords as you read the passage without elaboration
- Read the passage again, pause for silence, and answer the following question: Where does the content of the reading touch my life today?
- Read the passage once more, again pausing for silence, and complete this sentence: I believe God wants me to . . . .

Then Jesus told them this parable: . . .

> "Or suppose a woman has ten silver coins and loses one. Doesn't she light a lamp, sweep the house and search carefully until she finds it? And when she finds it, she calls her friends and neighbors together and says, 'Rejoice with me; I have found my lost coin.' In the same way, I tell you, there is rejoicing in the presence of the angels of God over one sinner who repents." —Luke 15:3, 8-10 (NIV)

October 28

LOVE IS THE FULFILLMENT OF THE LAW

Love does no wrong to a neighbor; therefore, love is the fulfilling of the law. —Romans 13:10 (NRSV)

There are more than six hundred laws throughout the Christian Old Testament. For the most part, these laws help set the people of God aside from their neighbors. The law teaches how a person should relate to God and to other people.

Jesus famously taught that he had come to fulfill rather than to abolish the Law, and he summarized the Law in two commands: that of loving God with all our being and loving our neighbor as we love ourselves. Paul, the traditional author of the letter to the Roman believers, fleshes out this teaching further. To love our neighbor is to do no wrong to or against them. This is following the law, and therefore this is fulfilling the law whether one interprets it through the old or new covenant.

For Christians to say that collectively we are no longer under the law is to utter a half truth. While we are no longer condemned for failing to uphold or follow the law, we are still called to live in such a way that the law, as it is summarized by Jesus Christ, is fulfilled. Indeed, loving others and God in action as well as through our words is a wonderful evangelistic tool.

It can be hard to love our neighbor. We are tempted to see the odd or frustrating things our neighbors do and allow those actions or words to frustrate us and keep us from showing love. Seek to reframe your view of others. Strive to see everyone you encounter as a beloved child of God, just as you are a beloved child of God, whether they know and accept this truth or not.

October 29

DOING GOOD BRINGS NO HARM

Now who is there to harm you if you are zealous for what is good? —1 Peter 3:13 (ESV)

There was a woman who had a heart for helping others. She moved into a neighborhood where she was immediately recognized as different. Her race, socioeconomic status, and almost every other discernible and outward classification was different from the people who lived in the neighborhood where she bought a home.

At first her home was ransacked and robbed regularly, yet she remained. Eventually it was discovered that she was sharing produce from her backyard garden with the elderly in the neighborhood. Slowly she began engaging with children and teens, building rapport with them. Once she had established a bond with the children, she began tutoring them in a local park or restaurant. Finally, when they were comfortable, she invited them to her home for a snack and tutoring.

As the neighborhood discovered the heart of this woman, the break-ins slowed and eventually stopped. Finally, the local community leaders on both sides of the law recognized this woman as an asset and worked to protect her and provide for her when she was in need, just as she worked to provide for the most vulnerable in the neighborhood.

You do not need to move, uprooting your own life, in order to do good. Further, doing good does not necessarily mean that you are protected all the time as was true, initially, for the woman in our story. However, when we do good and others see that good, we are perceived in a new light and the world responds positively to that goodness.

October 30

A PATIENT GOD

Now return to the LORD your God, for He is gracious and compassionate, slow to anger, abounding in lovingkindness and relenting of evil. —Joel 2:13b (NASB)

One of the most common failings witnessed in humanity in the twenty-first century appears to be our lack of patience with others. Whether we are driving down the road, standing in line, on hold with customer service, waiting on our toddler to pull up his pants or eat her food, or glancing at our smartphone's display as the pastor drones on from behind the pulpit, we appear to be an impatient society.

This makes sense given that so many things are geared toward immediate gratification, whether it is getting a quick bite at our favorite fast food restaurant, clicking the overnight or same-day delivery button in our favorite online retailer cart, or simply getting an email in lieu of another staff meeting at work. We are a society geared toward quick service.

While our patience appears to be thin, God's patience is long-lasting. Even though the ancient Israelites appeared to be wishy-washy, faithful at one moment and then quickly slipping back into sin, falling for the newest or most comfortable temptation, God remained patient. The same is true for modern Christians as well: God remains patient despite our sinfulness and failures in the face of temptation.

Offer thanks to God today for the patience to handle your sins and to continue to offer you forgiveness in and through Jesus Christ. Then strive to exercise a little more patience with others, following the Divine example revealed to us in Scripture.

October 31

RENEWING THE COVENANT

*There was not a word of all that Moses had commanded that
Joshua did not read to the whole assembly of Israel, including the
women and children, and the foreigners who lived among them.*
—Joshua 8:35 (NIV)

Joshua was renewing the covenant God made with the people of Israel while Moses had served as an intermediary. Following a defeat of the Israelites by some of the people living in the promised land, Joshua led the people in a renewing of the covenant between themselves and the Divine.

Notice that everyone was included in this renewal: the young, the old, men and women, and even the non-Israelites who happened to live among them. Was this foreshadowing of the inclusion of Gentiles in the new covenant through Jesus Christ? Perhaps.

It is significant that the people renewed their covenant with God. Renewing covenants, promises, vows, and other significant agreements is important in life. When we renew our minds on a specific task, it will often give us renewed energy to accomplish our goals associated with the agreement. Further, we may find that the act of renewing not only reenergizes us but also reminds us of the importance of the agreement and the relationships involved in it. For example, when a married couple renews vows, it is an outward symbol of their continued commitment to each other in their relationship. The same was true for the Israelites in today's verse. Reflect on your relationship with the Divine through the new covenant in Christ. How important is this relationship to you?

November 1

NEW RELATIONSHIPS IN CHRIST

Perhaps this is the reason he [Onesimus] was separated from you for a while, so that you might have him back forever, no longer as a slave but more than a slave, a beloved brother—especially to me but how much more to you, both in the flesh and in the Lord. —Philemon 15-16 (NRSV)

Onesimus was a slave of Philemon who ran away and encountered Paul in prison, only to convert to Christianity. Paul then wrote to his friend, Philemon, the owner of Onesimus, and encouraged his fellow Christian to accept the slave back—but as a brother in faith rather than a slave. Paul hoped that the newfound faith of Onesimus would bring a new understanding to the relationship between Onesimus and Philemon.

No matter our relationship or how we view one another, it is important to remember that God created all people and loves and cherishes them regardless of their sins or even their religious beliefs (or lack thereof). Further, when we believe in Jesus as the Christ and then encounter other people who share our faith, our relationship ought to be built on love and a shared faith. This is difficult if we had a tense prior relationship with the person in question and they have converted to the faith. They are our sibling, no matter what our relationship looked before their conversion.

Coming to faith in Jesus Christ gives us a clean slate with God, and it ought to give us a clean slate with other people, too. Reflect on your relationships with your siblings in faith. Have you done all that you can to ensure that these relationships are healthy and built on love?

November 2

ABIDING IN GOD

Whoever confesses that Jesus is the Son of God, God abides in him, and he in God. —1 John 4:15 (ESV)

Abiding in God and having God abide in you is one of the promises to those who confess faith in Jesus as the Christ of God. But what does it mean to abide? Simply put, it means to remain stable or fixed in a state or to endure without yielding. "Abide" is a "churchy" word that Christians often take for granted or utter without a full appreciation of its meaning—not unlike other words such as "grace" and "mercy."

There is great joy when one abides in God and especially when God abides with and in the people of God. As you confess your faith in Jesus Christ as your Savior, God remains with you, never wavering, not leaving, remaining fixed with you in your life through the various joys and challenges you face.

Reflect today on the truth that God is with you simply because you believe in the Son of God as your Savior. Your relationships with others may waver. They may ebb and flow with differing life circumstances that you and they face. Indeed, sometimes your relationship with another person may end because of a sin you have committed. However, God is always with you, abiding with you, remaining with you, and surrounding you with the Divine arms of love and support, no matter what you do that is sinful and foolish. Be encouraged to relish in this truth, and take some time today to simply abide with God.

November 3

SPIRITUAL EXERCISE: LECTIO DIVINA
(DIVINE READING)

On this day you are invited to practice a spiritual exercise, a "divine reading" of a select passage of Scripture. Please follow the guide provided as you meditate on this passage.

- Read the passage twice, pausing between each reading for a moment of silence. Identify keywords as you read the passage without elaboration
- Read the passage again, pause for silence, and answer the following question: Where does the content of the reading touch my life today?
- Read the passage once more, again pausing for silence, and complete this sentence: I believe God wants me to . . . .

> The LORD is slow to anger but great in power, and the LORD will by no means clear the guilty. His way is in whirlwind and storm, and the clouds are the dust of his feet.
> He rebukes the sea and makes it dry, and he dries up all the rivers; Bashan and Carmel wither, and the bloom of Lebanon fades.
> The mountains quake before him, and the hills melt; the earth heaves before him, the world and all who live in it. . . .
> The LORD is good, a stronghold in a day of trouble; he protects those who take refuge in him,
> even in a rushing flood. He will make a full end of his adversaries, and will pursue his enemies into darkness. —Nahum 1:3-5, 7-8 (NRSV)

November 4

CONSISTENCY IS KEY

Jehoshaphat walked in the way of Asa his father and did not turn aside from it, doing what was right in the sight of the LORD. The high places, however, were not taken away; the people had not yet set their hearts upon the God of their fathers.
—2 Chronicles 20:32-33 (ESV)

Jehoshaphat was king of Judah, the southern kingdom of the people of God prior to the Babylonian exile. He was relatively faithful to God, though he did fail in one major matter: he did not remove the shrines or "high places" to false gods throughout his kingdom. This was a major hindrance to his rule over the people because the Israelites' unfaithfulness to God was largely what led them to being exiled in the first place.

The people of God within the Christian Old Testament were often inconsistent in their faithfulness. To be successful in life, consistency is key. At work you must be consistent in your duties, at home you must be consistent in your relationships and paying your bills, and the list continues. Consistency does not mean boring, unimaginative, or bland. Instead, consistency means faithfulness and trustworthiness. Within the context of our Scripture verse, this is especially true.

Consider the areas in your life where you might be inconsistent. Why might this be the case? How can you better focus yourself to maintain a faithful level of consistency? Consider also your relationships with those closest to you and with God. Are there any inconsistencies on your part in any of those relationships? If so, seek to remedy them and deepen the relationship.

November 5

GOD THE FATHER AS CREATOR

And the LORD God formed man of the dust of the ground and breathed into his nostrils the breath of life; and man became a living being. —Genesis 2:7 (NKJV)

Creating things is often difficult and time consuming. Whether you are building something concrete such as your own home or a doghouse, baking a pie, or doing something less tangible like putting together a financial portfolio or brainstorming ideas for the next great novel, it all takes effort. No matter the project, the end goal is the same: to complete the project to the best of your ability. It is rewarding to create something new, unique, and all your own.

What is more satisfying than creating something of your own? Little can compare to this feeling of accomplishment; however, for a believer in God, the knowledge that we are creations of the Divine hands and that God's own spirit dwells within our being can be overwhelming.

Rest in the knowledge that the Creator of the vast universe, both large and small, formed you with God's hands and breathed into your nostrils God's own breath, a Divine breath that sustains life. Knowing that God intimately created each of us means that we are all loved dearly by God. The fact that God went to such lengths to shape and mold each of us individually means that God is willing to do anything to ensure that we have an abundant spiritual life, and that was revealed through God the Father's willingness to sacrifice God the Son for you, God's favored creation.

November 6

ATONEMENT THEN AND NOW

He shall put on the holy linen tunic, and the linen undergarments shall be next to his body, and he shall be girded with the linen sash and attired with the linen turban (these are holy garments). Then he shall bathe his body in water and put them on. —Leviticus 16:4 (NASB)

The book of Leviticus is full of commands regarding sacrifices, purity or cleanliness, relationships, and many other things that a modern reader might consider stiff, dry, and foreign. Chapter 16 deals with the Day of Atonement, a time to make the relationship between God and God's people right again. Much pomp surrounded the event, and specific steps were taken to make sure things went as God intended. The point of the complicated rituals was that the people needed to be cleansed.

Our relationship with the Divine is made right through our faith in the salvific work of Jesus Christ. Yes, repentance is necessary, and, if possible, baptism is preferred; however, we cannot do every single thing that is necessary to maintain personal holiness and ensure our own salvation. Christ alone secured our salvation. The more than six hundred commands of the Christian Old Testament have less to do with offering salvation and more to do with maintaining a right relationship with God and caring for other people. We still ought to strive to do these things today. Christ teaches as much when he summarizes all those laws into the two greatest commandments: love God with our whole being and love others as we love ourselves. Reflect on the similarities and differences between the old way to righteousness and the way of Christ.

November 7
A TOUGH MASTER

Now before faith came, we were imprisoned and guarded under the law until faith would be revealed. Therefore the law was our disciplinarian until Christ came, so that we might be justified by faith. —Galatians 3:23-24 (NRSV)

For the people of God, there have been two covenants: the first through Abraham and the second through Jesus Christ. The first was solidified in writing with the giving of the Law. The Law expanded to more than six hundred commands for the people of God who were under the old covenant to follow. These ensured that they could be holy or set apart from other people around them as God's chosen people. As Paul says in our verses for today, these commands were a tough disciplinarian.

Disciplinarians of Paul's day were slaves who followed the children of wealthy members of society to and from school and had the authority to discipline the children if they got out of line. Paul viewed the Law of God in this regard—as a powerful figure that held the people at its mercy.

And then came Jesus Christ. Christ took over as the primary mediator between humanity and God. The disciplinarian was no longer needed.

As you believe in Christ, you have been justified by that faith in Jesus Christ as your Savior and Mediator. Reflect today on this truth of Christianity. Upon reflection, what thoughts come to your mind? How will you carry yourself as you are reminded of your justification, not through the tough master of an overbearing disciplinarian but through the compassionate mercy of God in Jesus Christ?

November 8
DEEP LONGING

My soul yearns for you in the night; in the morning my spirit longs for you. When your judgments come upon the earth, the people of the world learn righteousness. —Isaiah 26:9 (NIV)

There are moments in this life when we long for something deeply—so deeply that the thought of having it, whatever or whomever it may be, consumes our minds day and night. We may even become physically ill from our deep longing. Typically, there is a great emotional attachment to the person or thing we pine over, and this can lead to a loss of sleep or an inability to focus.

Have you ever longed for something so deeply? Perhaps you long to see a loved one again, to visit a special place once more, to play with your favorite pet who has died, or even to recover a favorite item or trinket. Admittedly, all of these things pale in comparison to the longing for God that we ought to have, though that longing often does not come easily to us since we live in a society bent on needing tangible evidence to support claims—even the claim of faith.

Reflect on your relationship with the Divine. Do you ever long for that relationship when it seems that there is a divide between you and God? What helps in situations when you feel distant from God? Consider what other Christians are going through when they feel distant from God and how you may be able to support them in their longing.

November 9
GIVING AND TAKING

For to the one who has, more will be given, and from the one who has not, even what he has will be taken away. —Mark 4:25 (ESV)

Faith can be a fickle thing. To believe in something intangible like God, salvation from sins, and the life, death, and resurrection of a man some two thousand years ago—all to forgive humanity of our sins—is difficult at times. Jesus is speaking on faith in this series of proverbs that he presents from verses 20 through 25 of the fourth chapter in Mark.

This is a word on being generous versus being a miser. When we are generous with what we have, God will increase our faith. On the other hand, when we are stingy with what we have, the faith that we do have is taken from us. The idea seems to be that the faithful followers of God through Christ are generous with their gifts, whether those gifts are time, money, talents, or other resources. When we are generous with our gifts, the positive impact on our lives is that our faith continues to increase.

Be encouraged to be as generous with your gifts as you are able. Prayerfully consider how to use your gifts to help others and to continue to grow in your faith. As we share the blessings that God first gives to us, we begin to mature in our faith, understanding the Divine on a deeper level in ways that were previously closed to us. Be mindful of opportunities to share the gifts given to you.

November 10

SPIRITUAL EXERCISE: CELEBRATION

By contrast, the fruit of the Spirit is love, joy, peace, patience, kindness, generosity, faithfulness, gentleness, and self-control. There is no law against such things. —Galatians 5:22-23 (NRSV)

The result of practicing the spiritual disciplines and having them work in our lives is celebration. The purpose and hope of practicing any of the disciplines or exercises is to produce the fruit of the spirit. The fruit of the spirit and the spiritual disciplines go hand in hand. The fruit is peace, love, joy, patience, kindness, generosity, faithfulness, gentleness, and self-control.

The spiritual discipline of celebration is different from a celebration around a birthday, retirement, promotion, or any other reason to get together with friends and family. The spiritual exercise of celebration is the culmination of spiritual maturity in the life of a believer. This type of celebration is the result of a transformed life and a transforming mindset.

Spiritual celebration is the ability to see God in the minutia of life and find genuine joy in response to this ongoing discovery. The wonderful thing about this discipline is that it can be both large and small. Spiritual celebrations can rival an elaborate wedding ceremony and accompanying reception, or they can be as small and simple as taking an intentional walk with someone close to you and enjoying the time together.

Be encouraged to seek the lasting joy of God and find the Divine in all people and things. As you find this joy, you will be better able to celebrate in all things in this life, knowing that God loves you and that you are cherished no matter what. Start small in your celebrations. Spend some time intentionally connecting with nature, a loved one, or both simultaneously and celebrating the Divine spark in them and in yourself.

November 11

KNOWING THE LAW

The Pharisees were saying to Him, "Look, why are they doing what is not lawful on the Sabbath?" —Mark 2:24 (NASB)

Jesus' disciples were picking heads of wheat and eating them as they walked. They did this on the Sabbath day, a day that the Christian Old Testament set aside for rest and worship. The act of picking the wheat was considered work and, according to the Pharisees' interpretation of the Law, was forbidden.

There are laws of all sorts in our society. The intent of these laws seems to be to protect people and to maintain a sense of order and safety. Sometimes the laws are unjust. Looking back throughout human history will reveal that there have been unjust laws in most major societies, including slavery, inequality based on skin pigmentation and gender, and so on. Sometimes the history books are not needed for us to find unjust laws; we need only to glance at our own region's laws.

That is not to say that the laws of the Christian Old Testament were unjust, though some of them would cause many Christians to raise their eyebrows in concern or confusion. The intentions of those laws were to set the people of Israel apart from their neighbors and make them a holy people for God.

Be encouraged to know and understand the laws of the land but to ultimately follow the intent of the laws of God as summarized by Jesus Christ: love God with your entire being, and love others as yourself.

November 12

REMEMBERING GOD'S POWER

"Where were you when I laid the earth's foundation? Tell me, if you understand." —Job 38:4 (NIV)

Job has argued with his friends for the last thirty chapters of the book. Back and forth they went, with the friends insisting that Job was guilty of something for such tragedy to have befallen him. Job never relented, always insisting that he was innocent. He demanded that God come and reason with him, even saying that he wished to take God to court over the curses in his life.

God responds to Job in chapters 38 through 41. God begins by reminding Job of humanity's limited understanding and power, especially in the face of God, who brought the entirety of the created order, both things seen and unseen or known and unknown, into being.

There is nothing wrong with questioning why terrible things happen to us; it is a natural response. Even God is fair game in terms of our questioning. God is, after all, God and can take the questions of humanity often better than we can take questioning the Divine.

However, we should remember our place in the created order. In comparison to the Divine, we are small, and we lack understanding of many situations. There are circumstances in this life that we will never fully understand or appreciate.

Be encouraged to ask for clarity from God, but be prepared to receive answers that are unsatisfactory, if the answers come at all.

November 13

HOLISTIC CARE

He strictly ordered them that no one should know this and told them to give her something to eat. —Mark 5:43 (NRSV)

Jesus has just revived a young girl, bringing her back from the dead. Beyond following his usual pattern of telling the witnesses to remain quiet about this miracle, Jesus tells them to give the young girl something to eat. Throughout the Gospel accounts, Jesus is apparently concerned with the holistic health of those to whom he ministers.

Jesus' example of ensuring that this girl has food to eat following a traumatic experience shows both holistic care and good hospitality. These ministries are important for Christians to adopt in our daily lives, especially as we encounter other people suffering a traumatic loss, indignity, or another challenge.

This was not the only time in Jesus' ministry when he insisted that someone have something to eat after a difficult experience.

Given this trend in Jesus' ministry, what does it mean for modern Christian ministry? How important is it to offer holistic care to those in need? Has anyone ever offered you such care? If so, what was your response? Was it different compared to situations when you did not receive such care? How might you be able to offer more holistic care or ministry to others in your life moving forward? Consider these things today.

November 14
LIFE IS TOUGH

For we do not want you to be unaware, brothers, of the affliction we experienced in Asia. For we were so utterly burdened beyond our strength that we despaired of life itself. —2 Corinthians 1:8 (ESV)

Paul did not mince words in his letters. Often, he was writing to correct behavior, mediate a conflict, or otherwise settle a problem. However, in this portion of the opening of 2 Corinthians, Paul was admitting to something that is often overlooked by Christians: he was having a hard time. His circumstances were so bad that he and his companions were fed up with life.

Life is tough at times. Sometimes the children aren't sleeping well and are keeping everyone in the house up at night. Sometimes money leaves the bank faster than it goes in. Sometimes families get into heated arguments around the dinner table during the holiday season. Sometimes such difficulties come one at a time; other times they seem to come all at once or in successive waves. We can be overwhelmed to the point that we do not know what else we can do other than cry out to God or anyone who might listen and beg for some form of relief.

Life is hard, and sometimes the best thing to do is acknowledge this reality. If you know of someone going through a hard time and they turn to you, be a listening ear and affirm their struggles. If you are struggling, seek out a listening ear. Sometimes life is tough, and there is nothing to do about it aside from sitting in the ashes the way Job did.

November 15

BOLDNESS IN THE FACE OF ADVERSITY

For John had been saying to Herod, "It is not lawful for you to have your brother's wife." —Mark 6:18 (NASB)

John the Baptist, like Paul and like many other prophets in our Scriptures, was not one to mince words. He called things like he saw them and challenged those who would break the commands and laws of God, including the members of the ruling class of his day.

King Herod broke the commands of God, and John called him out on his unlawful union. Herod's wife was more upset than the king and eventually manipulated the king into beheading John and presenting his head on a plate to his wife via her daughter.

There are many people in this life who commit wrongdoings, whether they are officially legal or not according to the laws of the land. Morally and ethically questionable behavior is common among people of all socioeconomic classes, genders, vocations, and other classifications. It is important for Christians to be bold in standing up against such behavior when it is discovered, especially when this behavior may have an impact on those who are vulnerable in society.

Be bold in the face of opposition or adversity. If you are aware of immoral behavior on the part of another person, challenge them on this behavior with the intention of helping them correct it. Be bold in the face of injustice as well, whether you are the victim or not. Trust in God's guidance and wisdom as you encounter immorality or unethical behavior.

November 16

THE NAME OF JESUS

But Peter said, "I have no silver or gold, but what I have I give you; in the name of Jesus Christ of Nazareth, stand up and walk." And he took him by the right hand and raised him up; and immediately his feet and ankles were made strong. Jumping up, he stood and began to walk, and he entered the temple with them, walking and leaping and praising God. —Acts 3:6-8 (NRSV)

Peter and John began their ministry after receiving the Holy Spirit at Pentecost by following in Jesus' footsteps. Jesus healed and preached in the temple and synagogues throughout what is called the Holy Land. His apostles did the same thing in the beginning of their ministry after Jesus' resurrection and ascension.

Note that Peter heals the lame man by invoking the name of Jesus Christ of Nazareth. There is power in that name. Further healings and miraculous works are executed in the same manner, by calling on the name of Jesus Christ of Nazareth.

What's in a name? The name of Jesus is an important one. Some Christian traditions still use this method in their acts of worship, ceremonies, and even healings and exorcisms. This may or may not be a part of your faith tradition, and either way, that is fine. You are encouraged to remember the name of Jesus Christ of Nazareth today. Reflect on what it means. Jesus means "God is salvation." It is the same as the Old Testament name of Joshua. Names throughout Scripture carry significant weight. What is the significance of God in flesh going by this name?

November 17

SPIRITUAL EXERCISE: PSALM OF PRAISE

Today you are encouraged to reflect on the following psalm. What does the Spirit tell you through these words? Do you find it easy to offer praises to God today? If not, then commune with God and listen for the Divine voice. Can you identify what is preventing your ability to offer praises?

> *"Blessed be your glorious name, and may it be exalted above all blessing and praise. You alone are the LORD. You made the heavens, even the highest heavens, and all their starry host, the earth and all that is on it, the seas and all that is in them. You give life to everything, and the multitudes of heaven worship you. You are the LORD God, who chose Abram and brought him out of Ur of the Chaldeans and named him Abraham. You found his heart faithful to you, and you made a covenant with him to give to his descendants the land of the Canaanites, Hittites, Amorites, Perizzites, Jebusites and Girgashites. You have kept your promise because you are righteous. You saw the suffering of our ancestors in Egypt; you heard their cry at the Red Sea. You sent signs and wonders against Pharaoh, against all his officials and all the people of his land, for you knew how arrogantly the Egyptians treated them. You made a name for yourself, which remains to this day."* —Nehemiah 9:5b-10 (NIV)

November 18
HOSPITABLE TO ALL

Let brotherly love continue. Do not neglect to show hospitality to strangers, for thereby some have entertained angels unawares.
—Hebrews 13:1-2 (ESV)

Christians are called to a difficult life that includes being hospitable to all people. We are even to pray for our enemies! What a difficult task. However, the writer of the letter to the Hebrews reminds us that, if we are hospitable to all whom we may encounter, then we may be hospitable even to angels.

Whether you believe that angels are among us or not, the point of this passage is to encourage us to be consistent in our hospitality. Do not withhold hospitality from anyone, but instead share it with everyone. Yes, this is a difficult thing to do given that not everyone has the same mentality, whether fellow Christians or non-Christians.

What, then, is the point of being hospitable to others when they may not be hospitable toward us? It is a part of our calling as the people of God in and through the new covenant in Jesus Christ. Further, it is something that we, as mature believers, ought to do anyway.

What does it mean to be hospitable to others? It means being friendly, kind, generous, and pleasant as far as you are able. We cannot control what others think and do, but we can control ourselves and how we carry ourselves in relation to others. Be encouraged to show hospitality in small ways to others today, and be prepared to see the doors that this hospitality opens in their lives and in your own.

November 19

THE OVERCOMING WORD

Remember Jesus Christ, risen from the dead, descendant of David, according to my gospel, for which I suffer hardship even to imprisonment as a criminal; but the word of God is not imprisoned. —2 Timothy 2:8-9 (NASB)

Throughout Christian history there have been attempts to stifle the sharing of the gospel of Jesus Christ. In the first century, the early church was persecuted by other religious systems of faith as well as governmental officials and regulations. Continuing throughout history, particularly in regions of the world where Christianity is the minority, believers in Jesus Christ have been forced from their homes, imprisoned, had their businesses closed, and even been killed.

In regions where Christianity has become the faith of most of the population, the danger has been less severe in the here and now. The real danger to Christianity, which stifles its spread and growth, is stagnation or complacency.

Paul suffered mightily at the hands of non-Christians. He was beaten nearly to death, attempts were made on his life, other plots were concocted to kill him, and he was thrown in prison. Yet Christianity continued to spread, and those who believed grew in their faith.

The belief in the Divine man who is Jesus Christ—living, dying, and then rising from the dead again—could not and would not be stifled. Much like the Savior on whom the faith is centered, the faith would not be silenced or stalled, at least not for long. Be encouraged to meditate on how you might spread the Christian faith to others or how you might help others, and yourself, to enrich your faith in Christ.

November 20
GOD'S LISTENING EAR

"And will not God grant justice to his chosen ones who cry to him day and night? Will he delay long in helping them?"
—Luke 18:7 (NRSV)

Luke's Gospel account is known for flipping societal norms upside down. Throughout the third Gospel are numerous instances of the lowly being elevated and the high being humbled. Women are given a voice, the poor are made to feel important, and sinners are constantly shown forgiveness, while the righteous are revealed to be arrogant in their faith.

Today's verse is no different from the overarching theme. Those who long for justice, who have been oppressed and put down by society at large, by life circumstances, or some other trouble, are heard by God when they cry out for justice in the face of an unjust world. Two rhetorical questions are asked in the above verse. The answer to the first is "yes," and the answer to the second is "no." God does hear people's cries for help and will act in a timely manner for those in need of justice, whatever that justice looks like when they are oppressed.

Be encouraged to cry out for justice for those who face injustice in this life. Too often the powers that be—government, society, businesses, and even the church—have been silent in the face of oppression and have allowed injustice to flourish. If you are seeking justice, cry out to God for help and trust that God will send aid. If you are not the victim of an unjust circumstance, pray that God will prepare you to be an advocate of justice for those who have suffered under an unjust system. Pray for the boldness to stand for those who cannot stand for themselves and to help those who are otherwise helpless in this world. Be an active agent for Christ.

November 21

JUSTICE BEYOND THE GRAVE

"I know that my redeemer lives, and that in the end he will stand on the earth." —Job 19:25 (NIV)

Job saw his plight of losing his wealth, health, and children as a result of God's actions and accused God of attacking him. That is the context of today's verse. In response to this perception, Job calls out for justice, desiring even to take God to court and charge God with wrongdoing.

Job calls out for a vindicator or redeemer, one who might rescue Job from his plight. In the minds of the people of the Christian Old Testament, this figure would physically and literally rescue those in need of help. Job, though, speaks of this redeemer working even beyond his own life. The phrase "he will stand on the earth" can also be translated "he will stand on my grave." There is an assurance in the mind of Job that this rescuer will continue the work even after Job is dead and gone.

For Christians, the redeemer is working in the spiritual sense as much as, if not more than, in the physical and literal sense, though that does not mean our redeemer is not working in our physical lives. Jesus Christ is our redeemer and continues to work beyond Jesus' own grave and will work beyond ours whenever that time comes. We can rest in this assurance, trusting that our redeemer does not rest in terms of our salvation until we have tasted salvation in its fullest in the presence of God is sweet. Reflect on this today, on what it means to have a redeemer who has worked, is working, and will continue to work for the salvation of all who believe.

November 22

THE SUBVERSIVE
MESSIAH

*And Jesus answered them, "Go and tell John what you hear and
see: the blind receive their sight and the lame walk, lepers are
cleansed and the deaf hear, and the dead are raised up, and the
poor have good news preached to them." —Matthew 11:4-5
(ESV)*

John, like many of his fellow Jews of the first century, had been waiting for
the promised Messiah. He had spent his adult life preparing the way for
this promised Messiah and had baptized Jesus as a part of the beginning of
his earthly ministry. John suddenly found himself in prison and naturally
began to wonder whether the Messiah had come or not.

Jesus responded to John's wondering by telling John's disciples to send
a message, which is found in the reading for today. While not declaring
directly that he is the Messiah, Jesus reveals his identity to his cousin.
People are healed of all kinds of physical ailments, the dead are raised to life
again, and the poor receive the good news of salvation and, arguably, justice
in the here and now.

The long-awaited Messiah had arrived, albeit subtly. There was no
pomp and circumstance, no inauguration, and no coronation—just a
baptism, some fasting and prayer, and the selection of a dozen learners.
Granted, there was an awesome theophany when God spoke and a dove
descended onto Jesus from heaven, but that all happened in the wilderness
away from the eyes of the social elite. Reflect on the idea that the Messiah
subverted expectations. Also consider how Christianity ought to subvert
the expectations of our own society. How should you subvert expectations
as a follower of Christ?

November 23

CALL AND RESPONSE

For I command you today to love the LORD your God, to walk
in obedience to him, and to keep his commands, decrees and
laws; then you will live and increase, and the LORD your
God will bless you in the land you are entering to possess.
—Deuteronomy 30:16 (NIV)

There are many instances of call and response throughout Scripture. This essentially means that the people of God are called to an action and then are intended to respond accordingly. In the instance of our Scripture for today, the Israelites were called to faithfully follow the Law of God, which was intended to set them apart from the surrounding people groups and make them holy in the eyes of God.

For Christians, or people of the new covenant with God through Jesus Christ, there is a theological realization that we cannot do anything to make ourselves holy in the eyes of God. However, that does not mean we are without hope. Indeed, Jesus Christ is our hope. The people of the Old Testament were called to respond in faithful obedience to the Law of God. The people of the New Testament, including us, are called to respond in faith of the salvific acts of Jesus Christ.

Offer thanksgiving to God for the clear and free path to salvation through Jesus Christ. Reflect on the importance of being called to faith and then responding in faith to the gospel of Jesus Christ. Why is this significant to you as a Christian? How might you live out this faith today? How will you respond in faith to Christ so that you both reveal Christ to others in your life and enrich your own faith in Christ?

November 24

SPIRITUAL EXERCISE: GUIDED PRAYER

You are encouraged to enter a time of prayer and meditation. Thanksgiving is important for the spiritual and emotional maturity and intelligence of Christians. Being thankful for our blessings, both large and small, increases our appreciation of those blessings and further increases our contentment. Offering thanksgiving to God through active prayer is important because Christian theology teaches that blessings come from God. Consider the many things and people in your life that are blessings, and offer a prayer of thanksgiving as those blessings occur to you throughout your day.

Suggested Scripture: 1 Chronicles 16:34-35; Psalms 95:1-2; 105:1-3; John 6:11; 1 Corinthians 15:57; Revelations 11:17

Suggested Prayer:

Gracious God,
You who are the giver of all good things in life, I thank you today for the many blessings that you have given to me. For the things that sustain me, protect me, and shelter me, I give thanks. For the skills I have that allow me to provide for myself and my family, I give thanks. For the provisions that ensure that I have all I need, I give thanks. For the people in my life whom I love and care for and who love and care for me, I give thanks. For my salvation that I have through Jesus Christ, I give thanks. That you consider me worthy of your love and affection, I give thanks. For the people, even my enemies, in this life with whom I disagree, I give thanks. Thank you, oh God, for all that you have done, are doing, and will ever do for me. Amen.

November 25

DIVINE DISCIPLINE

Now, therefore, say to the men of Judah and the inhabitants of Jerusalem: "Thus says the LORD, Behold, I am shaping disaster against you and devising a plan against you. Return, everyone from his evil way, and amend your ways and your deeds." —Jeremiah 18:11 (ESV)

The Christian Old Testament is rife with messages of gloom and doom if the people of God do not repent of their sinful ways and return to God in faith. This does not mean that God is an unloving or unmerciful God. On the contrary, God warns the people of impending gloom and doom in order to correct them, much like a parent lovingly disciplines their child.

In our verse for today God warns the unruly Israelites to return to God and to turn away from—repent of—their sinful ways. Just as a parent warns a toddler not to stick her finger in the electrical socket, God warns the Israelites not to be unfaithful and worship false gods and idols. If children continue a destructive path, they must deal with the consequences of their actions. The same goes for the Israelites.

The decisions you make in this life carry consequences—some good, some bad, and others somewhere in between. As you face decisions today and throughout your life, think about the consequences of those decisions. Think also of how God would have you choose. Follow the guidance of the Holy Spirit, but when you fail, take comfort in knowing that God is a loving parent who will offer forgiveness and grace to you, the wayward child.

November 26

LORD, HAVE MERCY!

"But the tax collector, standing far off, would not even look up to heaven, but was beating his breast and saying, 'God, be merciful to me, a sinner!'" —Luke 18:13 (NRSV)

The parable of the Pharisee and the tax collector is one of opposites. On the one hand, there is the traditional, faithful follower of the will of God, at least on the surface. And on the other hand, there is the one considered a traitor to the Jewish people. Both went to pray in the temple. One stood in the middle of the gathering and spoke loudly for all to hear, while the other stood at a distance and took on a posture of humility. One offered a gaudy and self-righteous prayer, while the other offered a prayer saturated in meekness.

Paul teaches that we gain access to heaven not with our own righteousness but through our faith. James teaches that we perform good deeds through our faith.

With this parable, Jesus taught that the tax collector, the "sinner" and "traitor" to the Jewish people, went home justified before God. Humility not only makes you more attractive and bearable to your friends and family but is also preferred by God. Someone with a humble heart has the self-awareness to recognize their own sins and, instead of hiding them or pretending as though they do not exist, prays to God for mercy because of them.

Commune with God today and approach the redeemer humbly. As you commune with the maker of all things, remember that God's love for you covers your sins through your faith, but this does not allow you to treat the gift of salvation flippantly. Instead, be thankful that God has granted mercy to you as you approach the Divine today.

November 27

CHRISTIAN BOASTING

Therefore, since we have been justified through faith, we have peace with God through our Lord Jesus Christ, through whom we have gained access by faith into this grace in which we now stand. And we boast in the hope of the glory of God. —Romans 5:1-2 (NIV)

Boasting is often seen as a negative activity. No one likes a braggart, though plenty of people get caught up in the act of boasting about their abilities, their accomplishments, their possessions, their careers, their children, their pets, and so on. Naturally, this is a turnoff for those who are unfortunate enough to listen to it.

But what about boasting in something that is never ending, incorruptible, always valuable, and has great worth to everyone who lays claim to it? What about boasting in the hope that we, as Christians, have in the faithfulness of God through Jesus Christ? Even this type of boasting may grate on someone's nerves. However, this is not boasting rooted in arrogance. Neither is it an attempt to claim a sense of self-worth through an unenthusiastic "way to go" from our peers.

Reflect on your method of boasting in your hope for a future in the full presence of God. What does such boasting look like? Is it full of praise for God and thanksgiving for the love that God has shown, is showing, and will continue to show you?

November 28

AN ABSURD LEAP OF FAITH

*"I will put My Spirit within you, and you will come to life, and
I will place you on your own land. Then you will know that I,
the LORD, have spoken and done it," declares the LORD.*
—*Ezekiel 37:14 (NASB)*

Ezekiel had a vision where he saw God bring to life the dry bones of the
Israelites who had died in exile. Ezekiel's contemporaries, his fellow Israelites living in exile, had been through an ordeal. They were told that their
exile was a direct result of generations of unfaithfulness to God. Further,
they learned of the destruction of the temple in Jerusalem, and the prophets
of God gave them dire words of condemnation.

Yet now God, through Ezekiel, gives the people hope if only they will
listen and have faith. God is going to restore the people to their land, and
God can do it just as easily as God can breathe new life into dry old bones.

Christianity, like Judaism before it, has its fair share of callings to take
absurd leaps of faith, at least absurd to the rational mind of humanity. The
idea that God would come to earth in flesh, live among humanity, and then
die a humiliating death is scandalous to say the least and perhaps foolish at
worst. But this is what orthodox Christian theology teaches. It is the absurd
leap of faith that we are called to take as we join in union with our siblings
in faith in Jesus Christ.

Reflect on your spiritual journey thus far. Has it been difficult to
believe, or has it come naturally to you? Reflect on your answer, and pray
for continued faith as you journey alongside the risen Christ.

November 29

MUTUAL LOVE

Having purified your souls by your obedience to the truth for a sincere brotherly love, love one another earnestly from a pure heart, since you have been born again, not of perishable seed but of imperishable, through the living and abiding word of God.
—1 Peter 1:22-23 (ESV)

Many things in this life call for more than one person to accomplish. At least, more than one person may accomplish any number of tasks more easily than a single individual. The early church faced persecution in different forms and from different sides. The early church was often a minority among the religious pluralism of the first-century Roman Empire. This status, and Christianity's insistence on elevating Jesus as the Christ, ruffled the feathers of many religious leaders of other beliefs and led to widespread persecution.

In response, the leaders of the burgeoning church encouraged their fellow Christians to love one another mutually. This mutual love would manifest itself in support during imprisonment or other outward signs of oppression.

What about today, if you live in a society that does not persecute the Christian church? Mutual love still manifests itself in support of one another in times of crisis such as the death of a loved one, the loss of gainful employment, or some other life-shaking event. Be encouraged to love your fellow Christians, to support them when they suffer, and to seek their support when you suffer. There is no shame in calling on your siblings in faith to aid you or support you when you have been knocked down.

November 30

THE PROVIDING KING

God gives the desolate a home to live in; he leads out the pris-
oners to prosperity, but the rebellious live in a parched land.
—Psalm 68:6 (NRSV)

Throughout the Christian Old Testament, God is described as a King. The imagery goes beyond a royal individual who sits on a throne and executes judgment over the people of the kingdom. The imagery is one of provision. The ruling class of the Old Testament was intended to provide for the people, especially when the ruler was fair and just.

In Psalm 68, God is again described as a King, a provider for those oppressed by the system and who are faithful to God.

Jesus is the King of the New Testament and the new covenant between humanity and the Divine. As followers of this King, we are granted promises of provision, including the gift of the Holy Spirit, the Comforter and our guide throughout the here and now. We are also promised salvation and look forward with hopeful anticipation to the return of our King and for the fulfillment of the Messianic promise of the faithful people of God being brought together as one.

Find comfort in the idea of the Divine King. Find hope in the knowledge that Jesus Christ gives peace to his followers in this life and the next. Reflect on how you might also serve as an agent of the Divine King. How might you engage the world around you and provide for others, either in tangible ways or in spiritual support?

December 1

SPIRITUAL EXERCISE: GUIDED PRAYER

You are encouraged to enter a time of prayer and meditation. The season of Advent encompasses the four weeks leading up to Christmas Day. Advent means "coming in to" or "arrival." During this time, we celebrate the first coming of the promised Messiah whom Christians believe is Jesus of Nazareth. Many hundreds of years before Jesus was born in Bethlehem to his virgin mother, our Old Testament prophets like Isaiah were prophesying that the Messiah or "anointed one of God" would come and redeem the people of Israel and the world. During this season of waiting, you are encouraged to reflect on God's promises and faithfulness. Begin this season in prayer, thanking God for God's faithfulness and asking for endurance and patience as we await Christ's second arrival.

Suggested Scripture: Isaiah 7:10-25; Matthew 1:18-25

Suggested Prayer:
Faithful God,
During this season of waiting and preparation, I pause to reflect
on your faithfulness to me and the world. How wonderful it is
to know that your promises are never left unfulfilled. As I await
your Son's second arrival, give me patience and endurance.
During this season of busyness, shopping, traditions, feasting,
parties, and merriment, allow me to be an example of true joy
as I await the fulfillment of your ultimate promise in salvation
through Jesus Christ. Thank you for this hope and your love.
Amen.

December 2

THE REASON
FOR THE SEASON

The LORD said to Moses, "How long will these people treat me with contempt? How long will they refuse to believe in me, in spite of all the signs I have performed among them?" —Numbers 14:11 (NIV)

Rebellion, sin, hopelessness. None of these seem to fit with the theme of Christmas, at least not the theme that immediately comes to mind, whether you celebrate Christmas from a religious or secular point of view. However, these are the true reason for the season.

Jesus came to this world as God in flesh not because we were obedient, righteous, and hope filled. We, humanity, have turned our backs on God, chasing after other things that seem more appealing to our finite and limited senses and understandings. Therefore, we have Advent and Christmas. We rebelled and continue to rebel, so we need a Savior. We await that Savior's arrival and celebrate the truth that our relationship with God is repaired because of our Savior's work.

The trinkets that announce that "Jesus is the reason for the season" are right in that we celebrate this holiday because of Jesus' arrival. However, from a biblical and faith standpoint, the real reason for the season is spelled out, almost painfully, in Numbers 14. The people rebelled, even as they stood at the cusp of entering the promised land and poised to inherit blessings from God beyond measure.

Reflect on the reason for the season. Christ came so we might be saved from our own sinfulness. That is reason enough to celebrate this wonderful gift each year.

December 3
AN ARRIVAL
FOR THE AGES

"See, I am coming soon; my reward is with me, to repay according to everyone's work. I am the Alpha and the Omega, the first and the last, the beginning and the end." —Revelation 22:12-13 (NRSV)

Advent means "arrival" or "coming in to." As Christians, we celebrate two advent seasons. The first is celebrated in the four weeks leading up to Christmas Day. We sing carols, read Scripture, and recount the first advent of the promised Messiah story in plays and cantatas.

We did not live through that time—the time between the last of what we call the Old Testament Prophets and the final arrival of Jesus of Nazareth. What a time of expectation and long-suffering for the faithful people of God! We can empathize to a degree with our spiritual forebears, as we are now waiting for the second advent of Christ—the return that will usher in the kingdom or dominion of God in its fullest.

In our verses for today, Jesus declares that he is the Alpha and the Omega, the beginning and the end. We find ourselves somewhere in the middle of that beginning and end. We look back this Advent season and remember with hopeful expectation the first coming of the Christ as a child born to a virgin mother. We also look forward with the same hopeful expectation to the future coming of the Christ, not as a child again but as our Savior coming to bring us to our eternal home. Let us rest in that hope this Advent season and find joy in our assured salvation in and through the Christ child, our Savior.

December 4
ONE EXTREME

Hear this, you who trample the needy, to do away with the humble of the land, saying, "When will the new moon be over, so that we may sell grain, and the sabbath, that we may open the wheat market, to make the bushel smaller and the shekel bigger, and to cheat with dishonest scales . . . ?" —Amos 8:4-5 (NASB)

During the month of December, it seems that humanity is a little kinder, a little more willing to give to those in need. The motivation may be the tax write-offs, but it could also be the genuine kindness of humanity and, on the part of Christians, a desire to be the hands and feet of Christ in the here and now.

The people Amos was speaking to were greedy, selfish, and abusive, to say the least. They were corrupt and focused on gaining material wealth, even at the expense of others, particularly those in need. This is one extreme: the example of total disregard for other people. This is also something that is alive and well in our own society.

Be encouraged to avoid this extreme in your life. Yes, the ways of this world are tempting. It is tempting to use and abuse other people, particularly if there isn't a face to put to a name or situation. But this is not justice. It is not fair. It is not the way of God or the gospel of Jesus Christ. One extreme of human behavior is selfishness. Selfishness is on full display throughout the prophetic literature of our Old Testament. Avoid this extreme as best you can, and seek support from God and close friends or family to help you.

December 5

TWO EXTREMES

Remember this: Whoever sows sparingly will also reap sparingly, and whoever sows generously will also reap generously. Each of you should give what you have decided in your heart to give, not reluctantly or under compulsion, for God loves a cheerful giver.
—2 Corinthians 9:6-7 (NIV)

The people Amos spoke to were greedy and selfish. On the contrary, the people Paul wrote to were generous in their giving and were being encouraged to continue their activity of offering aid to others. In the case of giving, we ought to give generously as God has given to us generously.

Some of the greatest gifts Christians can offer have no monetary value. Look, for instance, at the gift of salvation that God has offered to us through Christ Jesus. It has no monetary value, but from a faith standpoint there is no gift of greater value to Christians than salvation.

The gifts we offer to others are hope, mercy, love, support, presence during traumatic chapters in life or joyous occasions, and the list goes on. If we are to fall into the category of being an extremist, let us be known as extremely merciful, kind, loving, and filled with hope.

Find ways to give throughout this season of Advent and into the new year. Remember, tangible things are great, but time spent with those who suffer, who are close to us, or who are alone is the greater gift. It is the way to put the gospel into action.

December 6
NO EXTREME

It is good to grasp the one and not let go of the other. Whoever fears God will avoid all extremes. —Ecclesiastes 7:18 (NIV)

In the larger section that contains today's verse, the writer of Ecclesiastes teaches that we ought to find middle ground between righteousness and wickedness. He had witnessed the righteous going to an early grave and the wicked prospering in their wickedness. Even so, Christians would be wise to err on the side of Christ when it comes to a decision between righteousness and wickedness.

In most things in life, however, moderation is key. When making financial decisions, when eating, when being physically active or inactive, we should maintain a healthy balance, not overexerting ourselves or lazing about.

We should be careful to avoid falling into the temptation to choose one side over another in conflicts as well. Often, the truth is somewhere in the middle, whether the conflict is on an international, local, or familial level. Seek the truth. Few issues in this life are black and white or offer clear-cut answers to our ponderings. From the Christian perspective, the only true black and white answer revolves around Jesus. He is the only source of salvation for the world.

Avoid falling into the temptation of choosing one extreme in this life over another. Seek instead the guidance of the Holy Spirit. Where is God in the situation that you are facing? How would God have you carry yourself in this situation?

December 7
THE GIFT OF PRAISE

Through him [Jesus] then let us continually offer up a sacrifice of praise to God, that is, the fruit of lips that acknowledge his name. —Hebrews 13:15 (ESV)

Exchanging gifts is one of the most exciting things about Christmas time for many people. Admittedly, I enjoy getting gifts for others, though it does produce a level of anxiety until I am sure that the person enjoys what they received.

During Advent, we await with excited anticipation the arrival of our greatest gift, the promise of salvation through the Messiah. This is our long-awaited gift from God. The tradition is to exchange gifts, so what does a finite being get for the Creator of all things?

Praise! This is what we may give to God, who has given us so much. Our praise falls far short of equaling the value of our gift from God. Thankfully, that is not how God sets up this gift exchange. There is no price limit. This is not a gift exchange party, after all; it is our eternal destination.

The author of Hebrews understood the importance of offering God praise and adoration to God for the gift of salvation through the life, death, resurrection, and glorification of Jesus Christ. Be encouraged to offer genuine praise to God on this day, throughout this joyous season, and for the remainder of your days in the here and now.

December 8

SPIRITUAL EXERCISE: REFLECTING ON LIGHT

We are taught in Scripture that Jesus is the Light of the World. In the birth narrative found in Matthew's account of the gospel, the light of a star led the wise men to the young Jesus and his family. Throughout Scripture, light is used as a symbol or metaphor for wisdom, hope, and salvation.

The month of December offers several special worship opportunities, often including a candlelight service. This service encourages participants to reflect on the idea that Jesus is indeed the Light of the World that pushes darkness away and gives hope to those who suffer and need salvation.

On this day, you are encouraged to meditate on the image of light. If it helps you to look at a candle, do so, whether lit or unlit. Even gazing at Christmas lights may be of help. What thoughts come to your mind? What images? What feelings? Do you have any new revelations regarding light and what it means to you as a Christian? Use the remainder of this page to make some notes about your experience in this exercise.

_____

_____

_____

_____

_____

_____

December 9

RESPONDING APPROPRIATELY

"They are like children sitting in the marketplace and calling to one another, 'We played the flute for you, and you did not dance; we sang a dirge, and you did not weep.'" —Luke 7:31 (ESV)

The verse for today may sound odd given that we are neck deep in the season of Advent, but the imagery Jesus offers in this teaching is appropriate.

Jesus challenges his audience, explaining that they have not behaved appropriately. They did not celebrate when it was time to celebrate, and they did not mourn when it was time to mourn. They saw John the Baptist as too severe in his religious practices and viewed Jesus as too extreme, though they both behaved appropriately for their roles in God's salvific plan for humanity.

We getting closer to one of Christianity's highest holidays, where we will celebrate the birth of our Savior. How should we respond to the coming of the Son of Man? We are given examples in both Matthew and Luke, the two Gospel accounts that offer us the birth narrative. We see that shepherds, angles, and wise men all came to worship and honor the Christ child.

Let us, too, respond appropriately to the coming of the Christ, through praise and adoration. Just as with the birth of any child, celebration is appropriate. We celebrate because this baby is God in flesh, our redeemer and savior. Be encouraged to offer praises to God, for that is appropriate and good.

December 10

THE COMFORT OF A HOPE-FILLED PROMISE

And not only the creation, but we ourselves, who have the first fruits of the Spirit, groan inwardly as we wait eagerly for adoption as sons, the redemption of our bodies. For in this hope we were saved. Now hope that is seen is not hope. For who hopes for what he sees? —Romans 8:22-25 (ESV)

The verses for today speak of the comfort brought by our hope in the promises of God. Our reading speaks of the hope in the second coming of Jesus of Nazareth, the Christ or Messiah, to bring us into the full presence of God the Father in the kingdom or dominion of God.

In this season of Advent, waiting expectantly is typical and part of the experience. Children anxiously await Christmas morning to see what goodies lie under and around the Christmas tree. Christians anxiously await the second advent of the Christ as we look back to his first advent with assurance in the promises of God.

Christians also look to Jesus' birth as the fulfillment of Divine promises. We then, with hope, look forward to the fulfillment of Jesus' own Divine promise in his return. For believers in Christ, this ought to bring comfort and hope as we wait. We know that God is true to God's promises; we need only wait in faith, which is, admittedly, a difficult task.

Be encouraged to wait patiently, not only for the second advent of Christ but also for all things in life that cause you to wait. It is difficult to be patient, especially with many of life's questions. Lean on God for this patience, and seek comfort in knowing that, no matter what this life presents to you, you may find comfort in God's hope-filled promise.

December 11

THE LONG-IN-COMING FULFILLMENT

*Comfort, O comfort my people says your God. Speak tenderly
to Jerusalem, and cry to her that she has served her term, that
her penalty is paid, that she has received from the LORD's hand
double for all her sins. —Isaiah 40:1-2 (NRSV)*

Our reading speaks of the hope and comfort associated with the eventual coming of the promised Jewish Messiah, whom Christians believe is Jesus of Nazareth. Israel had been in exile and longed for redemption. Our world, too, sits in exile and darkness, removed from the full presence of God. Christ is the bridge between the world and God the Father.

The Israelites waited over four hundred years to see the fulfillment of the Messianic prophecies. We have waited now for nearly two thousand years for Jesus' second coming, and we do not know when it will take place. We do know that God is faithful to God's promises, no matter how long it takes from our perspective.

Find comfort in God's promises today. Advent and Christmas are seasons of hope and comfort. Allow these reminders to stir your heart and ease your mind. There are indeed troubles all around in this life, yet God is faithful.

Be encouraged also to serve as a tangible reminder of God's love and faithfulness in this life. Remind others, through your own patient waiting, to cling to the hope that is found in God through Christ.

December 12

CHRISTIAN VIRTUES

*For if these qualities are yours and are increasing, they render
you neither useless nor unfruitful in the true knowledge of our
Lord Jesus Christ. —1 Peter 1:8 (NASB)*

Moral excellence, knowledge, self-control, perseverance, godliness, brotherly kindness, and love are but a few of the many Christian virtues. The list that Peter offers prior to our verse for today is worth remembering and applying to our own daily walk of faith. In our verse, Peter goes on to explain that, when applied to our lives, these virtues are not useless or unfruitful; rather, they lead to true knowledge of Jesus Christ.

Not only do these virtues lead to greater knowledge of Jesus Christ; they exemplify the behavior of followers of Christ. To be sure, these are not all the behaviors of Christians all the time. It is not realistic to expect any Christian to carry themselves in this manner every second of every day. Rather, these are examples for us to follow and strive for in our own lives.

It is important that we seek to apply these virtues to our daily walk in faith. However, it is equally important that we not beat ourselves up too severely when we fail to apply these virtues to our journey of faith. The Christian walk is a difficult path to follow, but it is one that is covered in grace. When we fail to be the virtuous Christians we ought to be, God's grace is there to cover our mistakes. Do not let that assurance hinder you from striving to be the most faithful and virtuous Christ follower that you can be this day.

December 13

ARE YOU THE ONE?

He [John the Baptist] sent them to the Lord to ask, "Are you the one who is to come, or should we expect someone else?" —Luke 7:19 (NIV)

John the Baptist is in prison at this point in Luke's account of the gospel. Naturally, the fiery preacher clothed in camel's hair was curious about his cousin, the one whom he had baptized and prophesied about, the one whom he and many others had placed their hope in as the Messiah. The problem for John, and many of his contemporaries, was a misunderstanding of what the Messiah would do. The common belief was that the Messiah would deliver the people of Israel from their oppressors.

It is true that all who follow Jesus the Nazarene as the Christ, or Messiah, will be delivered from their oppressors. However, there is a misconception as to the identity of the oppressor(s). Many of Jesus' contemporaries, including his cousin John, must have believed that Jesus would somehow lead a rebellion against Rome and expel the Roman government and military from Israel's borders, thus restoring the kingdom of David.

The true oppressors that Jesus delivers his followers from are sin and death. John was not sure about Jesus when he looked and saw the four walls of a jail cell surrounding him. In life's most difficult and dire moments, it may feel that our Messiah is not who we thought he was or should be. Rest assured that through all of life's challenges and hardships, Jesus Christ is indeed our Savior and will deliver us from the most serious of oppressors and longest-lasting consequences.

December 14

RESTORE US!

Restore us, O God; make your face shine on us, that we may be saved. —Psalm 80:3 (NIV)

Restoration is the all-encompassing theme of the story of Scripture. It begins with creation, moves to the fall of humanity, and muddles through the back and forth of God providing for God's people until, finally, restoration begins in the Gospels. In the psalms as well as elsewhere in Christianity's Old Testament, there are cries for restoration. God's people seek restoration to former glory, to former status, riches, and so on. Primarily, we ought to seek restoration between ourselves and God, and this comes through Christ Jesus.

The psalmist, or the author of our verse, seeks restoration and salvation. The writer of the psalm knows that the people of God have strayed and that God's face does not shine upon them because of their own foolishness.

"Restore us" is not a cry that is limited to God's people of the old covenant; it is a cry that carries over to God's people of the new covenant through Jesus Christ. We continue to seek restoration between ourselves and God; that is why we have faith in Christ. But we should not only seek restoration of the Divine-human relationship.

If you have trusted in Christ as your Savior, then you have sought restoration with God. How about your human relationships? Have you sought restoration between yourself and those who have hurt you or those you have hurt? Reflect today and seek restoration in your human relationships during this season, when we remember our restoration to God in Christ.

December 15

SPIRITUAL EXERCISE: PSALM OF PRAISE

Today you are encouraged to reflect on the following psalm. What does the Spirit tell you through these words? Do you find it easy to offer praises to God today? If not, then commune with God and listen for the Divine voice. Can you identify what is preventing your ability to offer praises?

> "My soul magnifies the Lord, and my spirit in God my Savior, for he has looked with favor on the lowliness of his servant. Surely, from now on all generations will call me blessed; for the Mighty One has done great things for me, and holy is his name. His mercy is for those who fear him from generation to generation. He has shown strength with his arm; he has scattered the proud in the thoughts of their hearts. He has brought down the powerful from their thrones, and lifted up the lowly; he has filled the hungry with good things, and sent the rich away empty. He has helped his servant Israel, in reembrace of his mercy, according to the promise he made to our ancestors, to Abraham and his descendants forever." —Luke 1:46b – 55 (ESV) (Mary's Song of Praise or "The Magnificat")

December 16

DIVINE PURPOSE

And you, child, will be called the prophet of the Most High; for you will go before the Lord to prepare his ways. —Luke 1:76 (ESV)

The overall section of our verse for today is Zechariah's prophecy concerning his son John, who would be called the Baptizer. John had a specific purpose in his life that was identified even before he was born. He would serve as the prophet and messenger for the Messiah, announcing that salvation has arrived for all who will believe.

We all have a purpose in this life. What that purpose is may not be as easily identifiable as John's purpose was. Divine encounters have a way of clarifying things for us like nothing else in life.

However, just because it is not as clear to us does not mean we do not have a specific purpose. Perhaps you have identified your call, or perhaps you are still struggling to come to terms with your call. Maybe you do not feel as though you have a specific call. Rest assured that you are called to something in this life by your Creator and God. For some it is a specific vocation, a job or career that seems to beckon.

No matter where you are in your life, what you are doing, planning on doing, or have done, there is a purpose for you. No one aside from God can promise to know what that is without Divine discernment. Be encouraged to seek that discernment today. Commune with God for the purpose of discovering what you will do with the time you have in this life.

December 17

THE PROMISE
TO THE FAITHFUL

They shall be mine, says the LORD of hosts, my special possession on the day when I act, and I will spare them as parents spare their children who serve them. —Malachi 3:17 (NRSV)

There are many promises throughout Scripture. Most promise from the Divine point to God's faithfulness; God has yet to fail to live up to a promise that God made. In this passage, God promises to spare those who are faithful to God, serve God, and have faith in God.

The "they" in today's verse are the faithful people of God who have continued to practice faith despite the surrounding circumstances. God's promise here is that these people will be spared harsh judgment.

Scripture is also rife with examples of what happens to both the people who remain faithful to God and those who are unfaithful. The Israelites were punished for their unfaithfulness. The biggest example is the Babylonian exile. Another example is being made to wander in the desert for forty years, waiting for the last of the unfaithful generation to die off before they could enter the promised land.

Now, through the new covenant, a promise is made to the faithful yet again: we will be in the full presence of God forevermore. You, as you believe in Jesus Christ, are one of God's special possessions, spared from separation and given the gift of love. Reflect on this today.

December 18

TOTAL TRUST

He [Jesus] told them: "Take nothing for the journey—no staff,
no bag, no bread, no money, no extra shirt." —Luke 9:3 (NIV)

Don't take any extra money, a change of clothes, food, luggage, or anything else that seems practical for a journey. This instruction flies in the face of the Boy Scout motto "Be prepared." Jesus says this to his disciples before sending them out into the world to do ministry, but it seems like bad advice.

That is not the case, though. Jesus was not teaching his disciples how to be more resilient and self-reliant. On the contrary, Jesus was teaching his disciples to be more reliant on God for their needs in this life.

The idea of it is terrifying. We would not send our children into the world without preparation. We would not embark on a long road trip without first ensuring that our engine was well maintained, our tires were inflated properly, and we had a full tank of gas. Why, then, would Christ not want his disciples to be prepared?

The passage further teaches that the disciples should rely on the generosity of those who welcome them into their homes on their missionary journeys. We are to rely on God for our needs as we do the work of God in the here and now. This flies in the face of the rugged individualism that is taught by so many in our society.

It is clear as we read through Scripture that Jesus' teachings often do not align with human expectations, desires, and logic. Reflect on your trust of God. Is there room to grow? Are you ready to drop all things and share the love of Christ without thought of being prepared?

December 19

A CLEAR PATH TO GOD

"Behold, I am going to send My messenger, and he will clear the way before Me. And the Lord, whom you seek, will suddenly come to His temple; and the messenger of the covenant, in whom you delight, behold, He is coming," says the LORD of hosts.
—Malachi 3:1 (NASB)

In the third chapter of Malachi, God is speaking through the prophet about one who will sit as a refiner of gold and silver, burning away the impurities and cleansing the Levites, or the priests, of Christianity's Old Testament.

This refiner is coming and will clear a path directly to the Lord, making all who approach God in worship ready to commune with God.

Christians have been purified. Like gold going through a refinery, our impurities or sins are burned away, and all that remains is what God intended in the beginning: a pure being that can share in communion with the Divine. It is God's desire for all people to be purified and come into the Divine presence without the burden of our sins.

What a message to cling to! We have the promise of God in flesh removing our sins from us so that we might enter the full presence of God the Creator. Malachi's audience was waiting for that messenger. Christians have received that messenger and now rest in the knowledge that we have been purified, are being purified, and will be purified. Praise be to God this day for our salvation.

December 20

HOPE NOT FOUND
IN THIS WORLD

*For we are the circumcision, who worship by the Spirit of God
and glory in Christ Jesus and put no confidence in the flesh.
—Philippians 3:3 (ESV)*

Christians are a people set apart. You may already know this, have been taught this, and believe this. However, do you live this? It is easy for us to get caught up in the ways of the world. To put our hope in our bank accounts. To dream big dreams based on our career aspirations and goals. To believe that our spouse will never let us down and that the difficulties of life like cancer, pink slips, and poverty only affect other people.

How wrong we are if we hold to any of these or other ideas about this life. We are not set apart from the world because of our faith to then dive back into the world around us, becoming consumed with the same thoughts, desires, and appetites that consume our secular neighbors.

Why not simply conform to the world? What harm would it do?

Our hope is not found in this world, so why be consumed with finite things that matter little in the long run? Yes, we need certain things for survival. We have responsibilities in the here and now. But our hope is not found in a bank account, in gifts under a tree, or even in our families. Our hope is found in Christ! That is what sets us apart from the world around us, both from other religions and from the secular clubs. Be encouraged to remember where your hope lies, and conform to that way of thinking rather than to the world's way.

December 21
LONG NIGHT OF WAITING

Who gave up Jacob to the spoiler, and Israel to the robbers? Was it not the LORD, against whom we have sinned, in whose ways they would not walk, and whose law they would not obey?
—Isaiah 42:24 (NRSV)

The winter solstice is the day when there is more darkness than on any other day throughout the year. Darkness is often connected with suffering, pain, and anguish. Those who are hurting use language like what is found in many of our Old Testament psalms and even the poem *Dark Night of the Soul* by Saint John of the Cross. That poem is synonymous with suffering for many, even those who have never read it.

The Israelites of Isaiah's day were suffering. They had been sent into exile. Granted, their own sinfulness and unfaithfulness to God served as the culprit. Their suffering was nevertheless real. Those many years must have felt like a single, continuous winter solstice. The people longed for the dawn, for hope, for restoration. Unfortunately, the original audience of Isaiah's messages of hope regarding the Messiah would never see it come to pass; it would be many hundreds of years between Isaiah's prophecies and Jesus' birth.

For us, though, that initial long night of waiting has come and gone, and the promise of the Messiah has begun. We now wait, perhaps during another long night, for the second advent of the Messiah. Be encouraged today as we wait for Christ's second coming. Look to the fulfillment of the first promise for a Messiah, and find comfort in your own long night.

December 22

SPIRITUAL EXERCISE: WORD FOCUS ON "IMMANUEL"

Therefore, the Lord Himself will give you a sign: Behold, a virgin will be with child and bear a son, and she will call His name Immanuel. —Isaiah 7:14 (NASB)

When translated, Immanuel means "God is with us." What a profound word! What a wonderful declaration and prophecy! This awesome concept is revisited every Advent and Christmas season. Matthew's account (1:23) quotes the Old Testament prophet Isaiah and explains that Jesus fulfills this prophecy, particularly in reference to his birth by a virgin mother.

Today you are encouraged to reflect on the meaning of Immanuel. What does "God is with us" mean to humanity? What does "God is with us" mean to you? During this Advent season, continue to reflect on this concept of "God is with us."

Hebrew: Immanuel (read from right to left), עִמָּנוּאֵל
Greek: Emmanuel (read from left to right), Ἐμμανουήλ

December 23

REJOICE, FOR SALVATION IS HERE

Rejoice in the Lord always. I will say it again: Rejoice!
—Philippians 4:4 (NIV)

Christmas is only two days away, another blessed reminder of the wonder of God's love for humanity. It is a time of much rejoicing, remembering hope, and preparing our hearts and minds to offer praise and thanks to God.

But why? Why do we rejoice? What is there to be so happy about? When we look underneath our Christmas trees, we see the gifts; when we look on our tables, we see the feast; when we look on the couch, we see our family. All these things are tangible. We can touch them and enjoy them in the here and now. We cannot touch salvation. We cannot see it and experience it with our senses. We cannot even truly comprehend what it means to have salvation. So why rejoice? Why the hubbub?

Simply put, we rejoice for this reason: we need not fear death, and we may look forward to eternity in the full presence of God. But what is the big deal? Christianity sometimes doesn't make any sense, so why bother?

We bother because we see the pain, experience the hurting, shed the tears, and long for something better. The gifts wear out, the feast is consumed, our family succumbs to illness, injury, and age. These are the reasons we rejoice. Our salvation does not have an expiration date. Our salvation does not end. It continues beyond infinity. Rejoice today, and every day, as you remember your salvation and the promise of hope through Christ Jesus.

December 24

THE EVE OF
A NEW COVENANT

*For to us a child is born, to us a son is given, and the govern-
ment will be on his shoulders. And he will be called Wonderful
Counselor, Mighty God, Everlasting Father, Prince of Peace.*
—Isaiah 9:6 (NIV)

Many hundreds of years before the birth of Christ, the prophet Isaiah lived and served with the people of Israel during a tumultuous time in their collective lives. The Israelites were amid a transitional period, one that saw many of the people enter what is called the Babylonian Exile. This meant that many were forced from their homes and into a foreign land. The people needed hope for their future.

God spoke through the prophet and offered the Israelites the promise of a coming new covenant and a coming Messiah who would rescue the people. This promise was not only for the Israelites, though; it was for all the world. All who believe in Jesus as the Christ may be counted in this new covenant. That time in between Isaiah's prophecy and Jesus' birth must have been slow in coming; many generations would come and go before Jesus would arrive.

This long waiting may drive people nuts. It can also cause people to become impatient, lose sight or focus, and maybe even lose hope that the promise will ever be fulfilled. That is not unlike children as they wait for Christmas Day to arrive. As you sit on the cusp of another celebration of Christmas Day with your many traditions, take a moment to enjoy the wait. Reflect on what it means to not yet have what has been promised to you, to not yet understand the joy that your hope for something promised brings you.

December 25
THE BIRTH OF
SALVATION

*"To you is born this day in the city of David a Savior, who is the
Messiah, the Lord."* —Luke 2:11 (NRSV)

Salvation has arrived! Praise be to God, for we who believe in Jesus of Nazareth as the long-expected Christ have received salvation from our sins and
death. Christmas Day is such a wonderful gift. Yes, it may not be the actual
day on which Christ was born; many of the celebrations and traditions
have roots in pagan traditions; and it has become a wildly consumer-driven
holiday in Western society. But Christians may rejoice because we have set
this day aside to praise God and celebrate the gift of salvation.

Undoubtedly you will have several traditions to enjoy today. You'll
probably visit family and friends, exchange gifts, and share in feasting and
fellowship. Do not lose sight of the reason we celebrate today. All those
family traditions are nice, and exchanging gifts can be fun if everyone has
the right spirit about it, but none of these things matter in the long run.
Please enjoy your traditions. Do not feel guilty about doing the various
things that you and your family do on Christmas to celebrate. But take
time to honor God too.

As Christians, there is only one day on our calendar that comes close
to Christmas in significance, and that is Easter. Easter probably surpasses
Christmas, but there would be no Easter without Christmas. Today, Christians celebrate the promise God made to Israel as it comes to fruition. God
has finally fulfilled what was promised by sending the Messiah to rescue us
from sin and death. Celebrate today the birth of salvation as well as your
own rebirthing into salvation.

December 26

NO JUDGMENT AGAINST YOU

The LORD has taken away the judgments against you, he has turned away your enemies. The king of Israel, the LORD, is in your midst; you shall fear disaster no more. —Zephaniah 3:15 (NRSV)

Have you ever seen the blue lights of a law enforcement vehicle flash in your rearview mirror? Have you pulled to the side hoping that they pass by only to learn that they are coming for you? If you have, and you received a citation, then you know the feeling of being caught doing something you should not have been doing. Whether you feel that the ticket was justifiable matters little to the officer; they caught you and pulled you over. Either you or a lawyer went to court and pleaded your case. Maybe you admitted guilt and paid the fine. Either way, a judgment was leveled against you, and you were labeled a criminal.

It hurts, doesn't it? Maybe you have never found yourself on the receiving end of a traffic citation, but there are instances in other areas of your life where you were in the wrong or were judged as though you were in the wrong—by an employer, coworker, friend, teacher, or someone else.

Remembering those feelings and then reading our verse for the day can bring relief if we reflect on what it means to have the judgments that are aimed squarely at us taken away.

What a blessed thing to know that you are being judged and found guilty, and then that judgment is taken away; the relief of knowing that you deserve punishment, yet you are spared or pardoned. The judgments against you have been taken away. Rejoice today and thank God.

December 27

SALVATION FOR ALL

"Therefore, I want you to know that God's salvation has been sent to the Gentiles, and they will listen!" —Acts 28:28 (NIV)

Paul was speaking to a group of Jews in his ministry, and they were not buying into this Jesus of Nazareth being the Messiah. How can the Messiah, the one who would lead the people from oppression and restore the kingdom of David, be crucified?

The message of salvation in and through Jesus was initially for the Jewish people. Some believed in that first century after Jesus' death and resurrection. Some did not. Paul, after ministering to the Jews, shifted his attention to the Gentiles or non-Jewish people groups. The plan of salvation was never intended to be for one people group. The message of the gospel is for all people. Nationality, language, race, sexual orientation, or other fabricated identifiers are moot when sharing the gospel.

Many Christian churches and denominations send mission teams out for short periods of time and collect shoe boxes for children in other countries. While these are well-meaning ventures, it is prudent for us as Christians to find more lasting methods of reaching all peoples as Paul did. Paul built relationships and spoke honestly and truthfully to his Gentile audiences. Salvation is for all; therefore, our work for Christ should be taken seriously, not done to pat ourselves on the back because we collected more boxes than last year or for the experience of going overseas on a mission trip. How will you bring the knowledge of salvation to others in a lasting, genuine way?

December 28

THE OFFERING
OF THIS BABE

By this will we have been sanctified through the offering of the
body of Jesus Christ once for all. —Hebrews 10:10 (NASB)

Christians have just celebrated the remembrance of the birth of Jesus of
Nazareth, the promised Messiah or Christ of our Old Testament. It is
sobering to think that this baby's birth would lead to the cross, a horribly
painful and effective means of execution. This, though, would lead to our
salvation.

The writer of the book of Hebrews goes to great lengths to express the
idea that Jesus Christ's death on the cross was a sacrifice for the forgiveness
of our sins. Essentially, Jesus served as an offering like in the sacrificial
system of the Old Testament, cleansing us of our sins the way an animal
would have before.

The difference is that the sacrifices of old were needed repeatedly. The
one giving the sacrifice would inevitably sin again and require another
sacrifice to atone for the more recent sins. Jesus' offering was different. No
other sacrifices would be necessary. Churches no longer have an alter on
which the blood of sacrifices is sprinkled to atone for the sins of the individual or community. Jews no longer do this either, but for Christians the
reason is Jesus Christ.

Take some time to reflect on what this means for you. All of your sins
have been, are being, and will be forgiven simply because Jesus died and
was resurrected and you have faith in these events.

December 29

SPIRITUAL EXERCISE: LECTIO DIVINA
(DIVINE READING)

You are invited to practice a spiritual exercise, a "divine reading" of a select passage of Scripture. Please follow the guide provided as you meditate on this passage.

- Read the passage twice, pausing between each reading for a moment of silence. Identify keywords as you read the passage without elaboration
- Read the passage again, pause for silence, and answer the following question: Where does the content of the reading touch my life today?
- Read the passage once more, again pausing for silence, and complete this sentence: I believe God wants me to . . . .

> And in the same region there were shepherds out in the field, keeping watch over their flock by night. And an angel of the Lord appeared to them, and the glory of the Lord shone around them, and they were filled with great fear. And the angel said to them, "Fear not, for behold, I bring you good news of great joy that will be for all the people. For unto you is born this day in the city of David a Savior, who is Christ the Lord. And this will be a sign for you: you will find a baby wrapped in swaddling cloths and lying in a manger." —Luke 2:8-12 (ESV)

December 30

PEACE LIKE A RIVER

For thus says the LORD: "Behold, I will extend peace to her like a river, and the glory of the nations like an overflowing stream; and you shall nurse, you shall be carried upon her hip, and bounced upon her knees. As one whom his mother comforts, so I will comfort you; you shall be comforted in Jerusalem." —Isaiah 66:12-13 (ESV)

A powerful Christian hymn titled "It Is Well with My Soul" begins with these words: "When peace like a river attendeth my way . . . ." God's peace is gentle and yet overwhelming. Both words, "gentle" and "overwhelming," may be applied to a river at different seasons or sections along its winding path through the landscape.

The Christmas season is a season of peace, a season during which the church gathers with a renewed sense of hope and awe at God's love for the world. As the season continues, be encouraged to reflect on what it means to be a member of the body of Christ, a loved individual, a creation of God who has accepted God's love of you and thus has received access to a calming peace.

There are untold reasons in this world that peace may elude us: disease, financial insecurity, familial conflict, national crises, violence, hatred, war, famine, and so on. Meditate on the peace of God today. Allow time in your life to commune with God, to find this Divine peace, and to be comforted by the assurance that God is indeed with you, even when the peace of God eludes you.

December 31

THE BEGINNING
AND THE END

I am the Alpha and the Omega, the first and the last, the beginning and the end. —Revelation 22:13 (NRSV)

As another calendar year ends and many around the globe prepare to usher in a new year with all the hopes, dreams, and promises that traditionally accompany such a celebration, take time to celebrate God having been a part of every day of your life over the last year, whether you realized it or not. Reflect on the blessings God has given to you throughout this last calendar year: new life brought into your family, a new job, new beginnings, or perhaps simply a new day of life as you greeted each morning throughout the year.

In the final chapter of the book of Revelation, Jesus declares that he encompasses all things from beginning to end. He is above all, through all, and in all things. He is the Divine conductor of the symphony that is creation, bringing forth new life in a great crescendo as with the climbing of instruments in a music hall. Major events in the lives of people punctuate the seemingly mundane and ordinary ebbs and flows of life like the angelic voices singing in staccato fashion. And he calls his people home with a steady decrescendo until we see his face at last, accompanied with an energetic fortissimo from the angelic host and the saints who have gone before.

As you close out the year and prepare for another, take time to praise God for the blessings, no matter how small, that you have been given throughout the year. Praise all three Persons of the Trinity for their presence in your life and that they are indeed both the Beginning and the End of all things. Look forward to this new year as well, taking courage in God through the challenges and praising God for the blessings.

BIBLIOGRAPHY

Augustine. *Confessions*. In vol. 1 of *The Nicene and Post-Nicene Fathers*, Series 1. Edited by Philip Schaff. 1886–1889. 14 vols. Repr., Peabody, MA: Hendrickson, 1994.

Holt, Bradley P. *Thirsty for God: A Brief History of Christian Spirituality*. Minneapolis, MN: Augsburg Press, 2005.

"Hunger Statistics." Food Aid Foundation (foodaidfoundation.org/world-hunger-statistics.html).

"National Sleep Foundation Recommends New Sleep Times" (sleep.foundation.org/press-release/national-sleep-foundation-recommends-new-sleep-times/page/0/1).

Peck, M. Scott. *The Different Drum: Community Making and Peace*. New York: Touchstone, 1987.

Satir, Virginia, quoted in "Have You Hugged Anyone Lately?" by Parveen Chopra, *Life Positive*, November 1996 (lifepositive.com/have-you-hugged-anyone-lately-/).

Soanes, Catherine, and Sara Hawker, editors. *Compact Oxford English Dictionary of Current English 3rd Edition*. Oxford: Oxford University Press, 2008.

Substance Abuse and Mental Health Services Administration (samhsa.gov/).

SCRIPTURE INDEX

A DAILY WALK WITH GOD

6:33	246	3:7	162	12:27	113
9:12	47	4:29	164	13:3-5	148
11:4-5	334	5:8	87	13:23	3
11:28	209	5:10b	100	13:34	135
12:33	70	6:27	171	14:1	262
16:13b-16	20	6:29a	173	14:6	142
18:21-22	80	7:19	335	15:1	144
19:14	13	7:31	351	16:33	114
25:23	237	7:48	51	17:20	67
25:35a	40	9:3	360	17:21	56
27:54	66	9:23	217	19:30	106
28:6	109	10:39-40	5	20:21	133
28:19	223	11:34b	27	20:25	189
28:20	151	12:6-7	267		
		15:3, 8-10	307	**Acts**	
Mark		15:27-28	131	2:42	19
1:24	111	16:4	273	2:46	170
1:35	81	17:6	53	5:31	224
2:24	323	18:7	332	5:38-39	238
3:13	8	18:13	338	9:21	259
3:23b-24	121	19:39-40	102	12:14	263
4:25	321	22:38	166	28:28	269
4:34	124	23:34	149		
4:36	145	23:44-45	202	**Romans**	
4:38	125	23:47	208	3:23	16
5:43	325	23:56b	107	4:5	110
6:3	127	24:1-8	108	5:1-2	339
6:18	327			5:8	15
6:56	132	**John**		5:19	128
8:31	134	1:1	1	8:26	228
9:24	98	1:14	92	12:2	203
10:18	178	3:16	211	12:18	194
14:50	231	3:17	212	12:21	37
		6:35	137	15:1	225
Luke		8:12	138	15:5	285
1:46b-55	357	10:7	139	16:1-2	230
1:76	358	10:10b	64		
2:11	367	10:11	140	**1 Corinthians**	
2:49	38	11:25	141	1:10-13, 17	236

A DAILY WALK WITH GOD

Made in the USA
Columbia, SC
21 November 2021

49474290R00211